I0836699

LIFE

OF

CHARLES SUMNER.

BY

JEREMIAH CHAPLIN

AND

J. D. CHAPLIN.

WITH AN INTRODUCTION

BY

HON. WILLIAM CLAFLIN.

BOSTON:
PUBLISHED BY D. LOTHROP & CO.
DOVER, N. H.: G. T. DAY & CO.
1874.

STEREOTYPED AT THE
BOSTON STEREOTYPE FOUNDRY,
19 Spring Lane.

PREFACE.

In the belief that a Life of Charles Sumner, our great Senator, written in a somewhat popular style, would be welcomed by the public, this work has been carefully prepared from the most authentic sources.

The writers have had access to private papers, and other sources of information, which have enabled them to give some hitherto unpublished incidents and letters.

The works of Mr. Sumner have been carefully examined, and fitting selections from his speeches have been incorporated in the biography. His addresses are an integral part of the history of the times in which he lived, and they largely reveal his character.

A full survey of Mr. Sumner's public career has not been attempted. To do that, would have been to transcend the limits of our plan, which was, rather, to dwell upon his connection with the one great subject which, above all others, called out his powers and developed his character. To the overthrow of American Slavery he gave his most earnest thought, and it was in this, his chief work, that his distinguished qualities of mind and heart are most conspicuous. He was a statesman in no narrow sense; he was not a man of but one idea; he was at home in all the business of legislation, in all foreign and domestic affairs. But he will be chiefly remembered as a philanthropist. Intellectually great, he was pre-eminently distinguished as a lover of justice, a defender of humanity. His moral endowments and humane achievements will chiefly endear him to mankind. From these are to be gathered the most valuable lessons, especially for the young.

Happy will it be for our country if her young men study his life, and emulate his example of unselfish devotion to the cause of humanity. Happy for her if her coming legislators believe that to be upright is to be practical, to be just is to be patriotic.

Properly to present Mr. Sumner's philanthropic services, it has been necessary briefly to sketch the progress of the anti-slavery enterprise up to the time when he became its foremost champion. Three chapters have, therefore, been given to the pioneers in that cause, and to the state of public sentiment upon the slavery question prior to Mr. Sumner's public life.

In sketching his career, it has been almost a necessity to cast his co-laborers into the shade. As we have not attempted a history of his times, but only of his special relation to the great question of the times, he seems to absorb to himself more than his share of attention. He was, indeed, a most conspicuous figure, great among the great, in some respects without a peer; but the names of many men and women will come to mind who gave the full measure of noble talents and sweet charity to the cause of the humble and oppressed — names that will never die. Without these to prepare the way, or to furnish the contemporary support of sympathy, of encouragement, of prayer, of sacrifice, Mr. Sumner could never have achieved those deeds which will make his name immortal.

The writings of Mr. Sumner abound in noble sentiments, and in the fruits of rich and varied culture. They are eminently worthy of perusal by the rising generation. But above all, his life, in which those sentiments found their most consistent and best illustration, deserves to be studied for its example of unwavering devotion to duty. To do right, to serve mankind, to obey God, was the high purpose for which he wrought. Such a life, in the inspiration which it imparts, in the lessons which it teaches, must be an abiding and ever-widening power in the world. It is grandly practical. It shows the path of true success.

To friends who have kindly and greatly aided our work by letters of Mr. Sumner, and by various valuable information, we here express our grateful appreciation of their help.

The invaluable work of Vice-President Wilson, Rise and Fall of the Slave Power in America, has been consulted in preparing a portion of this volume.

J. C.

J. D. C.

INTRODUCTION.

The people of the whole country realize, now, the loss they have sustained by the death of Senator Sumner. His place in the Senate cannot be filled from his native State, or any other.

While he lived, the people felt that there was one man in the national councils whose voice was ever ready in defence of the right, and in opposition to injustice or wrong. That voice is forever hushed.

The fame of the great statesman, orator, and philanthropist reaches all civilized lands; and all classes, here, desire to know his history from the beginning to the end of his life. This is not strange, when it is remembered that only two men exceeded his term of service in the Senate, and that neither of them held the position during a very eventful period in the history of the country, or made himself especially distinguished beyond his own immediate locality.

Few persons have used their opportunities for obtaining an education so faithfully as Mr. Sumner. Endowed by nature with great intellectual powers, possessing a genius for statesmanship and philanthropy of the first order, he early devoted himself to most diligent study of all matters relating to jurisprudence, international law, and the principles of government.

In the order of Providence he was kept from the first struggles of the party of freedom. He was preparing for the great work before him. When, therefore, he entered upon his career in the Senate, he was better fitted than any one of his associates to meet the tremendous responsibilities which soon pressed upon him.

He gave himself to the cause dear to him and to every lover of liberty, without the least reserve or hesitation. All private business was laid aside, that he might devote himself to the accomplishment of the object for which the people of his State sent him to the Senate.

The great political struggle in the legislature which resulted in his election had drawn the attention of the country to him. Nor were the people long kept in ignorance of his purposes and power. His first great speech showed the depth of his moral convictions, and his determination to leave nothing undone to free the land from the blighting curse of slavery.

Thenceforth there was no cessation of hostility to him and his measures on the part of the upholders of that system. All their denunciations, however, had no effect upon him. He was one of the foremost of the noble band of statesmen who deemed all other questions subordinate while slavery existed.

Although its abolition was paramount with him, yet there never was a greater mistake than to suppose that he was not a practical man in matters pertaining to his office. He was familiar with the whole machinery of government, and knew how to accomplish an object in the shortest possible time. This was attested, again and again, by those having business before Congress or the departments, in which it was proper to ask his influence and co-operation.

But if a doubtful scheme or claim was to be carried through, he was the most *im*practical of men. Professional lobbyists knew, well enough, that if a thing was right, he would favor it, but if questionable, no tactics, however skilful, would secure his support.

In all his long official life no one dared to impeach his integrity or question his motives. Entire devotion to duty, undeviating rectitude, and high moral convictions guided and controlled him.

The sudden termination of a life so intimately connected with the government, and so potent in its influence, makes impressive these traits, rarely found in the most distinguished statesmen of the world.

That a character so noble may be clearly brought before the masses, and especially before the young men who are soon to hold positions of honor and trust in the State and Nation, is the purpose of this volume.

Senate Chamber
10th May '70

My dear Mrs Claflin,

I needed no assurance from you to know that your husband had done for Mr Revels all that hospitality or sympathy could suggest.

I am glad to hear of Mr Revels's success &

yours the kindness be received. In this wel-come I catch the triumph of a new civi-lization.

Believe me
dear Mrs Claflin,
very faithfully yours,
Charles Sumner

"Humbly do I recognize the authority of Him who, when reviled, reviled not again; but His divine example teaches me to expose crime, and not to hesitate, though the Scribes and Pharisees, chief priests and money-changers, cry out."

"Liberty has been won; the battle for Equality is still pending."

"To be a man is a sufficient title-deed for the rights of man."

"Say, in lofty madness, that you own the sun, the stars, the moon; but do not say that you own a man, endowed with soul to live immortal, when sun, and moon, and stars have passed away."

LIFE OF CHARLES SUMNER.

CHAPTER I.

Birth of Charles Sumner.—His Parents.—His Ancestry.

An event so common as the birth of a child makes little stir in the busy world; and even when Heaven is so lavish of its blessings as to send two little ones to the same home at once, it brings joy only to the limited circle of relatives and friends who can enter into the happiness of the parents.

On the 6th day of January, 1811, Charles Pinckney Sumner and Relief, his wife, were gladdened by the birth of their first children, Charles and Matilda.

The little new-comers to the great, strange

world were frail and tiny specimens of humanity.* But they were born to live; one of them to grow to maidenhood, and to grace her home a few short years, and then to pass away like a flower; the other, with a frame scarcely large enough to carry life, was to develop into a strong man, whose name was to be a power in the land for whose freedom his fathers had fought.

The men of Boston read their papers on that 6th day of January, and discussed the plans and the broils at the seat of government, just as the men of Boston do to-day. They passed and re-

* Mrs. Winslow, a very aged widow, a member of the First Baptist Church, living in Charter Street, gives the following interesting facts: —

The Sumner family were neighbors of hers at the time their twins were born. She knew Mrs. Sumner well, and speaks of her as an excellent, kind person, and remembers when she made a public profession of religion. She states that on the third day after the birth of the twins, she (Mrs. Winslow) said to a neighbor, "Let us go over and see Mrs. Sumner's babies." They went, and were shown into the chamber where they lay. They were the smallest infants she had ever seen, weighing but three pounds and a half each. The clothes which would have fitted ordinary babies were so much too large that the little ones were simply wrapped up, and not dressed, at that time. Mrs. Winslow says she took both babes in her arms, and held them while there.

The house in which they were born was in May Street (now Revere Street), on the site now occupied by the Bowdoin School building. The family afterwards removed to 20 Hancock Street, which was long their home, and where Mrs. Sumner died.

RESIDENCE OF MR. SUMNER'S FATHER, HANCOCK ST., BOSTON

passed the house where lay sleeping the future senator — the little Samson, who was to take so large a part in slaying the lion that was threatening the life of the nation, and in pulling down the gates with which oppression had guarded her strong cities.

One of God's anointed had come to do a mighty work for him and for humanity. But he had appeared without the prophecy of seer, or the heralding song of rejoicing angels; and he lay there as little an object of terror to Southern oppression, as was the Babe of Bethlehem, on the night of his advent, to the imperious rulers of the East. And yet the birth of Charles Sumner was a great event to Massachusetts, to America, and, more than all, to millions of slaves groaning under the lash and trembling before the auction-block.

America had broken her own fetters, but she had gathered up the links and welded them anew on the limbs of defenceless strangers. But she was not quite at ease in her oppression. She was beginning to hear the voice of God — to be afraid.

Some men affect to despise ancestry, and even regard it as Democratic to boast of a low origin.

Men of noble heart and earnest life have, indeed, come up to bless the world from coarse and ignorant families; but their success has been in spite, rather than in consequence, of their origin. The Scriptures, which teach the truest humility, hold up to us the great blessing of an upright and godly ancestry. Wealth does not settle the question of pedigree. The noble of the earth are those who are moved by high moral principle and unselfish aims, let their worldly condition be what it may. We often see nobility under the garb of toil, and meanness beneath purple and fine linen.

The greatest and grandest specimen of humanity that ever walked the earth (for Jesus was as truly human as divine) wrought with the tools of the artisan, ate the bread of toil, and slept the sleep of the laboring man, which is sweet.

Decker, an old English poet, says, —

> "the best of men
> That e'er wore earth's garb about him —
> A soft, meek, patient, humble, tranquil spirit;
> The first true gentleman that ever breathed."

None will deny that it is a great blessing to have come of a long line of noble and honorable men, who, having served God and their generation, left to their descendants an inheritance of moral, physical, and intellectual strength. In such a parentage Charles Sumner was singularly blessed.

The ancestor who emigrated to this country was William Sumner, a sturdy Puritan, born in Kent, England, in 1605, and "made a freeman," that is, admitted to the privileges of citizenship, in Massachusetts, in 1637. Next comes his son Roger, and his grandson Seth, and then Job, the grandfather, and Charles Pinckney, the father of the great senator who has just passed away.

Job Sumner was a student at Harvard when the revolutionary war broke out. He dropped his books, gave up all his literary plans, at his country's call, and, immediately after the battle of Lexington, joined the army, in which he rose to the rank of major, and where he remained until the close of the war.

Charles Pinckney Sumner was a graduate of Harvard, a gentleman of high culture and stern integrity, accomplished in all the etiquette of society in his day, and noted for his free and genial hospitality. He was a lawyer of eminence, and was for some years sheriff of Suffolk County. It was during his term that Boston was disgraced by the anti-slavery riots, which opened her eyes to the true character of the slave power, and brought her into the front ranks in the battle for freedom.

In the year 1810 Mr. Sumner married Relief Jacobs, daughter of a substantial farmer of Hanover, in "the Old Colony," who became the mother of nine children.

She had many and deep afflictions. Two of her beautiful children fell at her side in their early years; two were lost at sea; others died in their full manhood; and for many years she knew the heart of a widow. But she bore her sorrows with strong trust and fortitude. Rev. Mr. Foote, of King's Chapel, who was her pastor in her declining years, says of her,—

"Mrs. Sumner was a woman of retiring simplicity of life, but of strong and heroic traits of character; and those who knew her could trace in the senator's noblest characteristics a direct inheritance from her. The lofty and resolute sense of duty by which she was governed was strikingly illustrated by the following incident, which occurred while she was on her death-bed. A few days before she died, as a friend bent over her to receive what she supposed to be her dying message to her son, then at Washington, during the session of Congress, she caught these words from the failing lips: 'Tell him his country needs him more than his mother does now.' He returned, however, instantly, on receiving tidings of her fatal illness, and had the satisfaction of being with her when she died." *

* Matilda (twin sister with Charles) died in March, 1832, aged 21 years; Jane died in October, 1837, aged 17 years; Mary died in October, 1844, aged 22 years; Horace was drowned in the wreck of the ship Elizabeth, on Long Island, July 16, 1850, on his return from abroad; Albert was lost with his family in the wreck of the Lyonnais, November, 1856; Henry died at Orange, N. J., in 1856; George died October 6, 1863, in Boston, aged 46 years. One child, Mrs. Julia Hastings, of San Francisco, is still living.

George Sumner was a man of varied accomplishments. He enjoyed the advantages of study at the foreign universities of Berlin and Heidelberg, and travelled in Europe, Asia, and Africa. Like his brother Charles, he was much interested in international law, and in the political, social, and philanthropic institutions of different countries. He was a strong foe to war and slavery. He wrote in favor of the Philadelphia Penitentiary System. In connection with Dr. S. G. Howe, he introduced into the United States the education of idiots. He wrote articles, not only for American, but for English, French, and German periodicals. He spent many years abroad, and was often consulted by foreign governments on questions of political economy. De Tocqueville spoke of him "as knowing the different parties and politics of Europe much better than any European with whom he was acquainted."

In 1859, within less than five months, he gave one hundred and

One who knew Mrs. Sumner, and who saw her when her son was rising to eminence, noticed the motherly pride which she would not conceal. When asked how he gained so many and great acquirements, she replied, "Charles, when a boy was a good scholar, and always diligent in his studies." Her pride was not vanity. She did not boast of his genius, but only of application and industry. Mrs. Sumner died in June, 1866, aged eighty-one.

But not to his mother alone belongs the glory of rearing such a son for his country and for humanity. His father was not only a gentleman and a scholar, but also a philanthropist of the purest type, whose talents were not spent for self-adulation or ambition, but were laid on the altar to whose smoking fagots the boy that bore his name was a new torch, to alarm the oppressor, and burn up, like chaff, his imaginary wealth. He was a strong anti-slavery man, when anti-slavery men were few and their principles unpopular.

two lectures in towns and cities of the United States. On July 4 of that year he delivered the Annual Oration before the municipal authorities of Boston, which was spoken of as an "admirable address." The orator censured in severe terms the Dred Scott decision of Chief Justice Taney.

He was also a great advocate of peace principles. From "The Compass, a Poetical Performance," delivered by him at a Literary Exhibition, in September, 1795, at Harvard University, we extract the following, which shows the seed that bore such rich fruits of justice, philanthropy, and peace in the heart of his son: —

> "We antedate the time
> When futile war shall cease through every clime,
> No sanctioned slavery Afric's sons degrade,
> But equal rights shall equal earth pervade:
> When fearless Commerce, by the compass led,
> On every wave her sacred flag shall spread;
> With liberal course to either pole shall run,
> Or round the zodiac travel with the sun;
> No narrow treaty sell the boundless sea,
> Which Nature's charter to the world made free;
> When all the compact which this globe shall bind
> Shall be the mutual good of all mankind."

Charles Pinckney Sumner was the last high sheriff who wore the antique dress which was till then here, as in England, the badge of office; and it is said that it accorded well with his commanding person and dignified bearing.

Descended from a hardy stock of old Kentish yeomanry, men noted for their fine physical development, their powers of endurance, their skill in athletic games, and their bravery in battle, —

and in later times from men who, to these advantages and qualities, added the learning of the schools and the graces of society, — Charles Sumner belonged to the aristocracy of nature and of education, rather than to that of blood or of wealth.

Increase Sumner, an eloquent man, an able judge, and one of the governors of Massachusetts, shows the principles of the Sumners, in which this one, their brightest ornament, was reared. Just before the revolutionary war he wrote, —

"The man who, regardless of public happiness, is ready to fall in with base measures, and sacrifice conscience, honor, and his country merely for his own advancement, must (if not wretchedly hardened) feel a torture the intenseness of which nothing in this world can equal."

In one of his charges as judge, he said, "America furnishes one of the few instances of countries where the blessings of civil liberty and the rights of mankind have been the primary objects of their political institutions; in which the rich and poor are equally protected; where the rights of conscience are fully enjoyed; and where merit and ability can be the only claim to the favor of the public. May we not, then, pronounce that man destitute of the true principles of liberty, and unworthy the blessing of society, who does not, at all times, lend his aid to support and sustain a government?"

This man — who was a prince and a ruler in the land in early times — was a cousin of Charles Pinckney Sumner, and was the son of a yeoman of Roxbury, who was noted, like the others of the name, for his physical strength, and also for his untiring energy and ambition in the sphere where God had placed him.

CHAPTER II.

Childhood. — School Days. — Story of a Stick. — Enters Harvard University. — Severe Application to Study and Reading. — Trip to a Brighton Cattle Show.

CHARLES SUMNER does not come before us in his boyhood as one of those precocious little book-worms or baby philosophers who now and then startle the world as intellectual monstrosities, but as a vigorous boy, naturally studious and thoughtful.

His splendid physical development, which made him, in manhood, a Saul among his fellows, proves conclusively that he did not in boyhood sit bowed and moping over his school books without exercise or recreation. He ran, full of glee, down Beacon Hill, and over the Common, drawing his sled to the coasting-ground or carrying his boat to the pond; shouting and hallooing at his success, just as the boys of to-day do in the same play and at the same places.

A story is told of him that illustrates one trait of his character, which "grew with his growth and strengthened with his strength."

There had been a dispute between him and some other boys about a stick of which he had possession, and a sharp contest ensued. The world was full of sticks, but that particular one was his by right, and he meant to keep it.

The others pulled, but he tightened his little fists about it, and held bravely on. One of his antagonists then tried a new game. He caught up a stone, and began pounding his knuckles, sure that the pain would cause him to relax his grip.

But little Sumner pressed his lips together, and still held on. Blow after blow fell on the delicate hands till the blood began to flow.

At sight of this, the little assailant fled in terror, and left Sumner in possession of the precious stick, and of the consciousness of having maintained his rights.

Little Sumner attended both private and public schools in Boston until he was ten years of age.

He read history, which was his delight, and, without advice or urgency from any one, he bought with his spending-money a Latin Grammar and Reader, and had made some little proficiency in the rudiments of that language before his parents knew that the books were in his possession. He studied for his own pleasure, rather than that he might stand well in his classes.

In his eleventh year, he entered the Boston Latin School, where his diligence soon gave him a high standing, under the instruction of Benjamin Gould, an eminent man of that day in his profession. Here young Sumner took prizes for English composition and Latin poetry, and on graduating received the Franklin medal.

He entered Harvard when only fifteen years of age, a strong, finely-developed and elegant-looking boy, and gave himself up to hard study with as much earnestness and zeal as if there was no such thing as boyish play in the world.

We should naturally expect that a youth of such striking appearance and studious habits would become at once a prodigy in college. But it was not so. He seems to have been remarkable there only for his correct deportment and his severe application to his chosen studies.

His aim was not for the first place in his class, but for a thorough education; else he might have gone up with the light of the rocket, and then vanished in sudden darkness, as do not a few who are much talked of in college, but are never heard of afterwards.

He applied himself not alone to his text-books; he read very widely, storing his mind with the history and the literature of many lands, thus transplanting into his wondrous memory the flowers with which the writings and speeches of future years are graced.

To these pursuits, which were foreign to his class studies, he devoted the early hours of morning, pilfering no time from the requirements of the appointed course for studies more congenial to his taste.

He also read far into the night, and when his less studious companions returned late from Boston, where they had been on social visits or to public entertainments, they always saw the light in Sumner's window, reminding them that there was one earnest student who could not be drawn away from his books by the allurements of pleasure. He was so wedded to his studies as to have almost no time for what is called "society" by collegians.

There were at Harvard at the same time with him several men who have since become distinguished as reformers, philanthropists, and in the world of letters; men, with whom the boyish friendship of that time deepened into a strong and sympathetic love, which encouraged and strengthened him in his subsequent battles for the right.

While we have no record of remarkable brilliancy at college, we know that he was studying with a purpose, and also that he kept himself entirely aloof from the follies and vices which were then regarded as almost inseparable from college life, but which social advance is now putting in their right place. His natural dignity, as well as his high principles, kept him from everything that would wound others or degrade himself.

He was the same gentleman at heart then as afterwards in the Senate, when he had acquired that perfect knowledge of society and its subtile etiquette for which he was so remarkable.

At that early period he was as considerate as

he was in after years. He tried every action by the standard of right. For example, while he was ever kind and obliging to his college mates, and ready to do any one of them a favor, there was one positive exception — no lazy fellow could persuade him to help his preparation for the recitations in Greek and Latin by translating his lessons for him. He thought it *wrong* to encourage laziness. A worker himself, he was ready to help others work in a good cause; but farther he would not go. In after years he had little patience with shirks and shams. He was genuine, and he honored genuine worth as above all price.

The only time we hear of his breaking college rules was when, very desirous of attending a cattle show at Brighton, he set out with a friend without permission.

On their way, the truants unfortunately were overtaken by two gentlemen bound in the same direction, who proved to be their fathers!

"Why, Charles," asked Mr. Sumner in surprise, "how came you here?"

"I wanted to go to the cattle show," was the reply of the young culprit.

"Had you permission to leave your classes?" asked the father.

"No; but we shall lose no recitations by our absence," replied the student.

And, like wise men, the fathers made no further objections. So the boys saw the cattle, and got back to Cambridge in season to avoid any trouble with the faculty.

There was, doubtless, then, in his nature, the incipient seeds of that delight in cattle which made him in after years such an adept in the science of stock-raising — a branch of study so widely differing from his life's work.

CHAPTER III.

Sumner's Law Studies. — Literary Work. — His First Great Sorrow. — Seeking for a Compliment. — Students changing Plans. — Failing Health.

CHARLES SUMNER graduated from Harvard in 1830, being then nineteen years old.

The following year was spent at home in private study and reading, and in preparation for his next step in life.

He entered the Cambridge Law School in 1831. Judge Story was not long in discovering those rare qualities and that untiring diligence which afterwards made him so great a favorite with that eminent jurist.

It would seem that the literature and principles of his future profession, rather than its practice, were the alluring charm to him, and to these he applied himself with characteristic ardor, amounting almost to a passion.

He was never satisfied with accepting anything second-hand, but invariably went to the original sources for the facts and arguments.

He read Kent's Commentaries in a way peculiar to himself, carefully looking up and examining every case referred to.

He began his researches in the law far back in the rude Norman, proceeding downward to the most recent authorities.

So familiar was he with the Law Library at Cambridge (of which he was librarian), that it is said he could go into it in the dark, and take any book he wanted from a shelf.

His great power of acquiring and retaining knowledge soon distinguished him above his fellows.

While yet a student, Mr. Sumner became a contributor to the literature of his profession, and published several articles in the "American Jurist" and "Boston Law Quarterly," all of which were marked by deep research, breadth of thought, and subtile ingenuity, which gave great promise of future usefulness.

In 1832 Mr. Sumner met the first great sorrow of his life. The sister, whose being was almost one with his own, who had been his playmate in babyhood and in childhood, his admiration, his pride, and his good angel in youth and dawning manhood, a girl remarkable for her personal beauty and for her loveliness of character, was removed by death, leaving a void such as is seldom felt in the heart and the life of a man by the loss of a sister.

We can imagine how dark a shadow the wing of death cast over every page of his books, and how the brightness of the future he had pictured for himself faded, now that his other self was no longer there to sympathize in his labor and to triumph in his success. Their double heart was divided, with bitter pangs to the living; and even when the keenness of the pain had passed away, and time had healed — as it always does in mercy — the gaping wound, the memory of that sweet face and that pure life was enshrined, almost as an idol, in the heart of the great man, coming back to him in his dreams, and softening the spirit which was in danger of being hardened by intercourse with bitter foes and wavering friends in his mighty struggle for principle.

Like most brilliant and ambitious students,

Sumner was possessed by a strong love of approbation; so marked at this time as to amount to almost a weakness.

A classmate, now one of the leaders of the Suffolk Bar, relates the following, which shows that, high as he stood with his instructors, he was not above the reach of an occasional rebuff from them.

The two students were together one day in Sumner's room, when they saw Professor Ashmun approaching. Sumner playfully remarked, "Now I am going to get a compliment from the professor."

He gave his teacher a polite reception, and when he was seated, offered him a cigar. As soon as Professor Ashmun was in a happy mood, Sumner began by saying, "There is a lawyer down on the Cape who says he can beat any man in the state at special pleading, but that — Ashmun."

An expression of pleasure passed over the professor's countenance, and Sumner proceeded.

He passed his hand over his forehead, with an air of discouragement, and said, "As for myself, I feel that I don't know anything," and then paused for the expected reassuring compliment;

when, to the amazement of both, the professor cried out, in a stern voice, "No, you don't know anything; and what's more, you never will."

This rebuke was so unlooked for and so crushing, that, although he must have known that it was spoken in the spirit of a joke, Sumner felt it keenly. His classmate, seeing this, came to his relief by changing the subject. That classmate never knew him to fish for a compliment again while in the Law School.

Mr. Sumner had a classmate who was from one of our most cultivated and wealthy families, and with whom he was on terms of the closest intimacy.

The difference in their circumstances — although Mr. Sumner was by no means poor — was very great. Not long before his death, in speaking of that friend, who was still a friend, he said, "I well remember the feelings I had when ——'s mother used to drive over to Cambridge to see her son in her fine carriage, as my mother could not do."

This friend had at that time a high ambition for being a statesman, and used to dwell on his plans, when Sumner's desire was to be a jurist, with no dream of the popular favor or the popular fickleness which he was afterwards to enjoy and to suffer, and which cried for years, "A god has come down to us in the likeness of a man;" and again, "He hath a devil," and almost robbed him of the coveted name of "patriot."

The young aspirant for honor in the higher walks of law became a statesman, and he who desired to shine in the forum has filled the no less noble sphere of a philanthropist; and although both changed their plans, they wrought through life, hand in hand, and shoulder to shoulder, in the mighty work for liberty and equality, and the living one now mourns for the dead as for a brother.

Mr. Sumner's fine constitution was not proof against the heavy burdens he was laying upon it by his close and unremitting study. At the first peep of day he was poring over his books, which he never closed till the small hours of the next morning sounded out their warnings from the clocks in the towers. He confessed afterwards that he always studied eighteen hours out of the twenty-four; so we need not wonder, especially when we know that members of his family have died with pulmonary disease, that his health gave way, and that he at one time seemed drawing near to the grave, with every symptom of consumption. This involved a suspension of study, and months of quiet and rest; after which he was able again to return to his work at Cambridge.

CHAPTER IV.

Returning Health. — Graduates from the Law School. — Enters the Law Office of Rand and Fiske. — His Aim in Life. — A Winter in Washington. — Attentions from prominent Men at the Bar. — Editorial Work. — Admission to the Bar. — Testimony by a Fellow-Student. — Love of Approbation. — Declines a Professorship at the Law School.

WITH the passing years, Mr. Sumner gained that great physical strength and vigor for which he was remarkable through life.

On leaving the Law School, he entered the office of Rand and Fiske. Mr. Rand was a profound lawyer and a voracious reader of law books. The Hon. G. W. Warren, a fellow-student in that office, speaks of Mr. Sumner as diligently improving the rare opportunities there afforded him of perfecting his legal knowledge, and in particular of becoming acquainted with the latest English law publications, which Mr. Rand regularly procured from abroad.

Judge Story was now a frequent visitor at the office, and there he and Mr. Rand discussed the contents of these publications and other legal questions.

A mind so earnest and receptive as Sumner's of course drank in with avidity the opinions of these masters in the law; his special object being at this time to acquire a knowledge of the practice of the law, which was, as we have seen, much less attractive to him than the study of principles.

His ambition was still to be a jurist. In his eulogy on Judge Story, delivered some twelve years after this, he reveals his own aspirations. He says, "The function of a lawyer or judge — both *practising* law — is unlike that of a jurist, who, whether judge or lawyer, examines every principle in the light of science, and, while *doing* justice, seeks to widen and confirm the means of justice hereafter. . . .

"Such a character does not live for the present only, whether in time or place. Ascending above its temptations, yielding neither to the love of gain nor to the seductions of ephemeral praise, he perseveres in those serene labors which help to build the mighty dome of justice, beneath which all men are to seek shelter and peace."

With these views, Mr. Sumner studied as a philosopher rather than as a lawyer, and looked on the law not so much as it is, but as it should be. The common law, though in its spirit favoring personal freedom, originated in a comparatively rude period, and was based not so much on the principles of right and justice as on convenience and expediency; and its rules are often arbitrary.

Mr. Sumner, in his philosophical spirit, seeking for the foundation of rules and statutes in justice, would almost certainly have failed to attain the highest distinction in the technical practice of the profession. Such men as he have a grand and beneficent work to do, which is more and more inspiring the higher class of students of the law, namely, to bring statutes and rules into closer harmony with the principles of right, and to infuse into the whole practice a higher and nobler spirit.

Although Mr. Sumner was, a few years after

this, summoned from his chosen path of serene speculation to the public strife of politics, yet he carried with him his lofty ideal of justice, and, as a statesman, rather than as a politician, gave the weight of his great and well-furnished mind to bring the national statutes and practice, both in our domestic and foreign relations, up to the standard of eternal right. This was his test of all laws and all measures.

About this time he spent a winter in Washington, little dreaming of the scenes through which he was there to pass, or the mighty work he was to accomplish in the halls of legislation. His personal presence and fine address won friends and admirers for him, young as he was, among the lights of the bar.

Much attention was shown him by the judges and practitioners in the Supreme Court. Even Chief Justice Marshall extended to him civilities very unusual for a man in his position to tender to a mere law student. He doubtless saw his future greatness through the veil of his youth.

Before being admitted to the bar, Sumner became chief editor of the "American Jurist," and conducted it with singular ability for a period of three years, doing much of the writing himself; bringing forth in his reviews of law books the varied stores of learning he had been gathering during his early and late hours of research at Cambridge.

He was only twenty-three years of age when, in 1834, he was admitted to the bar in Worcester, with the reputation of being the most learned young lawyer in the country.

He now opened an office in Boston, and set sail on the sea of life with a favoring breeze, and with a strong hand on the helm.

Not long after this he became reporter of the United States Circuit Court, and published three volumes of reports, the decisions being those of Judge Story, and known as "Sumner's Reports."

He had now formed an idea of going abroad, and, with this in view, held himself aloof from any engagements that would interfere with his purpose.

During three years he filled the place of Judge Story at the Law School, hearing recitations (for lectures had not yet been introduced in the Law School), and also performed, for a time, the duties of Professor Greenleaf, in his absence.

All this time he was unremitting in his labors, making constitutional law and the law of nations a specialty.

Soon after his service in the Law School, he was invited to a professorship at Harvard; and on his declining to accept it, the offer was repeated, with the additional inducement of a chair in the law faculty.

But much as Mr. Sumner appreciated the honor and usefulness of the position, he shrank from confining himself to those regular duties of a professorship which would interfere with the course of study and travel he had laid out for himself.

A lawyer, who was a student of Sumner's at this time, speaks of him as an admirable teacher, kind and fascinating in his manner, and possessed of a natural dignity, which had in it no trace of affectation. His ample store of learning, his rare power of communication, and his genial spirit won the respect and affection of the students. There was observable at the same time a measure of vanity, which, in his case, seemed to heighten one's estimate of his character, because it revealed that simplicity and truthfulness which could not conceal the pardonable weakness. In his subsequent life we shall have frequent occasion to see the real greatness of the man in that, while so desirous of the good opinion of others, he could sacrifice the dearest friendships and the most enticing social position, and incur odium and contempt, for the sake of his convictions; so overpowering was his regard for truth and justice.

We cannot doubt but the stand which he felt compelled to take, at different times in after years, against the wishes and expectations of his friends, and against his own seeming good, cost his sensitive spirit many a pang of agony; for he was not the cold, calculating, overbearing man that some have taken him to be. He loved to stand high in public esteem, to be caressed and honored; but he loved more to be true to conscience and to God.

Those who knew him in his youth and early manhood, who saw him in his most familiar hours, when his true character appeared without any temptation to disguise, assure us that he was singularly simple hearted and guileless. And as he was in his youth, so he was, in all his subsequent career. In this view we can hardly call his love of approbation an infirmity.

There are those who affect to disregard what others think of them, and glory in their independence of public opinion. But this, so far from being a virtue, or even an infirmity, is a grievous defect, and may become a vice. It is a sign of nobleness to desire the good opinion of the good; and he who really disregards it has a mean and despicable character. When, as in the case of Lord Bacon, vanity becomes an idol, demanding the incense which should be offered to honor and justice, it deserves only reprobation and contempt. But when a man is doing right, and desires that other men should know and appreciate his efforts, and honor him for them, it is, to say the least, pardonable, especially when his work, and not himself alone, is kept prominent.

CHAPTER V.

Visit to Europe.—Letter of Judge Story.—Incident in Westminster Hall.—Testimony of English Judges.—Baron Parke's Appreciation of Mr. Sumner's Learning.—In Paris.—In Germany.—In Italy.

FORTY years ago foreign travel for the purposes of enjoyment and study was the lot of a favored few, and not, as now, an event in the life of almost every literary and professional man.

In the fall of 1837, Mr. Sumner, then twenty-six years old, carried out his long-cherished plan of visiting Europe.

His previous studies had formed a fitting preparation for foreign travel. He was well read in the literature, the history, and the political institutions of England and the countries on the continent. In matters of art he had formed a taste, and knew what were the masterpieces and where they were to be found.

Full of scholarly enthusiasm, he longed to visit the world-renowned universities of Europe, to see and converse with its great men, — its scholars, its jurists, its statesmen, to examine its libraries and art treasures, and to inform himself more thoroughly as to the peculiar features of its civilization. The reputation for scholarship which he carried with him, his gentlemanly bearing, his unassuming modesty, his rare conversational powers, and the valuable letters he took from Judge Story and other gentlemen of European fame, gave him at once such access to the highest circles of society as is rarely enjoyed by so young a man in a foreign land.

The following is an extract from one of Judge Story's letters addressed to a gentleman in London, dated November 3, 1837: —

"Mr. Sumner is a practising lawyer at the Boston bar, of very high reputation for his years, and already giving the promise of the most eminent distinction in his profession; his literary and judicial attainments are truly extraordinary.

"His private character, also, is of the best kind for purity and propriety; but to accomplish himself more thoroughly in the great objects of his profession — not merely to practise, but to extend the boundaries in the science of law, — I am anxious that he should possess the means of visiting the courts of Westminster Hall under favorable auspices; and I shall esteem it a personal favor if you can give him any facilities in this particular."

Mr. Sumner first visited England, where he spent nearly a year, improving every moment in study, in careful observation of men and things, in attendance upon the debates of Parliament, the courts, and scientific associations; finding elegant and most congenial relaxation in the circles of the great and titled, where he was ever welcome.

More than once he was invited to sit with the judges in Westminster Hall. At one time, during the progress of a trial, a point arose where there seemed to be no precedent. The lord chief justice, turning to Sumner, said, "Can you inform me whether there are any American decisions upon the point in question?" "No, your lordship," was the reply; "but this point has been decided in your lordship's own court in such a case," giving him the citation. This remarkable readiness gave him éclat throughout the kingdom. The above is related by a former classmate, now a gentleman of standing in this city.

The letters which so close an observer wrote to his friends at home must have been full of interest. That they were of this character appears from the following letter written by Judge Story to Mr. Sumner, August 11, 1838:—

"I have received all your letters, and have devoured them with unspeakable delight. All the family have heard them read aloud, and all join in their expressions of pleasure. You are now exactly where I should wish you to be—among the educated, the literary, the noble, and, though last, not least, the learned of England, of good Old England, our mother-land, God bless her!"

Mr. Sumner spent several months in Paris, where, as in England, he was industriously employed in study and in converse with men eminent in literature and law. It was here that he met our distinguished countryman, Mr. Wheaton, with whom he had much conversation upon international law, and to whom he suggested the plan of the great work on that subject afterwards written by that eminent jurist.

It was there that he prepared an essay upon a subject then much discussed in foreign circles, namely, the north-eastern boundary of the United States, which was then in dispute between this country and Great Britain. The paper was, like all Mr. Sumner's efforts, exhaustive and satisfactory, and attracted much attention at home and abroad.

In Germany, and in particular at Heidelberg, he spent some time, and formed the acquaintance of eminent jurists and scholars, such as Savigny, Humboldt, and Ritter.

His visit to Italy was to him one of peculiar delight. It is said that here he used to spend all the day in the libraries and galleries of art, and nearly all the night in study, perfecting himself in the rich literature which had attracted Milton before him, a young and enthusiastic student like himself. One can easily imagine the pleasure which such classic scenes, where the ancient and the modern combine to make Italy, and especially Rome, so conspicuous in the annals of the world, in poetry, history, law, government, and art, must have awakened in Mr. Sumner's mind. He had all the tastes and instincts of a scholar, and in the serene pursuits of literature and law he was here, in his own purpose, laying the foundation of a career devoted to the quiet enlargement of human knowledge and human happiness.

Little did he then imagine that this cultivation of literature and art was to furnish but the bright gilding of a sterner life, engaged in heroic battling with the greatest wrong of the age, as the foremost champion of the poor and oppressed.

But so it was appointed, that Liberty, outraged in millions of slaves, was preparing for herself a leader, like Moses, "learned in all the wisdom" of the age, who should compel respect and consideration for a cause then intensely unpopular.

The reputation which Mr. Sumner left behind him in England appears from the following incident, referred to in Loring's "Hundred Boston Orators": —

On an insurance question before the Court of Exchequer, one of the counsel having cited an American case, Baron Parke, one of the oldest of the English judges, asked him from what book he quoted. "Sumner's Reports," he replied. "Is that," asked Baron Rolfe, "the Mr. Sumner who was once in England?" Being answered in the affirmative, Baron Parke replied, "We shall not consider it entitled to less attention because reported by a gentleman whom we all knew and respected."

The year after his return from England, the "London Quarterly Review," alluding to his visit, said, "He presents in his own person a decisive proof that an American gentleman, without official rank or wide-spread reputation, by dint of courtesy, candor, an entire absence of pretension, an appreciating spirit, and a cultivated mind, may be received on a perfect footing of equality in the best circles, social, political, and intellectual; which, be it observed, are hopelessly inaccessible to the itinerant note-taker, who never gets beyond the outskirts of the show-houses."

In the year 1840, Mr. Sumner returned home. As might be expected from his antecedents and his rare personal accomplishments, he was a welcome guest in the most refined circles. The literary notables of Boston and vicinity were proud of his acquaintance and friendship.

His foreign studies, especially in literature and art, had rendered the practice of the law still less attractive to him than before; and he was now chiefly known as an elegant scholar, and a devotee of the law in its literature and principles. His edition of Vesey's Reports, in twenty volumes, published from 1844 to 1846, show the bent of his mind and the affluence of his learning.

CHAPTER VI.

State of the Country. — Slave-Trade. — Missouri Compromise. — Change in Southern Sentiment. — Opposition at the North. — Change at the North. — Anti-Slavery Feeling.

Before entering upon the public life of Mr. Sumner, it will be proper to consider the state of the country, as regards the institution of slavery, previous to that period; for to the overthrow of that system his public life was mainly devoted. Where was the slavery question when he took it to his great heart?

Three years before his birth, the foreign slave-trade had ended. As it was still clandestinely carried on, the importation of slaves into the United States was, twelve years after, declared to be piracy, and made punishable with death. But the domestic slave-trade — that is, between the slave states — was still carried on, and with increasing vigor. It was attended with many horrors. Many free negroes fell a prey to kidnappers, and were reduced to slavery. No less than fifteen thousand slaves were annually imported from the more northern of the slave states into the distant South. Virginia, especially, became the "negro-raising state for other states."

After the war of 1812, "the demand for slave labor greatly increased, and the price of slaves was much advanced." The conscience of the South, which, in spite of slavery, had been, to no small extent, on the side of freedom, began rapidly to harden. As slavery became more profitable, it was viewed with less abhorrence, and its removal, which had been talked of even at the South as a most desirable event, at some future day, was now indefinitely postponed. Ere long slavery was declared to be a blessing to the negro race. It was a "patriarchal," it was a "missionary" institution. By these cheats practised upon conscience, the South became more and more wedded to slavery. The great curse of our nation was gaining new strength every day.

When young Sumner was nine years old, an important event occurred, which afterwards, when the lad had grown to be a man, and was a senator at Washington, became the occasion of calling forth his indignant eloquence. We refer to the Missouri Compromise, as it was called, which was effected in 1820. This Compromise was the result of a mighty struggle between the free North and the slaveholding South. The Territory of Missouri had applied for admission as a state. The North wished to exclude slavery, the South to allow it. The contest was waged long and fiercely. It ended in a compromise, by which something was granted to freedom, but much more was gained by slavery. Missouri came in as a slave state, and slavery was forever prohibited north of thirty-six degrees thirty minutes north latitude; but this did not express the whole result. The Compromise was a real triumph for the South. It was simply a politic measure on their part for effecting a new extension of slavery. When another extension was desired, a new compromise could be concocted, or the old one annulled — which was actually done in 1850.

"The Missouri struggle, which so aroused and called into action the vital forces of freedom and slavery, demonstrated the startling fact that the race of Southern statesmen who believed slavery to be a temporary evil, to be abolished at some future day, and in some unforeseen way, had passed away." Even Jefferson, who had pictured the evils of slavery in the darkest colors, and who "had once prepared a plan for the prohibition of slavery in all the territory from the Lakes to the Gulf, became alarmed, and shrunk appalled before the fury of the strife, declaring that it fell upon his ear 'like the fire-bell at midnight.'" * So with Madison and Monroe.

On the other hand, the people of the entire North, without respect to party, were aroused by this new attitude of the slave power. They were alarmed by the further extension of a system which they had fondly hoped would gradually disappear. The future assumed a more gloomy aspect.

"The legislature of Pennsylvania unanimously opposed the existence of slavery in Missouri. Their resolutions declared 'that they are persuaded that to open the fertile region of the West to a servile race would tend to increase their number beyond all past example,

* Rise and Fall of the Slave Power in America, by Henry Wilson.

would open a new and steady market for the lawless venders of human flesh, and render all schemes for obliterating this foul blot upon the American character useless and unavailing.' . . . And they invoked the several states, 'by the duty they owe to the Deity, by the veneration which they entertain for the memories of the founders of the republic, and by a tender regard for posterity, to protest against its adoption, to refuse to covenant with crime, and to limit the range of an evil that already hangs in awful boding over so large a portion of the Union.' "

These remonstrances against the organization of new slave states, and the extension of the curse of slavery, were sincere and earnest; but when, after a struggle, victory fell to the South, the moral effect was disastrous. The free sentiment of the North, thus baffled and humiliated, began to show signs of weakness and discouragement. "Freedom became timid, hesitating, yielding; slavery became bolder, more aggressive, and more dominating. Freedom retreated from one lost position to another; slavery advanced from conquest to conquest. Several years of unremitted despotism of the slave power followed the consummation of the Missouri Compromise. The dark spirit of slavery swayed the policy of the republic. Southern legislatures repealed the more humane acts of their slave codes, . . . and enacted statutes still more inhuman." But the spirit of freedom and humanity was still alive and growing in many hearts. Amidst general defection there was a precious remnant. There were men and women who learned their duty at a higher source than shifting public opinion, who listened to the "still small voice" of God, the Father of all. Their hearts were saddened — overwhelmed by the condition of the country. The cries of millions of slaves were to them an irresistible appeal for help. They pondered the question of duty, they prayed for light and strength, and then they went fearlessly forward in open and direct resistance to slavery. To human sight theirs was an unequal, almost profitless task. They were a handful of weak, obscure individuals, against a power which seemed well nigh omnipotent. But they were inspired and sustained by a serene faith in the ultimate triumph of truth.

Among the pioneers of direct anti-slavery effort, Benjamin Lundy, a native of New Jersey, of Quaker parentage, deserves the foremost place. He was a true philanthropist — tender-hearted, self-sacrificing, fearless, and yet prudent. "His heart was troubled at the sad condition of the slave. He enjoyed, he said, no peace of mind, and came to the conclusion that he must not only feel, but act, for the suffering bondmen. Calling a few friends together at his house, he unbosomed his feelings. An anti-slavery organization was formed, called 'the Union Humane Society.'"

This was in 1815, when Charles Sumner was a boy of four years. Six years later, in 1821, Lundy commenced, in Ohio, a monthly paper, The Genius of Universal Emancipation. In 1824 he transferred his paper to Baltimore. In 1828, on a visit to the Eastern States, he accomplished perhaps the greatest work of his life; he formed the acquaintance, in Boston, of a young man of twenty-three, and won him at once to his views. The young man was William Lloyd Garrison.

Charles Sumner was then in his second college year, seventeen years of age.

When Lundy returned to Baltimore, he did not

forget young Garrison. Evidently the acquaintance had deeply impressed his mind. He came back to Boston in search of his friend. But Garrison had left the city, and was editing a paper in Vermont. Thither Lundy pursued him. Mr. Garrison, afterwards writing of this visit, said, "He had taken his staff in hand, and come all the way to the Green Mountains. He came to lay it on my conscience and my soul that I should join him in this work of seeking the abolition of slavery." Lundy prevailed. The next year they joined hands in Baltimore in the warfare against slavery. Mr. Garrison outstripped his partner — not in devotion to the cause of emancipation, but in the fiery energy with which he assailed slavery. "In his first issue, he insisted on immediate and unconditional emancipation as the right of the slave and the duty of the master, and disclaimed all temporizing, all make-shifts, all compromises, condemning colonization, and everything else that involved or implied affiliation or sympathy with slaveholders." The Democratic slave-trade he denounced as "Democratic piracy." He branded as pirates the men — calling them by name — who carried on this traffic between Baltimore and New

Orleans. The result was a fine, and imprisonment for forty-nine days. Released by the generosity of a friend, who paid the fine and costs, Mr. Garrison returned to Boston, to resume his weapons against slavery.

CHAPTER VII.

"The Liberator" established by Mr. Garrison.— Its Boldness.—Excitement at the South.— Demand on the Mayor of Boston.

WHILE Mr. Sumner was engaged in his quiet studies, the year after his graduation from college, Mr. Garrison, six years his senior, commenced the publication of The Liberator, in Boston. The first number appeared in January, 1831.

The history of this newspaper teaches us "not to despise the day of small things." No beginning could be more humble. No funds, not a single subscriber, the partner, Mr. Knapp, who was the printer, as poor as the editor, "a dingy room of sixteen feet square, at once his sanctum, workshop, and home." What could be more unpromising or insignificant? But behind all this poverty and meanness was an ardent, indomitable soul, conscious of a great mission, resolved to be heard.

We have seen Mr. Garrison's spirit, truth-loving and fearless, in Baltimore. From prison he came to Boston to deal heavier blows against the greatest wrong of the age. The establishment of The Liberator was the inauguration of a new era in the anti-slavery cause. It was the era of calling things by their right names. Listen to the introductory announcement:

"During my recent tour for the purpose of exciting the minds of the people by a series of discourses on the subject of slavery, every place that I visited gave fresh evidence of the fact that a greater revolution in public sentiment was to be effected in the free states — and particularly in New England — than at the South. I found contempt more bitter, opposition more active, detraction more relentless, prejudice more stubborn, and apathy more frozen than among slaveholders themselves. Of course there were individual exceptions to the contrary. This state of things affected but did not dishearten me. I determined, at every hazard, to lift up the standard of emancipation in the eyes of the nation, within sight of Bunker Hill, and in the birthplace of liberty. That standard is now unfurled; and long may it float, unhurt by the spoliations of time or the missiles of a desperate foe; yea, till every chain be broken, and every bondman set free. Let Southern oppressors tremble; let their abettors tremble; let all the enemies of the persecuted blacks tremble.

"I am aware that many object to the severity of my language; but is there not cause for severity? I will be as harsh as truth, and as uncompromising as justice. On this subject I do not wish to think, or speak, or write with moderation. No! No! Tell a man whose house is on fire to give a moderate alarm; tell him to moderately rescue his wife from the hands of the ravisher; tell the mother to gradually extricate her babe from the fire into which it has fallen; but urge me not to use moderation in a cause like the present. *I am in earnest; I will not equivocate; I will not excuse; I will not retreat an inch.* AND I WILL BE HEARD! The apathy of the people is enough to make every statue leap from its pedestal, and to hasten the resurrection of the dead.

"It is pretended that I am retarding the cause

of emancipation by the coarseness of my invective, and the precipitancy of my measures. *The charge is not true.* On this question, my influence, humble as it is, is felt at this moment to a considerable extent; and it shall be felt in coming years — not perniciously, but beneficially — not as a curse, but as a blessing; and POSTERITY WILL BEAR WITNESS THAT I WAS RIGHT. I desire to thank God that He enables me to disregard the fear of man, which bringeth a snare, and to speak truth in its simplicity and power; and I here close with this dedication: —

'Oppression! I have seen thee, face to face,
And met thy cruel eye and cloudy brow;
But thy soul-withering glance I fear not now —
For dread to prouder feelings doth give place
Of deep abhorrence! Scorning the disgrace
Of slavish knees that at thy footstool bow
I also kneel — but with far other vow
Do hail thee and thy herd of hirelings base;
I swear, while life-blood warms my throbbing veins,
Still to oppose and thwart, with heart and hand,
Thy brutalizing sway — till Afric's chains
Are burst, and Freedom rules the rescued land,
Trampling Oppression and his iron rod.
Such is the vow I take — so help me God!'"

When were braver words ever spoken — to be followed up by corresponding words and acts?

When accused of using hard language, he replied: "I admit the charge. I have not been able to find a soft word to describe villany, or to identify the perpetrator of it. The man who makes a chattel of his brother — what is he? The man who keeps back the hire of his laborers by fraud — what is he? They who prohibit the circulation of the Bible — what are they? They who compel three millions of men and women to herd together, like brute beasts — what are they? They who sell mothers by the pound, and children in lots to suit purchasers — what are they? I care not what terms are applied to them, provided they do apply. If they are not thieves, if they are not tyrants, if they are not men-stealers, I should like to know what is their true character, and by what names they may be called. It is as mild an epithet to say that a thief is a thief, as it is to say that a spade is a spade."

Mr. Garrison had said, "I will be heard;" "Let Southern oppressors tremble." He was heard, and that speedily. The sound of his trumpet, issuing from that dingy attic, reached even Southern ears. There was alarm throughout Slavedom. Southern fears at once comprehended the full measure of this new foe. While as yet quite unnoticed at the North, he was famous at the South. Southern ears, accustomed to alarms, were quicker to discern coming danger. There was something in these clear, ringing tones that told of "a Daniel come to judgment." There was a spirit in the man which they felt could not be intimidated or blinded. Accordingly, measures were taken to avert the threatened peril.

"Before the close of the first year, the Vigilance Association of Columbia, S. C., 'composed of gentlemen of the first respectability,' offered a reward of fifteen hundred dollars for the apprehension and conviction of any white person detected in circulating in that state 'the newspaper called The Liberator.'"

The corporation of Georgetown, D. C., passed an ordinance rendering it penal for any free person of color to take from the post-office the paper, published at Boston, called The Liberator, the punishment for each offence to be twenty dollars fine, or thirty days imprisonment. In case the offender was not able to pay the fine, or the fees for imprisonment, he was to be sold into slavery for four months. The grand jury of Raleigh, N. C., at the instigation of the attorney general, made an indictment against the editor and publisher of The Liberator for its circulation in that county. The legislature of Georgia passed an act offering a reward of five thousand dollars for the arrest, prosecution, and trial to conviction, under the laws of the state, of the editor or publisher of a certain paper called The Liberator, published in the town of Boston, and State of Massachusetts.

Truly compliments were showered upon our poor editor!

A certain Southern magistrate thought to beard the Northern lion in his very den. He requested the Hon. Harrison Gray Otis, "the wealthy and aristocratic Mayor of Boston," *to suppress The Liberator.* The mayor had probably never heard of, certainly never read, the paltry abolition sheet. But, as a good and faithful peacemaker, he set about the task demanded of him. In due time he reported that his officers "had ferreted out the paper and its editor, whose office was an obscure hole, his only visible auxiliary a negro boy, its supporters a few *insignificant* persons of all colors," &c., &c.; and he assured the complainant that there was no possible cause for alarm! The South knew better, and kept up a standing premium on his head.

CHAPTER VIII.

Fears of Slaveholders. — Slave Conspiracy at Charleston. — Nat Turner's Insurrection. — His Execution. — Abolitionists in the Virginia Legislature. — Pro-Slavery at the North. — American Anti-Slavery Society. — Riots in New York and elsewhere. — Mr. Garrison Mobbed in Boston. — Wendell Phillips. — Mobs. — Elijah P. Lovejoy. — A human Ear. — Rifling the Mails. — Right of Petition. — John Quincy Adams.

THE South was disturbed not only by Northern fanatics; within in her own border, the spirit of liberty, which dwells in every human heart, an inextinguishable spark from heaven, not seldom roused her bondmen to recover their stolen rights. As far back as 1812, John Randolph, of Virginia, in opposing the proposed invasion of Canada, lest it might expose the Southern coast to British troops, and stir up a servile insurrection, said, "While talking of Canada, we have too much reason to shudder for our own safety at home. I speak from facts, when I say that the night bell never tolls for fire in Richmond, that the frightened mother does not hug her infant more closely to her bosom, not knowing what may have happened."

In Charleston, S. C., years after, an extensive conspiracy was formed for murdering the whites, and only the fortunate betrayal of the plot, almost at the last moment, by a female slave to her mistress, to whom and her family she was much attached, prevented its execution. The inhabitants of that city trembled when they learned how very near to them had come a terrible tragedy.

A slaveholder said to the writer, many years since, "We are dwelling on the sides of a volcano, which may burst upon us at any moment."

In 1831 occurred the Southampton insurrection in Virginia. It was headed by Nat Turner, a religious fanatic, who had been possessed from childhood with the idea that he was a prophet of the Lord, charged, like Moses, with the mighty work of delivering his people from bondage. His austerity of life and manners, and the magic power he exercised over his associates, influenced not a few of them to believe that he was indeed divinely inspired. In his statement before his execution, he said, "On the 12th day of May, 1828, I heard a loud noise in the heavens; and the Spirit instantly appeared to me, and said, 'The serpent is loosened, and Christ has laid down the yoke he bore for the sins of men, and I should take it up and fight against the serpent, for the time is fast approaching when the first shall be last and the last shall be first, and that by signs in the heaven that He would make known to me when I should commence the great work, and until the first sign should appear, I should conceal it from the knowledge of men.'"

The eclipse of February, 1831, he regarded as the token that the seal was removed from his lips, and that he was to call his forces together, slay the whites around them, and so give liberty to the enslaved. This was to take place on the 4th of July; but he fell sick in view of the awful task laid upon him, and the day passed by. But "the sign" appeared again, and on the 21st of August he and some fifty associates, mounted, and armed with guns, swords, axes, and clubs, went from house to house, and beginning with the owner of Nat Turner, massacred some sixty whites. They were, however, soon fired upon. As the result of the insurrection, one hundred negroes were either shot or captured.

The whole state was thrown into alarm, which ran like wildfire through all the slave states.

The next session of the legislature of Virginia was occupied with speeches, and plans, and arguments, called forth by this shocking event. Governor Floyd asserted that the plans for treason, insurrection, and murder had been designed and matured by unrestrained and designing fanatics in the neighboring states. He also denounced the negro preachers as instigators of revolt, and expressed his conviction that the safety of the public required that they should be silenced, and the free people of color banished from the state.

Petitions now began to pour into the legislature. Some of them were from slaveholders, praying for the removal of the free negroes; and others from the Quakers, asking for the emancipation of the slaves.

The discussions which followed woke up a spirit little looked for, and developed the fact that there were many anti-slavery slaveholders in the body. One member asserted that "the free negro population was a nuisance," but added, "There is another and a greater nuisance — slavery itself." He called the system "the greatest curse that God, in his wrath, had ever inflicted on a people." He asserted that men were forced to lock their doors at night and to open them in the morning to let their servants in to light the fires, with a pistol in their hand, and said, "Under such circumstances, life is a burden, and it were better to seek a home in some distant realm, and leave the graves of our fathers, than endure so precarious a condition."

Another member called slavery "the greatest curse ever inflicted upon the state," while yet another, using still stronger language, spoke of "its irresistible tendency to undermine and destroy everything like virtue and morality in the community," and declared that the purpose of the master was to see that the ignorance of his slaves shall be as profound as possible; and he vowed to do henceforth all in his power to restore to this oppressed people, their God-given rights. Another member called slavery "the bitterest drop from the chalice of the destroying angel."

It might seem that Virginia, at least, was on the eve of an act of emancipation. But the anti-slavery sentiment, which was so strong in Western Virginia, among the mountains, where freedom is wont to dwell, was overpowered by the eastern portion of the state, where lived the great slaveholders. The danger from which they had just escaped made these men only the more fanatical in their defence of slavery, and the more bitter in their hostility to those who sought its overthrow. New safeguards must be thrown around the "patriarchal" institution, new and more stringent laws enacted, a sharper watch maintained against abolition emissaries, and the national government made to take slavery more directly under its protection.

The free North, united to the South by social, political, commercial, and ecclesiastical ties, departed, to a fearful extent, from her better traditions, and joined in the crusade against abolitionists. "Great is Diana of the

Ephesians!" Great and ever to be defended is American slavery!

From that time onward, the opposition to anti-slavery increased in intensity both at the North and South. For several years mob-law had the ascendency. Free speech was put under the ban. Slavery must not be mentioned in sermons and orations, except in terms of commendation or extenuation. The press was muzzled. Public prayers for those who were in bonds was treason against the government. These mandates of slavery were enforced with unrelenting rigor. Abolitionists were the objects of constant abuse, and often their lives were in peril.

But, nothing daunted, these peaceable friends of human liberty resolved to proceed to more effective measures in the cause to which they had sacredly sworn themselves. In the winter of 1833, a convention assembled in Philadelphia for the formation of an American Anti-slavery Society. This meeting has been recently described in a very graphic manner by John G. Whittier, himself an active participator in the proceedings. Sixty-two delegates were in attendance, among whom were Beriah Green, William Lloyd Garrison, Samuel J. May, Lewis Tappan, and John Rankin.

The society was organized under circumstances of peculiar solemnity. Their work completed, the president, the Rev. Mr. Green, addressed the members, as they were about to separate, in touching and prophetic words. "Brethren," he said, "it has been good to be here. In this hallowed atmosphere I have been revived and refreshed. . . . But we must now retire from these influences and breathe another atmosphere. The chill hoar-frost will be upon us. *The storm and tempest will rise, and the waves of persecution will dash against our souls.* Let us be prepared for the worst. Let us fasten ourselves to the throne of God as with hooks of steel. . . . Let us be assured that our only hope in grappling with the bony monster is in an Arm that is stronger than ours. Let us fix our gaze on God, and walk in the light of his countenance. If our cause be just, — and we know it is, — his omnipotence is pledged to its triumph. Let this cause be entwined around the very fibres of our hearts. Let our hearts grow to it, so that nothing but death can sunder the bond."

Mr. Whittier adds, "He ceased, and then, amidst a silence broken only by the deep-drawn breath of emotion in the assembly, lifted up his voice in a prayer to Almighty God, full of fervor and feeling, imploring his blessing and sanctification upon the convention and its labors. And with the solemnity of this supplication in our hearts, we clasped hands in farewell, and went forth each man to his place of duty, not knowing the things that should befall us, as individuals, but with a confidence, never shaken by abuse and persecution, in the certain triumph of our cause."

Thus was born into life the first national anti-slavery organization.

The "storm and tempest" did rise. There had been pro-slavery mobs in New York city. The cry was raised in 1833, "Ten thousand dollars for Arthur Tappan." Valuable men were those abolitionists! But in 1834 the "waves of persecution" dashed more furiously. An anti-slavery celebration on the 4th of July was broken up by ruffians, crying, "Treason, treason!

Hurrah for the Union!" Alas that the United States were reduced to the humiliation of having such defenders! The leading journals of the city praised the rioters, who, for several days, committed their outrages unrebuked. At midnight, on the 9th, the dwelling of Lewis Tappan was broken open by a mob, his furniture carried into the street and consigned to the flames. The next day several churches had their doors and windows broken; one was "badly shattered, and one nearly destroyed, as were a school-house for colored children, and many dwellings inhabited by negroes. *None of the rioters were ever punished.*" It was a reign of terror. In Philadelphia there was a three-days' riot, in which the colored people suffered terribly by assaults upon their persons and dwellings.

New England was disgraced by similar scenes; for the slave-fiend had poisoned the moral atmosphere of the whole country. In Massachusetts, at Worcester, in 1835, an anti-slavery lecturer was assaulted in the midst of the meeting. Similar disturbances occurred in many villages. At Boston, October 21, 1835, a large and *most respectable* mob, composed in good part of merchants, assailed a meeting of the Female Anti-slavery Society, while its president was at prayer, and dispersed it.* Brave men were they! Mr. Garrison, being discovered, "was seized, a rope put round him, his hat knocked off his head and cut in pieces, and his clothes torn from his body. Dragged through Wilson's Lane into State Street, he was rescued by the mayor, his posse, and several respectable citizens, and taken into the mayor's room in the Old State House. From this place he was conveyed in a carriage to Leverett Street Jail, to save him from the fury of the mob." In order to effect Mr. Garrison's admission to the jail, the kind-hearted deputy-sheriff, Mr. Parkman, got out a warrant against him as "a disturber of the peace." Mr. Parkman attempted to get into the carriage with the *criminal*, but could not for the crowd. Hastening to his own carriage, he fortunately reached the jail just as Mr. Garrison arrived. The warrant was presented, the jail door was thrown quickly open, and Mr. Garrison was safe from the howling mob. There he remained for the night. As he was a prisoner for no crime, he could not be detained,

* The American Conflict, by Horace Greeley.

and the next day an order was issued for his appearance before the court, to secure his release. But it was not considered safe that so much publicity should be given to the affair; and accordingly, as Mr. Garrison could not go to the court, the court came to him! The judge went to the jail, and informed Mr. Garrison that he was free to go "as a blameless citizen." But before departing, he inscribed these words upon the walls of the prison: "William Lloyd Garrison was put into this cell on Monday afternoon, October 21, 1835, to save him from the violence of a respectable and influential mob, who sought to destroy him for preaching the abominable and dangerous doctrine that all men are created equal, and that all oppression is odious in the sight of God."

Among the spectators of that riot of the 21st was a young lawyer, of rare gifts, and of high promise — Wendell Phillips. Up to that day he had had no thought of linking himself with the abolitionists. His only ambition was eminence in his profession or as a statesman. That sight of savage brutality suddenly changed the whole purpose and current of his life. From that time he became a reader of The Liberator, and a co-laborer with its hounded editor, in the anti-slavery cause.

The same year, in November, at Northfield, N. H., Rev. George Storrs, while in prayer, preliminary to an anti-slavery lecture, was dragged from his knees, on a warrant issued by a justice charging him with being "a common rioter and brawler." *

In 1837, in Alton, Illinois, Elijah P. Lovejoy, a man of culture and much moral worth, an editor of an anti-slavery paper, was subjected to a series of annoyances and persecutions, resulting in the destruction of his press and type, and finally his murder by a mob. These are a few specimens of the pro-slavery spirit in the free states.

At the South, abolitionism was the unpardonable sin, to be visited with summary vengeance. A New Orleans paper declared that every anti-slavery emissary of the South would "be burned at the stake." Such was the voice from Georgia,

* The year 1835 may be called the year of mobs. Many had occurred the preceding year, but this was the culminating period. "A reign of terror prevailed throughout the free states. Churches and public halls were assaulted, life and limb were endangered, anti-slavery speakers were roughly handled, and often placed in circumstances of imminent peril."

Mississippi, and everywhere else. In the United States Senate, in 1838, a member from South Carolina said, "Let an abolitionist come within the borders of South Carolina, if we can catch we will try him, and, notwithstanding all the interference of all the governments of the earth, including the federal government, we will HANG him."

So great was the hatred and dread of abolitionists at the South, that the mails were searched, and rifled of anti-slavery documents; and the postmaster general, in a letter to the postmaster of Charleston, S. C., said, "I cannot sanction, and *will not condemn*, the step you have taken."

The writer remembers being once at the house of a gentleman of high standing, whose name was then an abomination at the South, when a large letter arrived from South Carolina. It contained *a dead and withered human ear and a bit of rope!* The letter read something like this: "Knowing that you are much interested in our negroes, I send you the ear of a slave, cut off for attempting to escape to the North. The rope is a hint of what awaits you if we can get you in our power."

Further, in order to effect its purpose, the slave power trampled on the sacred right of petition.

The existence of slavery and the slave-trade in the District of Columbia was especially offensive to the North. That horrid traffic was carried on in sight of the national Capitol, and under circumstances of extreme cruelty. Slave-pens were there, filled with human merchandise, and gangs of slaves, handcuffed and chained, were a spectacle of constant occurrence.

Liberty was outraged in the sight of the whole world. The United States were disgraced by such unspeakable hypocrisy — a free republic legalizing the buying and selling of human beings. It was not ashamed to expose its nakedness.

It was natural that such a state of things should provoke indignation in the free North. In the name of decency, as well as of humanity, let slavery cease to flaunt its flag at the common capital of the nation. Such was the growing feeling at the North. Numerous petitions were sent to Congress, in 1835, for the removal of these abominations. But the right of petition was denied by Congress, and a rule was passed excluding anti-slavery petitions.

In 1842, John Tyler being president, John

Quincy Adams, representative from Massachusetts, who had, in previous years, manfully defended the right of petition, secured a great triumph over the slave power. The subject was discussed for nearly two weeks, amidst the most intense excitement. The boldness and persistency of Mr. Adams were intolerable. A resolution censuring his conduct was introduced. But as it was a very serious matter, the pro-slavery members decided to take further thought before final action. A meeting for deliberation was held in the evening, and a chivalrous young member, Thomas Marshall, of Kentucky, was selected to bring forward resolutions. The wish was, to expel the venerable ex-president; but they feared to take that step. It was decided to be content with something less. The next morning, after the reading of the journal, Mr. Marshall submitted, according to the programme, three resolutions, declaring that the act of Mr. Adams might be held to *merit expulsion;* that the House deemed it an act of mercy and grace when they only inflicted upon him the *severest censure* for conduct so unworthy of his past relations to the state and his present position, and that this they did for the maintenance of their purity and dignity; and for the rest, they *turned him over to his own conscience and the indignation of all American citizens!* The resolutions in which Mr. Marshall charged Mr. Adams with high treason were followed by an eloquent and forcible speech. But the "old man eloquent" was far more than a match for the brilliant young orator and all his associates. With irresistible power of argument and sarcasm, he vindicated the right of petition, charged the South with aiming at the subversion of the fundamental rights of freemen, and assailed slavery itself as a tremendous evil. Southern members used every parliamentary artifice to stop him, but in vain. No one understood parliamentary usages and rights so well as he. He replied to his assailants with terrible severity. Referring to the charge of treason, he thanked God that it was not left to the "puny" mind of the gentleman from Kentucky to define that crime — the Constitution had done it. He said that if he were Mr. Marshall's father, he would "advise him to return to Kentucky, and take his place in some law school, and commence the study of that profession he had disgraced." Mr. Adams "carried the war into Africa" with such vigor that he overwhelmed his opponents. They had begun the onset with the full purpose to humble him. For several days the contest raged. But the veteran statesman, conscious of his innocence, and resolved to maintain the right, fearlessly stood his ground, and compelled his enemies to surrender. They dared not carry out their plan. Their carefully concocted resolutions were laid on the table! It was a grand triumph of liberty.

At the next session, Mr. Adams, as chairman of a committee on rules for the government of the House, omitted in his report the twenty-first rule — the rule which excluded anti-slavery petitions. Weeks were spent in discussing the subject, and Mr. Adams was violently assailed. "Mr. Dillett, of Alabama, quoted these words from a speech of Mr. Adams's to the colored people of Pittsburg: 'We know that the day of your redemption must come. The time and manner of its coming we know not. It may come in peace, or it may come in blood; but whether in peace or in blood, let it come.' Mr. Adams said, with emphasis, 'I say now, let it come.' Mr. Dillett replied, 'Yes, the gentleman now says, Let it come, though it costs the blood of thousands of white men.' Mr. Adams quickly responded, 'Though it cost the blood of *millions* of white men, let it come!'"*

The right of petition was not, however, now secured. At length, after ten years' struggle, Mr. Adams, in the second session of the twenty-eighth Congress, in 1844, effected the abolishment of the tyrannical "rule."

During all this time the friends of freedom were gaining strength and influence. In 1840 the Liberty party was organized, and in 1844, with James G. Birney as its candidate for president of the United States, it cast more than sixty thousand votes. It was a small beginning, but it led on to great results.

* Wilson.

CHAPTER IX.

Annexation of Texas. — Mr. Sumner's First Public Appearance. — Fourth of July Oration on "The True Grandeur of Nations." — Its Effect. — Scene at the Dinner. — Extracts from the Oration. — Opinions of John A. Andrew and John Quincy Adams.

THE year 1845 found Mr. Sumner quietly engaged in the pursuits of literature and the practice of his profession. Early in that year occurred an event which was destined to agitate the whole country — the annexation of Texas. That region was claimed by Mexico as a part of her territory, even after it had proclaimed independence as a republic, bearing on its flag a "lone star." The people of Texas, large numbers of them colonists from the Southern States, and slaveholders, at length desired to be united with the United States — a project into which the South entered with all its heart. To receive it would be to risk a war with Mexico; but its annexation was a foregone conclusion, provided its friends could secure the sanction of Congress. At the South it was not a subject of discussion, but of desperate determination. The area of slavery must be extended, its power strengthened. Every possible influence was brought to bear upon the two great political parties to commit them to the measure. As was usual then, the slave power carried the day. Thenceforth it became more defiant and exacting, more unscrupulous and domineering.

The North was beginning to be aroused, fearing whereunto all this would grow. But abolitionism was an unpopular doctrine.

As yet Mr. Sumner had taken no active part in the cause to which, not long after, he dedicated his life. But he had been doing a great deal of thinking. And he was not without deep convictions, even then, upon the stirring questions of the day. The great principles of right, which so early took deep root in his nature, were already working out their legitimate results. We know that from the year 1834 he had been a reader of Mr. Garrison's Liberator — a course of tuition decidedly stimulating to ardent and thoughtful minds. Horace

Mann, fifteen years his superior in age, also had no little influence in shaping young Sumner's course of thought and life. The two were always warm friends, of kindred opinions and sympathies.

The friends of anti-slavery in the city were aware of Mr. Sumner's principles. They had listened to his earnest, generous utterances in private, and knew that if an opportunity were given him for a fuller expression of his views, he would employ no uncertain words. It so happened that two, at least, of the board of aldermen of the city of Boston at this time, Deacon S. G. Shipley and Dr. Ayer, were abolitionists. They were on the committee to procure an orator for the anniversary of the Fourth of July, under the direction of the city government. They thought of Charles Sumner, the pride of Boston, who was as yet known to the general public only as a most promising young lawyer, of extraordinary attainments, literary and legal, and to a select circle as a gentleman of refined tastes, elegant manners, and fascinating social qualities.

But the committee knew him as more than this. Calling upon him, they obtained his consent—much to their delight. To a friend whom they met just after this, they said, "We have succeeded in getting Charles Sumner, a grand fellow, and a sturdy abolitionist." Had the board of aldermen known this, perhaps they would have had some misgivings.

And now is to be revealed to the world what Mr. Sumner had been deeply pondering in his mind during the past quiet years.

At last, full-armed in principles and purpose, he steps forth into public life. The city fathers are in their place of honor in the church; the solid men, the aspiring young men, the children of the public schools, are there, the last, to sing the songs of freedom. The flag that floats proudly that day bears the motto, "*Ense petit placidam sub libertate quietem*" — the glory of the sword. The assembly are sure of a rich treat from the learned and eloquent young lawyer. He announces his theme — "The True Grandeur of Nations." The occasion is one which, by the grace of long and honored custom, is to call forth a patriotic eulogy of the heroes of '76.

Mr. Sumner soon undeceived the expectant multitude — all but that committee. He had girded himself for a mighty onset upon war, and through a long and elaborate discourse he exposed that system as cruel, wasteful, irrational, repugnant to Christianity. He seriously proposed that all nations, our own setting the example, should disband their armies, and agree to settle their mutual disputes by friendly arbitration.

The audience sat respectfully through the delivery, but the feelings with which many of them entered the church, and the feelings with which they went out, were about as wide asunder as possible. The wiseacres, the leaders of the ton, the political managers, shook their heads at the rashness of the orator. He had got altogether too far out of the beaten track. He had put the presumptuous question, "Who believes that the national honor would be promoted by a war with Mexico?" and had added, "A war with Mexico would be mean and cowardly;" and again, towards the close, had said, "And when the day shall come (may these eyes be gladdened by its beams!) that shall witness the peaceful emancipation of three million fellow-men, guilty of a skin not colored as our own, now, in the land of jubilant freedom, bound in gloomy bondage,—then will there be a victory by the side of which that of Bunker Hill will be as the farthing-candle held up to the sun." He had seemed to manifest a leaning towards the ranting abolitionists. He had virtually said to the great Whig party, of which he was a hopeful scion, You must set yourself against the extension of slavery, against the retention of Texas; you must declare for emancipation, — which the great Whig party was not at all inclined to do, regarding even the suggestion as most disloyal to the party and unpatriotic to the country. And so, when the great men of the city met, after the oration, at the dinner table in Faneuil Hall, they gave vent to their displeasure. The Daily Advertiser of that time gives a brief account of the scene. One speaker said that he could not fully sustain the doctrines of the oration. Wars were sometimes necessary. Robert C. Winthrop, then a Whig representative in Congress, having in mind the annexation of Texas, and a probable war with Mexico, proposed as a toast, "Our country — however bounded, still our country — to be defended at all hazards." John C. Park took occasion to vindicate the military institutions of the country, against what he considered the doctrines of the oration. Judge Rogers gave as a sentiment, "That high and honorable feeling which makes the citizen a soldier, and the soldier a citizen." Not a word in commendation of the young orator. He stood alone. But he does not appear to have been at all daunted. He calmly rose, and, in a spirit in harmony with his theme, said that he would not follow with a single word the apple of discord which he seemed to have thrown that day, but would call their attention to that part of the performance in the church with regard to which there could be no difference of opinion, referring to the part taken by the children, and would speak of the public schools of the city.

It may be remarked that Mr. Sumner does not seem to have taken a stand against war as a defence in case of actual aggression, but against it as an established method for the settlement of international difficulties. Who can refuse his assent to such sentiments as these, from the oration?

"Stripped of all delusive apology, . . . war falls from glory into barbarous guilt, taking its place among bloody transgressions, while its flaming honors are turned into shame. . . . Amidst the thunders of Sinai God declared, 'Thou shalt not kill;' and the voice of these thunders, with this commandment, is prolonged to our day in the echoes of Christian churches." Referring to the maxim, "Our country, *right or wrong*," and to another, "Our country, our whole country, and nothing but our country," he said, "Cold and dreary, narrow and selfish would be this life, if *nothing but our country* occupied the soul; if the thoughts that wander through eternity, if the infinite affections of our nature, were restrained to that place where we find ourselves by the accident of birth. . . . In the faithful record of the future, recognizing the true grandeur of nations, the Muse of history, inspired by a loftier justice, and touched to finer sensibilities, will extend to universal man the sympathy now confined to country, and no war will be waged without arousing everlasting judgment."

He boldly proposed that the enormous sums expended in preparation for war in the time of peace should be devoted to objects of beneficence — to schools, colleges, churches, hospitals, libraries, — and that our army should be, not soldiers, but the teachers of youth and the ministers of religion. "This is the cheap defence of nations. In such intrenchments, what Christian soul can be troubled with fear? Angels of the Lord will throw over the land an invisible but impenetrable panoply: —

'Or, if Virtue feeble were,
Heaven itself would stoop to her.' "

And again: " True greatness consists in imitating, as nearly as possible to finite man, the perfections of an Infinite Creator, — above all, in cultivating those highest perfections, justice and love. . . . The true grandeur of humanity is in moral elevation, sustained, enlightened, and decorated by the intellect of man. The surest tokens of this grandeur are that Christian beneficence which diffuses the greatest happiness among all, and that passionless, godlike justice which controls the relations of the nation to other nations, and to all the people committed to its charge."

If the general voice was adverse to the doctrines of Mr. Sumner, John A. Andrew was not slow to write to his friend his hearty indorsement: "I cannot help expressing my gratitude that here, in our city of Boston, one has at last stepped forward to consecrate to celestial hopes the great day which Americans have, at least heretofore, held sacred only to memory." And from his home in Quincy, the venerable John Quincy Adams, some months later, wrote to Mr. Sumner these remarkable words: "Casting my eyes backward no farther than the Fourth of July of last year, when you set all the vipers of Alecto a-hissing by proclaiming the Christian law of universal peace and love; and then casting them forward, perhaps not much farther, but beyond my own allotted time, *I see you have a mission to perform. I look from Pisgah to the promised land; you must enter upon it.*"

From England, Richard Cobden, the great Liberal leader, wrote to Mr. Sumner, with reference to that oration, "You have made the most noble contribution of any modern writer to the cause of peace."

In a letter to the author, the poet Samuel Rogers wrote, "What can I say to you in return for your admirable oration? I can only say with what pleasure I have read it, and how truly every pulse of my heart beats in accordance with yours on the subject. . . . Again and again must I thank you."

CHAPTER X.

Meeting in Faneuil Hall.— Speech against the Admission of Texas as a Slave State. — Lyceum at New Bedford. — Lecture before the Boston Lyceum. — Eulogy on Pickering, Story, Channing, and Allston, before the Phi Beta Kappa Society, at Harvard College. — Washington Allston. — "No Battle-Piece!" — True Province of Art.

MR. SUMNER was now fairly before the public, and had given no doubtful indication of the drift of his future course. His lofty ideal was Right — Right, as applied to the improvement of mankind. He had already tried War by this test, and found it wanting; he was now to assail Slavery as radical injustice. He wanted Peace and Freedom for the whole world — nothing less. He would cry aloud and spare not, against all forms of oppression and cruelty.

In doing so he had no desire for political

office, and several years were yet to elapse ere he should be forced into such a position. But he had openly committed himself to the stream of conflict, which was every day growing more troubled and tempestuous; and he was not the man to desert the ship, or to haul down his flag.

And so, four months after his disquieting oration against war, we find him lifting up his voice in opposition to the admission of Texas as a slave state. The slave power had become alarmingly defiant. Having secured Texas as a Territory, it was resolved to have it fully equipped as a champion of slavery on the floor of Congress, and in the government of the nation. A meeting of all who were opposed to this movement was held in Faneuil Hall, November 4, presided over by Charles Francis Adams. There Charles Sumner stood beside William Lloyd Garrison and Wendell Phillips. Among the resolutions, which were drawn up by Mr. Sumner was the following: "Be it resolved, in the name of God, of Christ, and of humanity, that we, belonging to all political parties, and reserving all other reasons of objection, unite in protest against the admission of Texas into the Union as a slave state."

Mr. Sumner followed with a speech, in which he said, "Congress is asked to sanction the constitution of Texas, which not only supports slavery, but contains a clause prohibiting the legislature of the state from abolishing slavery. In doing this, it will give a fresh stamp of legislative approbation to an unrighteous system; it will assume a new and active responsibility for this system; it will again become a dealer in human flesh, and on a gigantic scale. At this moment, when the conscience of mankind is at last aroused to the enormity of holding a fellow-man in bondage, when, throughout the civilized world, a slave-dealer is a by-word and a reproach, we, as a nation, are about to become proprietors of a large population of slaves."

In answer to the objection that Massachusetts might stand alone in her opposition, he said,—"But we cannot fail to accomplish great good. It is in obedience to a prevailing law of Providence, that no act of self-sacrifice, of devotion to duty, of humanity can fail. It stands forever as a landmark, from which, at least, to make a new effort. . . . Massachusetts must continue foremost in the cause of freedom; nor can her children yield to deadly dalliance with slavery."

It was a stormy night on which this meeting was held, and the slave power took occasion from that circumstance, the next day, to growl out its wrath against those who had dared to question its infallibility, through the Daily Times, a Democratic paper of Boston. "The elements seemed determined not to sanction any such traitor-like movement, and interposed every obstacle to its success. It was proper that such a foul project should have foul weather as an accompaniment."

A few weeks later, Mr. Sumner was invited to lecture before the Lyceum at New Bedford; but he refused to go, as Mr. Phillips and George William Curtis had done before this, for the reason that colored persons were not allowed to purchase tickets, and were only admitted, free of expense, provided they would sit in "the north gallery." In his letter to the committee, Mr. Sumner said, "One of the cardinal truths of religion and freedom is the equality and brotherhood of man. In the sight of God and of all just institutions, the white man can claim no precedence or exclusive privilege from his color. It is the accident of an accident that places a human soul beneath the dark shelter of an African countenance, rather than beneath our colder complexion. Nor can I conceive any application of the divine injunction, 'Do unto others as you would have them do unto you,' more pertinent than to the man who founds a discrimination between his fellow-men on difference of skin. It is well known that the prejudice of color, which is akin to the stern and selfish spirit that holds a fellow-man in slavery, is peculiar to our country. It does not exist in other civilized countries. In France, colored youths at college have gained the highest honors, and been welcomed as if they were white. At the law school there, I have sat with them on the same bench. . . . All this was Christian; so it seemed to me."

This rule was soon after rescinded.

In February of the next year, Mr. Sumner lectured before the Boston Lyceum on the Employment of Time — a paper replete with valuable suggestions.

"The hours spent in listlessness or squandered in unprofitable dissipation, gathered into aggregates, are hours, days, weeks, months, years.

The daily sacrifice of a single hour during a year comes, at its end, to thirty-six working days, allowing ten hours to the day — an amount of time, if devoted exclusively to one object, ample for the acquisition of important knowledge, and for the accomplishment of inconceivable good. Imagine a month dedicated, without interruption, to a single purpose, — to the study of a new language, an untried science, an unexplored field of history, a fresh department of philosophy, or to some new sphere of action, some labor of humanity, some godlike charity, — and what visions must not rise of untold accumulations of knowledge, of unnumbered deeds of goodness!"

Referring with praise to the valuable precepts of Franklin, in favor of industry and economy, he adds, —

"It cannot fail to be regretted, that the lessons taught by Franklin are so little spiritual in their character — that they are so material, so mundane, so full of pounds, shillings, and pence. 'The almighty dollar,' now ruling here with sovereign sway and masterdom, was placed on the throne by Poor Richard. When shall it be dethroned? When shall the thoughts, the aspirations, the politics of the land be lifted from the mere greed of gain, with an appetite that grows by what it feeds on, into the serene region of inflexible justice and universal benevolence?"

Addressing the young, he said,—

"The image of God is in the soul, and the young must take heed that it is not effaced by the neglect of any of the trusts they have secured. They must bear in mind that there are debts other than to their profession or business, which, like gratitude, it will ever be their pleasure, 'still paying, still to owe,' which can be properly discharged only by the best employment of all the faculties with which they are blessed, so that life shall be improved by culture and filled with works for the good of man."

On the 6th of August, Mr. Sumner pronounced before the Phi Beta Kappa Society of Harvard College, a eulogy on four distinguished Americans, John Pickering, the scholar, Joseph Story, the jurist, Washington Allston, the artist, and William Ellery Channing, the philanthropist. It was an elegant and eloquent tribute to their worth. But it is particularly interesting as showing how thoroughly Mr. Sumner's mind was possessed by the idea of justice, and how clearly it perceived the grand duty of men of culture to consecrate their acquisitions to the good of the race. These great men, of whom he was speaking, "lived for knowledge, justice, beauty, love. . . . They were all philanthropists, for the labors of all were directed to the welfare and happiness of man."

In that part of the address which speaks of Allston, we notice how eagerly Mr. Sumner seized the opportunity to expatiate on the highest aim and duty of Art. Before a literary audience, he still presses the paramount claims of humanity. The assault on war, which, a year before, had exposed him to sharp and vipery criticism, he now renews in a selecter presence with equal earnestness: "Allston was a Christian artist; and the beauty of expression lends uncommon charm to his colors. All that he did shows purity, sensibility, refinement, delicacy, feeling, rather than force. His genius was almost feminine. As he advanced in years, this was more remarked. His pictures became more and more instinct with those sentiments which form the true glory of art. Early in life he had a partiality for pieces representing *banditti;* but this taste does not appear in his later works. And when asked if he would undertake to fill the vacant panels in the rotunda of the Capitol at Washington, . . . he is reported to have said, 'I will paint only one subject, and choose my own. *No battle-piece!*'

"Admitting the calamitous necessity of war, it can never be with pleasure — it cannot be without sadness unspeakable — that we survey its fiendish encounter. The artist of purest aim, sensitive to these emotions, withdraws naturally from the field of blood, confessing that no scene of battle finds a place in the highest art, — that man, created in the image of God, can never be pictured degrading, profaning, violating that sacred image. . . . There are tragedies which History enters sorrowfully, tearfully, in her faithful record; but this generous Muse, with too attractive colors, must not perpetuate the passions from which they sprang, or the griefs which they caused. Be it her duty to dwell with eulogy and pride on all that is magnanimous, lovely, beneficent; let this be preserved by votive canvas, and marble also. But *No battle-piece!* . . . The time is at hand when religion, humanity, and taste will concur in rejecting any image of human strife. Lais and Phryne have fled. Bacchus and Silenus are driven reeling from the scene. Mars will soon follow, howling, as with that wound from the Grecian spear before Troy. . . . In the mission of teaching to nations and to individuals wherein is true greatness, Art has a noble office. If not herald, she is at least handmaid of Truth. Her lessons may not train the intellect, but they cannot fail to touch the heart. Who can measure the influence from an image of beauty, affection, and truth? The Christus Consolator of Scheffer, without a word, wins the soul."

It is worthy of mention, that among the pictures with which, years after, Mr. Sumner adorned his house at Washington, no battle-scene had a place, but there was a St. Mark descending from the skies to rescue a slave in the slave-market.

When Mr. Sumner came to speak of Channing, he came again upon war and slavery. He well knew that many present would consider those subjects wholly out of place at such a time, and hence he said, with what seems like a

8

kind of grim humor, "All will see that I cannot pass these on this occasion; for not to speak of them would be to present a portrait in which the most distinctive features were wanting." With that graceful excuse he dealt some more lusty blows at "those two terrible scourges," including a reference to the annexation of Texas, a war with Mexico, and the extension of slavery.

Towards the end of the oration, Mr. Sumner, having spoken of the subjects of his eulogy as all philanthropists, added, —

"In their presence how truly do we feel the insignificance of office and wealth, which men so hotly pursue! What is office? and what is wealth? Expressions or representatives of what is present and fleeting only, investing the possessor with a brief and local regard. . . . They who live for wealth, and the things of this world, follow shadows, neglecting realities eternal on earth and in heaven. After the perturbations of life, all its accumulated possessions must be resigned, except those only which have been devoted to God and mankind. What we do for *ourselves* perishes with this mortal dust; what we do for *others* lives coeval with the benefaction."

A marked quality of Mr. Sumner's character was hopefulness as to the triumph of truth and justice. However dark the present aspect, or bitter the strife, he never doubted that success would come to the right. A short poem which he introduced into this oration well indicates this firm, serene faith in the good and the true: —

"There's a fount about to stream,
There's a light about to beam,
There's a warmth about to glow,
There's a flower about to blow,
There's a midnight blackness changing
Into gray:
Men of thought and men of action,
Clear the way!

Aid the dawning, tongue and pen!
Aid it, hopes of honest men!
Aid it, paper! aid it, type!
Aid it, for the hour is ripe,
And our earnest must not slacken
Into play:
Men of thought and men of action,
Clear the way!"

Such was Mr. Sumner's message to the then conservative Harvard and conservative Boston, and such his endeavor to kindle a generous enthusiasm for humanity among the young scholars of the land. Those ringing words, "Clear the way," were as the sound of a trumpet. With what dismay must they have fallen upon the ears of men who loved soft words of compromise, and dreaded above all things agitation! Doubtless they inspired some younger hearts with a noble ambition to "clear the way" for liberty throughout the land.

CHAPTER XI.

Whig State Convention. — Duty of the Whig Party. — Appeal to Daniel Webster. — Mr. Winthrop. — White Slavery. — Public Schools. — Prison Discipline.

We have seen Mr. Sumner making a literary festival serve the great interests of humanity. Letters, with him, were not an end; they were an elegant accomplishment and recreation, the ornament and grace of life, and helps to more complete and effective work in the great field of human improvement. And so he gracefully passes from the Academy to the Forum.

About a month after this, September 23, 1846, his voice is heard at a Whig State Convention in Faneuil Hall. He was a member of the Whig party, and anxious to have it maintain its integrity. His associations with it had been of the most friendly character. In his opinion, it had been the party of freedom and progress.

He still believed that it might be kept true to its patriotic and liberal principles.

But, in order to that, the friends of freedom must bestir themselves. The time for neutrality was past. The Whig party must demand the repeal of slavery under the constitution and laws of the national government. They must "choose *men* who will devote themselves earnestly, heartily to the work, — who will enter upon it with awakened conscience, and with that valiant faith, before which all obstacles disappear, — who will be ever loyal to truth, freedom, right, humanity, — who will not look for rules of conduct down to earth, in the mire of expediency, but with heaven-directed countenance seek those great 'primal duties' which 'shine aloft like stars,' to illumine alike the path of individuals and of nations. They must be true to the principles of Massachusetts. They must not be Northern men with Southern principles, nor Northern men under Southern influences. They must be courageous and willing on all occasions to stand alone, provided right be with them. . . . There are a few such now in Congress. Massachusetts has a venerable representative, whose aged bosom still glows with inextinguishable fires, like the central heats of the monarch mountain of the Andes beneath its canopy of snow. To this cause he devotes the closing energies of a long and illustrious life. Would that all might join him!"

All which was like a bracing north wind. Would the Whig party turn towards it its already feverish face, and be quickened to a new life? Alas for the fond dreamer! He was piping to a party that would call him an enthusiast, and before long a fanatic. Its very tower of strength had already become a leaning tower, destined to an ignominious fall.

But as yet there was hope. And Mr. Sumner pleaded with Daniel Webster to be true to freedom. "There is," said he, "a senator of Massachusetts we had hoped to welcome here to-day, whose position is of commanding influence. Let me address him with the respectful frankness of a constituent and friend. Already, sir, by various labors, you have acquired an honorable place in the history of our country. By the vigor, argumentation, and eloquence with which you upheld the Union, and that interpretation of the constitution which makes us a nation, you have justly earned the title of *Defender of the Constitution*. . . . Pardon me if I add that there are yet other duties claiming your care, whose performance will be the crown of a long life in the public service. Do not forget them. Dedicate, sir, the years happily in store for you, with all that grand experience which is yours, to grand endeavor in the name of human freedom, for the overthrow of that terrible evil which now afflicts our country. . . . Do not shrink from the task. . . . Assume, then, these unperformed duties. The aged shall bear witness to you; the young shall kindle with rapture, as they repeat the name of Webster; the large company of the ransomed shall teach their children and their children's children, to the latest generation, to call you blessed; you shall have yet another title, never to be forgotten on earth or in heaven, — *Defender of Humanity*, — by the side of which the earlier title will fade into insignificance, as the constitution, which is the work of mortal hands, dwindles by the side of man, created in the image of God."

We cannot wonder that this eloquent and

faithful appeal to Webster was "received with great applause." Would that its admonitions had been heeded by the great statesman to whom they were addressed.*

They are remarkable words, as describing to the life his own course in after years as the successor of Webster, and the glorious reward of his faithful service for humanity, of which the earnest has already come. The blessings of "the ransomed," which he hoped might crown another's head, have fallen upon his own. The nation, regardless of party, delights to honor him as the *Defender of Humanity.*

This speech, with its warning to the great senator, was followed, a month later, by a letter to another distinguished Massachusetts Whig,

* This warning proved not to be unnecessary. For it is useless to deny that Daniel Webster did falter in his duty in the treatment of the slavery question, and that he was guilty of a great error and wrong, when, in an hour of temptation, he suffered himself to be betrayed into that most unfortunate speech in the United States Senate, March 7, 1850, in which he advocated the infamous Fugitive Slave Bill. It was against all the better instincts of his heart and the real convictions of his judgment. In this he was false to himself. He had done grand service to his country. His previous speeches abound with noble sentiments, powerfully and eloquently expressed, and are well worth the study of every American. His life, by Rev. Joseph Banvard, D. D., is a very interesting and instructive volume for the young.

then a representative in Congress — Robert C. Winthrop.

As a consequence of annexing Texas, war with Mexico had come, and Mr. Winthrop had voted for the Mexican War Bill, and defended it with much ardor. As a brother Whig, as a constituent, as a friend, Mr. Sumner administers what he believes to be a wholesome rebuke.* He wonders that a son of Massachusetts could have sanctioned an aggressive war upon Mexico, and in the interests of slavery.

To the question, What shall be done? Mr. Sumner is at no hesitation for an answer. Retreat, recall the troops, acknowledge our wrong to an unoffending neighbor.

Such was the lofty Christian morality which Mr. Sumner brought to bear upon the subject. He saw no shame in doing right, in confessing and repairing a wrong. It was noble and Chris-

* Mr. Winthrop is well known as a gentleman of eminent ability and culture, of great private worth, and of pure and patriotic purposes; but his political course, like that of other public men, is open to criticism. Mr. Sumner — and in this he was far from being alone — believed Mr. Winthrop to have made a sad mistake in his treatment of slavery, especially as connected with the Mexican war. But that gentleman has lately borne generous testimony to Mr. Sumner's worth, and has said that their differences of opinion related more to measures than to ends.

tian. "Aloft on the throne of God, and not below in the footsteps of a trampling multitude, are the sacred rules of right, which no majorities can displace or overturn."

Mr. Sumner's bold opposition to the war for slavery awakened a desire, among those who sympathized with his views, that he would allow himself to be a candidate for representative against Mr. Winthrop. His name was proposed, but he would not consent to let it stand. He did not wish for office, and he would not "suffer the force of his denunciations of the war and of slavery to be weakened by the suspicion that he was influenced by selfish motives." He would not have it said that he used pious words as a cloak for ambition. This was in 1846. And for five years longer he fought with the wild beasts of war and slavery in a private capacity. If ever there was a man who was not a demagogue, Mr. Sumner deserves that honor.

Mr. Sumner had put his hand to the plough, and would not look back. Being invited to lecture before the Boston Mercantile Library Association, which he did early in 1847, he chose for his theme, "White Slavery in the Barbary States."

So long as slavery existed in our country, he felt that its suppression ought to be the one great idea with every American. But "before a promiscuous audience, it was at that time a subject too delicate to be treated directly," and Mr. Sumner ingeniously discussed white slavery, which, of course, every white person, of whatever party, or of whatever opinion about negroes, was ready to condemn. Thus would he catch his hearers "by guile." The transition was not difficult from white slavery to black slavery.

Mr. Sumner cited instances of efforts to escape from Algerine captivity, as for instance, that of Cervantes, the illustrious author of Don Quixote, and also those of American citizens — for Americans were reduced to slavery, down to the year 1816. What hearer, with such cases before him, would not sympathize with these glowing words? — "Endeavors for freedom are animating; nor can any honest nature hear of them without a throb of sympathy. Dwelling on the painful narrative of unequal contest between tyrannical power and the crushed captive, we resolutely enter the lists on the side of freedom; and beholding the contest waged by a few individuals, or, perhaps, by one alone, our sympathy is given to his weakness as well as to his cause. To him we send the unfaltering succor of good wishes. For him we invoke vigor of arm and fleetness of foot to escape. Human enactments are vain to restrain the warm tides of the heart."

The lecture was repeated in many parts of Massachusetts, and was an important means of training the people, in a way not calculated to arouse their prejudices, for the struggle that was before the country.

But Mr. Sumner's thoughts were not wholly given to slavery. He was a philanthropist in the broadest sense. Hence we find him giving much attention to the cause of Education, especially in the public schools of Boston, whose improvement he earnestly favored.

At this time there prevailed what was called the "double-headed system"—two masters over each school. Now, it has always been found difficult, from ancient times to our own, to have "two Cæsars in Rome." It was so in Boston. The masters often disagreed, and as each was the equal of the other, confusion and trouble were the result.

Rev. Rollin H. Neale, D. D., a member of the school committee, was the first to propose and advocate a change of system. He would cut off one of the heads, leaving a single one to be "master of the situation." He also urged the employment, to a large extent, of female teachers.

Both these proposals were for a time received with much disapprobation, by a majority of the directors of the schools. The innovation was preposterous. But among the advocates of the change was Charles Sumner. His voice was ever on the side of improvement. Tradition and prescription had no charm for his active and enlightened mind.

Mr. Sumner was also much interested in Pauperism and Prison Discipline. Upon the latter subject he wrote an able article for the Christian Examiner.

To this, as to every benevolent cause in which he was engaged, he brought that strong sense of right, that earnest love of truth, which we have seen to characterize his political action. And thus it happened, that, as in the Whig party, so in the Boston Prison Discipline Society, he was regarded by many very much as a "thorn in the flesh." His idealism was troublesome. He was not content that the annual report of the secretary should be meekly received with an annual satisfaction. He thought that the spirit of the secretary was narrow and illiberal, and he said so. It was wedded to a particular system, and would give no ear to arguments in favor of any other. This was offensive to his progressive and liberal mind. He wanted the society to be more active and more open to conviction, to be ready for information and advice from any quarter.

It seems strange to us that so reasonable a demand should have provoked so much opposition, controversy, and ill-feeling for a series of years. But so it was. The secretary favored the Auburn or social system, Mr. Sumner the Philadelphia or separate system. Boston was proud of her method, and was not willing to learn from Philadelphia. Mr. Sumner was a Bostonian, but he did not believe that Boston was all the world. He wanted fair play, and an open, generous policy. And so, parties were formed, there was private and public controversy, the newspapers took up the quarrel, and foreign countries became interested in the debate.

Among those who sympathized with Mr. Sumner were Dr. Samuel G. Howe, Mr. Hillard, and Dr. Francis Wayland, president of Brown University, and these were styled "intruders."

The difficulty began early in 1845, and in June, 1847, at a public meeting of the society in Tremont Temple, a committee, of which Mr. Sumner was one, brought forward a report embodying his views. These were explained and defended in a speech, courteous but plain-dealing. The system which Mr. Sumner favored he thus briefly described: "1. Separation of the prisoners from each other; 2. Labor in the cell; 3. Exercise in the open air; 4. Visits; 5. Books; 6. Moral and religious instruction. Its fundamental doctrine, and only essential element, is *separation of prisoners from each other*, on which may be ingrafted solace of any kind needful to health of body or mind."

Alluding to the practical working of the society, Mr. Sumner said, "Look at our grandiose organization. We have a president, with forty vice-presidents, or, borrowing an illustration from

Turkey, 'a pacha with forty tails.' Then we have a large body of foreign correspondents, whose names we print in capitals,—fancy men, as they have been called, because they are for show, I suppose, like our vice-presidents. Then there are scores of directors, and a board of managers. Now, I know full well, that, of these, very few interest themselves so much in our society as to attend its sessions. At the meeting last year for the choice of officers, there were *ten* present. We *ten* chose the whole army of vice-presidents and all. And then, too, the secretary politely furnished us printed tickets bearing their names and his own. Certainly, sir, something should be done to mend this matter. We must cease to have so many officers, or they must participate actively in the duties of the society."

Who does not sigh for such an inspector of some of our more modern "grandiose" organizations? Would he be deemed an "intruder"?

Such Mr. Sumner did not cease to be considered when he transferred his investigations from the Boston society to the nation. That sentiment of Right was destined to startle conservatives out of their propriety, and to be a terror to evil doers. He was indeed a terrible "intruder."

It should be added, that doubtless the men who stood in the opposition to Mr. Sumner, in the above controversy, were as honest and honorable as himself. They were good and true men. But, like many other good and true men, they were, it would appear, morbidly conservative. There was needed a new element, and Mr. Sumner's treatment of the case, though not for the present joyous but grievous, was calculated to work the peaceable fruits of less parade of names, and more liberality and energy.

CHAPTER XII.

Address at Amherst College. — " Fame and Glory." — Young Men. — True Object of Life. — Whig Meeting at Boston. — Whig State Convention. — The Whig Party "found wanting." — Party of Freedom. — Enthusiastic Meeting at Worcester. — At Union College. — " Law of Human Progress."

Mr. Sumner's heart and hands were now full of work. Less than two months after *intruding* upon the Prison Discipline Society, he responded to a call from the young men of Amherst College to address them at Commencement. What more could he desire? The year before, he had spoken at Harvard no uncertain words; now, to another company of young scholars, he would repeat the cry, " Clear the way." His theme was, *Fame and Glory* — a theme hackneyed enough, often written about by school-boys and sophomores; but how, under the master's touch, it glows with new brightness!

The times were stirring, great events were at hand, there was an open field for generous ambition, and Mr. Sumner wished to tune the spirits of his auditors, the future hope of the country, to the demands of the times.

Some words of his, written at a later period, well express his present feelings: "Especially do I invoke the young. They are the natural guardians of liberty. Thus has it been throughout all history; and never before in history did liberty stand in greater need of their irresistible aid. It is the young who give spontaneous welcome to Truth, when she first appears an unattended stranger. It is the young who open the soul with instinctive hospitality to the noble cause."

Having this end in view, he showed that the love of fame, a divinely implanted principle, was peculiarly liable to perversion. He pointed out the dangers to be avoided, the true use and end of the desire for glory, how it was to be controlled by, and subordinated to, higher principles.

"Whatever," he said, "may be temporary applause, or the expression of public opinion, it may be asserted, without fear of contradiction, *that no true and permanent fame can be found except in labors which promote the happiness of mankind.* If these are by Christian means, with disinterested motives, and with the single aim of doing good, they become that rare and precious virtue whose fit image is the spotless lily of the field, brighter than Solomon in all his glory."

Referring to several military heroes, he said, "There is little of true grandeur in any such career. None of the beatitudes showered upon them a blessed influence. They were not poor in spirit, or meek, or merciful, or pure in heart. They were not peacemakers. They did not hunger and thirst after justice. They did not suffer persecution for justice's sake."

In honorable contrast to these men, and to all the fame of military achievements, he referred to John Howard, who said, "*Hearing the cry of the miserable, I devoted my time to their relief;*" and to Clarkson, who, while yet in the university, his heart stirred by the horrors of the slave-trade, exclaimed, "*It is time some person should see these calamities to their end!*" "Such are exemplars of true glory. Without rank, office, or the sword, they accomplished immortal good. While on earth they labored for their fellow-men; and now, sleeping in death, by example and works they continue the same sacred office. To all, in every sphere or condition, they teach the universal lesson of magnanimous duty. From the heights of their virtue they call upon us to cast out the lust of power, of office, of wealth, of praise, of a fleeting popular favor, which 'a breath can make, as a breath has made,'—to subdue the constant, ever-present suggestions of self, in disregard of neighbors, near or remote, whose welfare should never be forgotten,—to check the madness of party, which, so often, for the sake of success, renounces the very objects of success,—and, finally, to introduce into our lives those sentiments of *conscience and charity* which animated them to such labors.

"Nor should these be holiday virtues, marshalled on great occasions only. They must become part of us, and of our existence,—present on every occasion, small or great,—in those daily amenities which add so much to the charm of life, as also in those grander duties which require an ennobling self-sacrifice. The former are as flowers, whose odor is pleasant, though fleeting; the latter are like the costly spikenard poured from the box of alabaster upon the head of the Lord. . . . Their [men's] worship in the future must be the true God, our Father, as he is in heaven, and in the *beneficent* labors of his children on earth. Then farewell to the siren song of a worldly ambition! Farewell to the vain desire *of mere literary success or oratorical display!* Farewell to the distempered *longing for office!*"

A few weeks later, and we find Mr. Sumner in a Whig meeting at Boston, urging the adoption of resolutions against the annexation of any territory by conquest, and against the extension of slavery. *They were laid on the table!*

A fortnight after, a Whig state convention was held in Springfield (September 29). Mr. Webster was there, Mr. Winthrop, Mr. Palfrey, Mr. Charles F. Adams, Mr. Sumner, and other notables. It was the last time of Mr. Sumner's appearance at a Whig meeting. The strong current of the party was proved to be in the direction of compromise. All real heart had gone out of it. It refused to place itself across the path of the slave power. It was in fact joining hands with it, and becoming partaker of a great crime. Its days were numbered.

But Mr. Sumner was hopeful, and made one more appeal. In support of the resolution of Mr. Palfrey, "That the Whigs of Massachusetts will support no men for the office of President and Vice-President but such as are known by their acts or declared opinions to be opposed to the extension of slavery," Mr. Sumner said: "Be assured, sir, whatever the final determination of this convention, there are many here to-day who will never yield support to any candidate who is not known to be against the extension of slavery, even though he have freshly received the sacramental unction of a 'regular nomination.' We cannot say, with detestable morality, 'our party, *right or wrong*.' The time has gone by when gentlemen can expect to introduce among us the discipline of the camp. Loyalty to principle is higher than loyalty to party. The first is a heavenly sentiment, from God, the other is a device of this world. Far above any flickering light or battle-lantern of party is the everlasting sun of Truth, in whose beams are the duties of men."

Having borne his testimony, but in vain, he felt himself free to act in any new direction which duty should point out. He that day ceased to be a Whig. And the "old line" Whigs gave him up as a disagreeable "intruder," an incorrigible, impracticable fanatic.

The Whig party was proved to be unequal to the emergencies of the hour. A new step was necessary. There must be a party of freedom, which should represent the moral sentiments of the country, which should gather within its ranks all, of whatever previous political name, who would not bow the knee to the Baal of slavery. There must be a party to represent the fundamental ideas of justice and human equality declared in the Declaration of Independence. The time for such an organization had now fully come. Accordingly, about one month after the unsuccessful attempt at Springfield to commit the Whig party to the cause of freedom, a mass convention was held in Worcester (June 28, 1848), to effect a union among men of all parties against the slave power and the extension of slavery.

It was an enthusiastic gathering, in every respect most memorable. It was the dawn of a new day for America, and for the world. Five thousand people were assembled on the Common, for no hall could hold the multitude, brought there by a common and resolute purpose to resist the further encroachments of slavery. Many of the most prominent Whigs were there, ready to cut loose from the past, and take a fresh start in the interest of freedom and humanity. The words that were spoken that day were not the stale, stereotyped, guarded phrases learned in party schools, but the free, fresh, warm utterances of souls inspired by noble sentiments. It was as if a new gift of tongues had been vouchsafed. Men spoke freely, boldly, grandly, as reason and conscience prompted. Once more politics and morals joined hands. There was a feeling of responsibility to God. There was a new love for humanity. "All the speakers," it is said, "united in renouncing old party ties." None did this better than Charles Francis Adams, who concluded his remarks by saying, "Forgetting the things that are behind, I propose that we press forward to the high calling of our new occupation; and, fellow-citizens, whatever may be the fate of you or me, all I can now add is, to repeat the words of one with whom I take pride in remembering that I have been connected: 'Sink or swim, live or die, survive or perish,' to go with the liberties of my country is my fixed determination."

Mr. Sumner said, "In the coming contest I wish it understood that I belong to the party of freedom — to that party which plants itself on the Declaration of Independence and the Constitution of the United States."

In answer to the objection that by voting for a separate candidate, — rejecting Cass and Taylor, — the new party, as being now small, would throw away its votes, and its opposition would fail, Mr. Sumner said, "Fail, sir! *No honest, earnest effort in a good cause can fail.* It may not be crowned with the applause of men; it may not seem to touch the goal of immediate worldly success. But it is not lost. It helps to strengthen the weak with new virtue, . . . to animate all with devotion to duty, which in the end conquers all. Fail! Did the martyrs fail, when, with precious blood, they sowed the seed of the church? Did the discomfited champions of freedom fail who have left those names in history that can never die? . . . Assurances here to-day show that we need not postpone success. It seems already at hand. The heart of Ohio beats responsive to the heart of Massachusetts, and all the Free States are animated with the vigorous breath of freedom. . . . From this demonstration to-day, and the acclaim wafted to us from the Free States, it is easy to see that the great cause of liberty, to which we now dedicate ourselves, will sweep the heart-strings of the people. It will smite all the chords with a might to draw forth emotions such as no political struggle ever awakened before. It will move the young, the middle-aged, and the old. It will find a voice in the social circle, and mingle with the flame of the domestic hearth. It will touch the souls of mothers, wives, sisters, and daughters, until the sympathies of all swell in one irresistible chorus of indignation against the deep damnation of lending new sanction to the enslavement of our brother man."

Thus was born the Free Soil party, from whose loins afterwards sprang the Republican party.

Before saying more about this important movement, we will follow Mr. Sumner to another college anniversary — this time at Union College, Schenectady, N. Y.

These literary festivals were times of seed-sowing. And it was a cheering indication of better, wholesomer days, that the young men of the country were ready to listen to such a teacher as Mr. Sumner. The high-toned, Christian morality which he inculcated, and which he insisted should be applied to politics, as everywhere else, was welcomed by young and ingenuous minds not yet blinded and hardened by the maxims of worldly expediency.

Having spoken at Harvard and Amherst, now again in July, 1848, having just assisted in forming a new party of progress, he discourses at Union on the *Law of Human Progress.* "I would, if I could," he said, "utter truth which, while approved by the old, should sink deep into the souls of the young, filling them with strength for all good works." Mr. Sumner had before him a grand ideal of truth and right, and also of humanity. He would teach the young not to be content with present attainments and the present condition of the world. There was a divine law of human progress running through and shaping all history, and working out a glorious future. "The earnest soul, enlightened by history, strengthened by philosophy, nursed to childish slumber by the simple prayer, 'Thy kingdom come, thy will be done on earth as it is done in heaven,' confident in the final, though slow, fulfilment of the daily fulfilling promises of the future, looks forward to the continuance of this progress during unknown and infinite ages, as a *law* of our being. . . .

"Christianity is the religion of progress. Here is a distinctive feature which we vainly seek in any heathen faith professed upon earth. Confucius, in his sublime morals, taught us not to do unto others what we would not have them do to us; but the Chinese philosopher did not declare the ultimate triumph of this law. It was reserved for the Sermon on the Mount to reveal the vital truth, that all the highest commands of religion and duty, drawing in their train celestial peace, and marking the final goal of all progress among men, shall one day be obeyed. 'For verily I say unto you,' says the Saviour, 'till heaven and earth pass, one jot or one tittle shall in no wise pass from the law till all be fulfilled.'"

This progress of humanity embraces people of every race, and demands for all the means of every kind of improvement. Bigotry, or conservatism, opposes this movement; but in vain. "Thus ever has Truth moved on — though opposed and reviled, still mighty and triumphant. Rejected by the rich and powerful, by the favorites of fortune and place, she finds shelter with those who often have no shelter for themselves. It is such as these that most freely welcome moral truth, with its new commandments. Not the dwellers in the glare of the world, but the humble and lowly, most clearly perceive this truth, — as watchers placed in the depths of a well observe the stars which are obscured to those who live in the effulgence of noon. Free from egotism and prejudice, whether of self-interest or of class, without cares and temptations, whether of wealth or power, dwelling in the mediocrity or obscurity of common life, they discern the new signal, and surrender unreservedly to its guidance. The Saviour knew this. He did not call upon priest, or Levite, or Pharisee to follow him, but upon the humble fishermen by the Sea of Galilee."

Mr. Sumner warned his hearers against impatience and rashness. "Cultivate a just moderation. Learn to reconcile order with change, stability with progress. This is a wise conservatism; this is a wise reform. Rightly understanding these terms, who would not be a conservative? who would not be a reformer? — a conservative of all that is good, a reformer of all that is evil, — a conservative of knowledge, a reformer of ignorance, — a conservative of truths and principles whose seat is in the bosom of God, a reformer of laws and institutions which are but the wicked or imperfect work of man, — a conservative of that divine order which is found only in movement, a reformer of those earthly wrongs and abuses which spring from a violation of the great law of human progress?"

Thus did Mr. Sumner seek to build up a new party on the highest grounds, and to enlist in its support the young men of the land.

CHAPTER XIII.

Object of the Free Soil Party. — Free Soil Convention at Buffalo. — Martin Van Buren and Charles Francis Adams. — Speech by Mr. Sumner. — Address on Peace. — Colored Children in Public Schools. — Mr. Sumner's Argument before the Supreme Court. — Mr. Clay's Compromise Measures. — Fugitive Slave Bill. — Its Effect in the Free States. — Meeting of Protest in Faneuil Hall. — Terror of the Colored People. — William and Ellen Crafts. — Mr. Sumner's Opinion of Slave-Hunters.

THE Free Soil party now entered fully upon its work. Its purpose was to prevent the further extension of slavery, and to secure its abolition wherever it existed within the national domain, as distinguished from State jurisdiction. It did not propose to touch slavery in the States.

A large number of persons, who were distinctively known as Abolitionists, and who, to a great extent, took no part in political action against slavery, were seeking the overthrow of that system throughout the whole country. But the political movement was more limited in its aim. It was, however, a necessary step in the great cause of emancipation.

The Free Soil party aimed to do all that could then be done aside from mere moral means. It would forbid slavery in the District of Columbia and the Territories, and the formation of new Slave States; would liberate the general government from any responsibility to maintain slavery in the States where it already existed; and thus shut up slavery within its own special boundaries, to take care of itself as best it could. It would have the Free States free from any complicity with slavery. They should be "free indeed."

To perfect the organization of such a party, a convention was held at Buffalo, August 9, 1848, at which Martin Van Buren, who had already once been president, was nominated as President of the United States, and Charles Francis Adams as Vice-President.

At a public meeting held in Faneuil Hall, August 22, this nomination, with the platform, was ratified. The list of speakers and of other friends to the new cause shows that it had drawn to itself many of the choicest spirits of the North. In fact, the best portion of the two great parties which had hitherto carried sway, came over to the new organization, which alone represented true American principles.

On this occasion Mr. Sumner was chosen presiding officer, and made an eloquent speech. He declared that not banks and tariffs, and such mere material interests, were now to give their tone to the policy of the country. "Henceforward, PROTECTION TO MAN will be the true American system. . . . The old and ill-compacted party organizations are broken, and from their ruins is now formed a new party, *the Party of Freedom.* There were good men who longed for this, and died without the sight. John Quincy Adams longed for it. William Ellery Channing longed for it. Their spirits hover over us, and urge us to persevere. Let us be true to the moral grandeur of our cause. Have faith in Truth, and in God, who giveth the victory."

During the campaign which followed, Mr. Sumner spoke at many places in the State. A speech delivered in Faneuil Hall, October 31,

1848, is said to have been one of "surpassing ability and eloquence," and to have been received with "tumultuous shouts" of applause. But it was not reported.

In Mr. Sumner's view, war and slavery were kindred evils. Their fundamental idea was force, violence. Being invited by the American Peace Society to speak at their anniversary, in Boston, May 28, 1849, he did not regard it as an interruption to his work in behalf of freedom. In an Address on the War System of the Commonwealth of Nations, he once more, as in 1845, urged "the abolition of the institution of war, and of the whole war system, as an established arbiter of justice in the commonwealth of nations."

Resuming his pen in behalf of freedom, he prepared an Address to the People of Massachusetts — which was afterwards adopted by the Free Soil convention at Worcester, September 12, 1849 — in vindication of the new organization. It contains the germ of his great speech in Congress in 1852, showing that the Freedom party is a national party, as opposed to sectional.

At this time, while Massachusetts was thus awaking to new opposition to slavery, she was herself holding her colored citizens in a position of inferiority. Colored children were not allowed to attend the public schools in company with the white. They had separate schools. The subject came before the Supreme Court of the State, December 4, 1849, under an action brought by a colored child, only five years old, who, *by her next friend*, as the law term is, sued the City of Boston for damages on account of a refusal to receive her into one of the common schools. Mr. Sumner undertook her case, and argued in a most thorough manner the unconstitutionality of the discrimination on account of race or color. He claimed for every person "equality before the law" — a term now for the first time introduced from the French. He denounced the separation of children in the schools, as in the nature of *caste*, that odious system, which no Christian could sanction. He declared it to be injurious, also, to the whole system of common schools. "The law," he said, "contemplates not only that all shall be taught, but that *all* shall be taught *together*. . . . All are to approach the same common fountain together; nor can there be any exclusive source for individual or class. The school is the little world where the child is trained for the larger world of life. . . . And since, according to our institutions, all classes, without distinction of color, meet in the performance of civil duties, so should they all, without distinction of color, meet in the school, beginning there those relations of equality which the constitution and laws promise to all. . . .

"Nothing is more clear than that the welfare of classes, as well as of individuals, is promoted by mutual acquaintance. Prejudice is the child of Ignorance. It is sure to prevail where people do not know each other. Society and intercourse are means established by Providence for human improvement. They remove antipathies, promote mutual adaptation and conciliation, and establish relations of reciprocal regard. Whoso sets up barriers to these, thwarts the ways of Providence, crosses the tendencies of human nature, and directly interferes with the laws of God."

Addressing himself directly to the judges, he said, "The Christian spirit I again invoke. Where this prevails, there is neither Jew nor Gentile, Greek nor barbarian, bond nor free, but all are alike. From this we derive new and solemn assurance of the equality of men, as an ordinance of God."

Here we see one feature of the Civil Rights Bill, which Mr. Sumner so earnestly pressed Congress to pass, as an act of justice to the blacks, and of benefit to the whole country.

The court, in the present case, did not see fit to annul the discrimination in the common schools.* But in 1855 the legislature threw the door open to all children alike. So we trust the national legislature will do for the whole country.

The year 1850 is memorable for the series of compromises, originating with Henry Clay, of Kentucky, which were designed to allay and forever settle the controversy about slavery. Alas! the "conflict" was "irrepressible."

It was now a period of extreme irritation between the Free and the Slave States. The annexation of Texas, as a slave state, in 1845; the war with Mexico, begun in 1846; the acquisition, as the result of it, of the vast territory of New Mexico and California, which the South were laboring to throw open to slavery, — all this had seriously alarmed the North. On the other hand,

* Chief Justice Shaw decided that the claim of equality before the law meant "only that the rights of all, as they are settled and regulated by law, are equally entitled to the paternal consideration and protection of the law for their maintenance and security."

the growing opposition to slavery at the North, the determined spirit of the abolitionists, the rise of the Liberty party in 1840, of the Free Soil party in 1848, and the fear entertained at the South that, after all, New Mexico and California were likely to be non-slaveholding, had aroused the people of the Slave States to a fearful pitch of exasperation. Then came forward the great compromiser, with his panacea of peace — his last public act. It was discussed amid great excitement, in and out of Congress, from January to September, in which month California was admitted as a Free State, New Mexico and Utah were organized as Territories with no provision for or against slavery, the slave-trade was prohibited in the District of Columbia, and a stringent Fugitive Slave Law was passed.

"Now," said President Fillmore, "we have been rescued from the wide and boundless agitation that surrounded us, and have a firm, distinct, and legal ground to rest upon."

But he was crying peace when there was no peace. Specially obnoxious to the North was the Fugitive Slave Bill. It was a shameful statute, not only as designed to rivet more firmly the shackles of the slave, and as carrying terror into every colored home in the Free States, but as turning the free North into a legalized hunting-ground for fugitives, and as visiting with "bitter penalties of fine and imprisonment the faithful men and women who rendered to the fugitive that countenance, succor, and shelter which Christianity expressly requires;" thus, "from beginning to end," setting "at nought the best principles of the constitution, and the very laws of God."

The most odious features of this bill were the following: it ordained a "summary process" — a legal proceeding intended to *protect* human freedom, but which in this case was wickedly perverted to the very opposite.

It violated the fundamental right of *trial by jury*, which the constitution of the United States grants in suits at common law, where the value in controversy shall exceed twenty dollars — the liberty of a man being made of less account than the recovery of a horse.

It provided that "in *no* trial or hearing under this act shall *the testimony of such alleged fugitive be admitted in evidence*." He might be a white man or a free negro, but he could bring forward no proof of the fact. The claimant with a bribe in his hand might enter into collusion with the commissioner, and between them the innocent victim might be reduced to slavery.

It placed the liberty of the alleged fugitive *at the mercy of one man*, from whose verdict there was no appeal.

The government *offered a premium for kidnapping*, for it allowed the commissioner twice as much in case he surrendered the alleged fugitive to the claimant, as he should receive if he released him — ten dollars for declaring a man a slave, five dollars for declaring him a freeman!

It authorized the ministers of the law — the mockery of law — to "summon and call to their aid the bystanders, or *posse comitatus* of the proper county," and it "COMMANDED" *all good citizens* to aid and assist in the prompt and efficient execution of the law, under the penalty of fine and imprisonment.

In the last provision, it seemed as though the slave power was resolved to press to Northern lips the bitterest cup of abomination which it could possibly concoct.

No wonder it awakened a feeling of indignation and horror, not only among the blacks, but among multitudes of the liberty-loving people of the Free States. Many, even, who were little concerned for the miseries of the colored people, revolted at the thought of being themselves "commanded" by the slave power to act the part of slave-catcher — in fact, to become slaves.

Meetings for protesting against the outrageous act were held in different places. One of the most note-worthy was held in Faneuil Hall, just one month after the passage of the bill, for the special purpose of taking measures for the protection of the colored people of the city, and of fugitives from slavery. It was an enthusiastic gathering. In the opening prayer, Dr. Lowell said, "Thou who art no respecter of persons, who art love, and dwellest in love, look in mercy upon those of our brethren on whose behalf we are now assembled — fugitives from slavery."

It was necessary that something should be done, for, immediately upon the passing of the bill, slave-hunting began all over the North, and was prosecuted with fearful activity. Spies were everywhere. Slave-hunters became familiar characters. In New York, one Sunday morning, a slaveholding clergyman, just arrived, was seen riding on the top of a stage, perched aloft for the purpose, perhaps, of discovering his victim. The first case under the act, September 28, was that of James Hamlet, who was seized in New York, and hurried off to a woman in Baltimore who laid claim to him. In many cases, the execution of the law was attended with circumstances of peculiar aggravation. Families which had long enjoyed peace at the free North were now invaded by the slave power, and either broken up, or forced to the most heart-rending separations. Large numbers fled to British soil. "Within the first year of its [the bill's] existence, more persons, probably, were seized as fugitive slaves than during the preceding sixty years."

The first fugitives whom the act sought to arrest in Boston were William and Ellen Crafts, in 1850. In their case no attempt was made to conceal them. William was ascertained to be a man of pluck, who would make a stout resistance, and whom it might be dangerous to approach. There was at this time a Committee of Vigilance and Safety, composed of prominent abolitionists, to look after the interests of fugitives. At one of their meetings, which were usually held in Stacy Hall, on Washington Street, Mr. Lewis Hayden, a well-known resident of Boston, himself a fugitive, came in under great excitement. The case now pending was becoming more critical. The question was, whether Crafts should be secretly sent to Canada, or whether he should be advised to remain and defy the "law."

Mr. Hayden, at whose house William and Ellen Crafts were stopping, and who knew the spirit of the former, immediately on entering the hall, poured out the fullness of his heart, taking the ground that Crafts should not be sent away. In his earnestness, he had scarcely noticed who were present; but suddenly pausing, and seeing what men he was addressing, — John C. Park, Theodore Parker, Francis Jackson, Ralph Waldo Emerson, Charles Sumner, Timothy Gilbert, George Thompson, and other members of the committee, or friends of the cause, — he instantly dropped into his seat. Mr. Sumner at once arose, and took up the case where Mr. Hayden had left it, urging, that as Crafts had given proof of his manhood, it would be wrong to hasten his escape; that it was his duty to remain, and make a stand against the infamous law. The kidnappers must be driven from Boston.

The character of his remarks at this time may also be gathered from what he said in a public meeting in November: "From a humane, just, and religious people will spring a public opinion to keep perpetual guard over the liberties of all within our borders. Nay, more like the flaming sword of the cherubim at the gates of Paradise, turning on every side, it shall prevent any SLAVE-HUNTER from ever setting foot in this Commonwealth. Elsewhere he may pursue his human prey, employ his congenial bloodhounds, and exult in his successful game; but into Massachusetts he must not come. Again, let me be understood. I counsel no violence. I would not touch his person. Not with whips and thongs would I scourge him from the land. The contempt, the indignation, the abhorrence of the community shall be our weapons of offence. Wherever he moves, he shall find no house to receive him, no table spread to nourish him, no welcome to cheer him. The dismal lot of the Roman exile shall be his. He shall be a wanderer, without roof, fire, or water. Men shall point at him on the streets and in the highways.

> 'Sleep shall neither night nor day
> Hang upon his pent-house lid;
> He shall live a man forbid;
> Weary, sevennights nine times nine,
> Shall he dwindle, peak, and pine.'

"Villages, towns, and cities shall refuse to receive the monster; they shall vomit him forth, never again to disturb the repose of our community."

Thus would Mr. Sumner arrest the action of the "law" at the outset.

William and Ellen Crafts were not apprehended. Their would-be kidnappers retired without their victims. At length the fugitives were sent to England, where Crafts became a sort of commercial agent to the kingdom of Dahomey. He is now living in Georgia.

At the public Free Soil meeting, to which reference was just made, November 6, 1850, before the annual election, Mr. Sumner denounced the Fugitive Bill as "cruel, unchristian, and devilish." It was unconstitutional also, and ought not to be obeyed.

After stating, in his speech, that he himself

held the office of commissioner by appointment, the year before, of Judge Story, — an office whose duties he had seldom exercised, — yet, said he, "I cannot forget that I am a *man*, although I am a commissioner. . . . For myself, let me say, that I can imagine no office, no salary, no consideration, which I would not gladly forego, rather than become in any way the agent in enslaving my brother man. Where for me were comfort and solace after such a work? In dreams and in waking hours, in solitude and in the street, in the meditation of the closet and in the affairs of men, wherever I turned, there my victim would stare me in the face. From distant rice-fields and sugar-plantations of the South, his cries beneath the vindictive lash, his moans at the thought of liberty, once his, now, alas! ravished away, would pursue me, repeating the tale of his tearful doom, and sounding, forever sounding, in my ears, 'Thou art the man!'"

Speaking in more general terms, he said, "We have seen what Congress has done. And yet, in the face of these enormities of legislation, . . . we are told that the slavery question is settled. Yes, *settled*, — *settled*, — that is the word.

Nothing, sir, can be settled which is not right. Nothing can be settled which is against freedom. Nothing can be settled which is contrary to the Divine law. God, nature, and all the holy sentiments of the heart repudiate any such seeming settlement."

As an encouragement to fidelity in the cause of freedom, he said, "To every laborer in a cause like this, there are satisfactions unknown to the common political partisan. . . . Whatever may be existing impediments, his is the cheering conviction that every word spoken, every act performed, every vote cast for this cause, helps to swell those quickening influences by which truth, justice, and humanity will be established upon earth. He may not live to witness the blessed consummation, but it is none the less certain. Others may dwell on the past as secure. Under the laws of a beneficent God, *the future also is secure,* — on the single condition that we labor for its great objects."

With reference to the election of suitable men to represent the cause in the State and the Nation, he said: "Admonished by the experience of timidity, irresolution, and weakness in our public men, amidst the temptations of ambition and power, the friends of freedom cannot lightly bestow their confidence. They can put trust only in men of tried character and inflexible will. Three things at least they must require ; the first is *backbone;* the second is *backbone;* and the third is *backbone.* . . . Wanting this, they all want that courage, constancy, firmness, which are essential to the support of PRINCIPLE. Let no such men be trusted." And then, referring to his own purpose, he added, "To vindicate freedom and oppose slavery, so far as I may constitutionally, — with earnestness, and yet, I trust, without personal unkindness on my part, — is the object near my heart. . . . Rejoicing in associates from any quarter, I shall be found ever with that party which most truly represents the principles of freedom. . . . Whenever I forget them, whenever I become indifferent to them, whenever I cease to be constant in maintaining them, through good report and evil report, in any future combinations of party, then may my tongue cleave to the roof of my mouth, may my right hand forget its cunning ! "

Now that he has gone from us, his work completed, we can say of him, that he never forgot these principles, but to the very last, even with his latest breath, redeemed every pledge here made.

This speech was received with great enthusiasm by one class, but denounced by another as "treasonable." It awakened deep feeling throughout the country, so bold and determined was its stand against a congressional statute. It doubtless had an important influence in the election which was about to take place for United States senator, to fill the place made vacant by the appointment of Daniel Webster as secretary of state.

CHAPTER XIV.

The "Coalition." — Nomination of Mr. Sumner for the United States Senate. — Scenes in the Legislature. — Mr. Bartlett's Proposition. — Lack of Envelopes. — Talking against Time. — Election of Mr. Sumner. — Letter of John G. Whittier to Mr. Sumner. — The Apple-Woman. — Feeling among the Whigs. — Treatment of Mr. Sumner. — Address to the Legislature. — Horace Mann.

WE have now reached a very important period. Hitherto Mr. Sumner has acted only as a private citizen; he is now to take a public office, and to become a public man, in a degree accorded to but few of this or any generation. The whole course of his life is henceforth to run in a channel far different from that marked out by himself. Yet, in a deeper sense, it was not different. He was still to be Charles Sumner, the same foe to war and slavery, the same friend of peace and freedom, the same lover of truth and justice, only in a wider sphere.

At this time there were three political parties in Massachusetts, the Whig, the Democratic, and the Free Soil. The two latter were neither of them strong enough to carry an election over the Whigs, but by a combination they hoped to secure their object.

The Democrats wished to conquer the Whigs, the Free Soilers wished to promote the cause of freedom. Among the former, also, there were a considerable number who were willing that the slave power should be rebuked. Many such afterwards became valiant Republicans.

It was accordingly agreed that most "of the state officers chosen by the legislature should be Democrats, and the United States senator a Free Soiler." This was the famous "coalition."

Henry Wilson, Free Soiler, was selected as candidate for President of the Senate; N. P. Banks, Democrat, for Speaker of the House; George S. Boutwell, Democrat, for Governor; and Charles Sumner, Free Soiler, for United States senator, all of whom were elected.*

* It is worthy of remark, that this legislature of 1851 contained an unusual number of members who have since risen to positions of eminence in the commonwealth or in the national government. Three have been governors of the State, N. P. Banks, H. J. Gardi-

To Mr. Sumner this was a wholly unexpected and undesired nomination. But he yielded to the importunities of the friends of freedom, who insisted that, for the sake of the cause, he ought to forget his personal preferences.

The choice of United States senator proved to be a three months' race between Mr. Sumner and Mr. Winthrop.

The Senate proceeded to ballot on January 22, 1851, with the following result: Charles Sumner, 23; R. C. Winthrop, 14; Beach, 1. Mr. Sumner received, therefore, a majority of the votes at the first ballot, and the Senate did not vote again. In the House the first ballot stood thus: Sumner, 186; Winthrop, 167; scattering, 28; blanks, 3. Whole number, 381; necessary to a choice, 191. There was no choice.

The voting in the House was not continuous from day to day, as is the present rule, but was carried on amid several postponements, sometimes for a fortnight at a time.

ner, and William Claflin; several have represented the State in Congress; three have been speakers of the House in the State legislature; one is the present state treasurer; one has been mayor of Boston; one has sat on the bench of the Supreme Court at Washington; and one has held many important offices under the general government, being at present our minister to Spain. Others have held influential positions.

It was a period of intense excitement within and outside the General Court, enlivened now and then by amusing incidents. One member, living in the vicinity, but generally confined at home from sickness, was brought into the House whenever voting was to be done, and then carried back. Every man was expected to "do his duty," even if he died in the attempt.

And so it went on till March 12, when an exciting debate took place, in the course of which Caleb Cushing, of ancient and modern renown, being then a member from Newbury, said that "he would cheerfully confront any personal extremity, he would be content to relinquish forever all aspirations as a statesman or a man, he would think no personal sacrifice too great, if he might thereby avoid such a death-stab to the honor and welfare of the Commonwealth, and such a stain and disaster to the Union as the election to the Senate of the United States of a one-idea abolition agitator to represent the people of Massachusetts." *

* In generous contrast with the above, we gladly insert the following later testimony from Mr. Cushing: "I think the speeches, discourses, and miscellaneous papers of Mr. Sumner eminently deserve to be collected and published in a complete form. Whatever

From this we infer that Mr. Cushing was not a party to the coalition.

The session had now reached the 24th of April without an election. Trial had been made of voting *viva voce* and by open ballot, without securing for any one the requisite majority. Somebody, it appeared, was casting two votes. Each side suspected the other of foul play. At length Sidney Bartlett, an eminent lawyer, of the Whig party, thinking that by another method their candidate might gain an advantage, moved, that "in the further balloting, the ballot be placed in an envelope; and that, where two votes for one person are found in the same envelope, one shall be rejected; and that, where two votes for different persons are cast, both shall be rejected; the envelopes to be of a uniform character, furnished by the sergeant-at-arms."

For once the shrewd lawyer committed a blun-

difference of opinion there may be in the country concerning the various political doctrines which, in his long senatorial career, he has so earnestly and so steadily maintained, certain it is that his productions constitute an essential part of our public history, as well in foreign as in domestic relations; and they are characterized by such qualities of superior intellectual power, cultivated eloquence, and great and general accomplishment and statesmanship, as entitle them to a high and permanent place in the political literature of the United States."

der. The Free Soil members were delighted at the motion, which was carried at once.

But there were not envelopes enough in the State House for the unusual demand, and a messenger was hurried off to a stationer's for a supply.

Meanwhile the Free Soilers were in an agony lest, because of the readiness with which the proposition had been received, a reconsideration might be called for, and one of their number set himself to the task of talking against time. It was an immense relief when the messenger appeared with his box of envelopes, which were to work such wonders for the Whig party.

Immediately the twenty-sixth vote was taken, when, to the dismay of the author of the infallible panacea and his compatriots, Charles Sumner was declared to have received one hundred and ninety-three votes, and to be United States senator for six years; it having required ninety-three days to effect a concurrence of the House with the Senate's vote of January 22d.

At that moment the breath of life went out of the Whig party in Massachusetts. A little longer it had a "name to live," but "was dead."

The Democratic party had gained a temporary triumph, but it was by putting forward its most powerful future antagonist.

The real victor was the little party of freedom, which had obtained a leader, who, through "evil report and good report," and through "deaths oft," was to uphold their cause in the national Senate with a consistency and a firmness hitherto unparalleled on the floor of Congress.

His election was a national triumph. Congratulations came in from all the Free States, and from the friends of humanity abroad.

John G. Whittier, an "original" abolitionist, was among the first to express his gladness at the event. "I rejoice," he wrote to Mr. Sumner, "that, unpledged, free, and without a single concession or compromise, thou art enabled to take thy seat in the Senate. I never knew such a general feeling of real heart-pleasure and satisfaction as is manifested by all except inveterate Hunkers, in view of thy election. The whole country is electrified by it. Sick abed, I heard the guns, Quaker as I am, with real satisfaction."

"Thank God, we have at last got a Governor *that can walk*," said an old apple-woman, in the year 1797, as Increase Sumner, a cousin of Charles Sumner's father, a man of athletic frame and majestic appearance, passed from the Old South Church after the election sermon. His predecessors, Adams and Hancock, had been crippled by gout or infirmity.

Thank God, Massachusetts had at last got a *Senator that could walk,* and with the firm and upright step of a real man. "*Laus Deo,*" wrote Mr. Chase when he heard of the event, and all lovers of freedom re-echoed the sentiment.

Mr. Sumner heard of the election while at the house of Hon. Charles Francis Adams, in Boston, and there received the first congratulations. A proposition for a public demonstration at his own house in the evening he discountenanced, saying, that, while feeling grateful to friends for their kindness, he was unwilling to do or say anything that could be construed by any one as evidence of personal triumph, — that it was the triumph of the cause, but that his heart dictated silence. The account given in the second volume of his Works, further states, that "in the evening there was a meeting for congratulation in State Street, where speeches were made by Hon. Henry Wilson and others." The crowd in State Street moved to the house of Mr. Sumner, but he had left the city.

A well-known colored man of the city, Lewis Hayden, who had been a fugitive slave, says that towards evening he met Mr. Sumner in Cambridge Street, who said to him, "I am doing what you did once — running away. I am a fugitive — from my friends." He was on his way to Cambridge, to his friend, Mr. Longfellow.

Besides other considerations, the solemn responsibilities, which he well knew were awaiting him, may also have weighed heavily upon Mr. Sumner's mind.

He was, further, making another great sacrifice. We have seen how, at an earlier period, in 1845, and again during the discussions on Prison Discipline, he had lost caste, in distinguished social circles, for his radical novelties, and his crossing the path of older and most reverend worthies in church and state. But now, doors which had been partially closed were to be shut in his face. He had allowed himself to be a competitor with a gentleman whom conservative Boston delighted to honor, and had actually taken possession of that dignified position of senator, which had seemed made vacant on purpose for Mr. Winthrop. This was not to be endured.

Most of Mr. Sumner's immediate literary friends, to whom he had been closely bound, now, with very few exceptions, turned their backs upon him. Among the exceptions were Mr. Prescott and Mr. Longfellow, whose friendship was immovable. One friend, distinguished for his classical attainments, would not, from this time, speak to Mr. Sumner, nor recognize him when they chanced to meet in the street; though in after years a hearty reconciliation took place. Such treatment must have saddened Mr. Sumner's heart, though it could not turn him from his high purpose. Not Plato, but Truth.

Through all these transactions we see the genuine greatness of the man. He did not seek office. Office sought him. "No man," says a journal of that day, "ever accepted office with cleaner hands than Charles Sumner. He consented to receive the nomination with extreme reluctance. His pursuits, his tastes, his aspirations, were in a different direction. He earnestly entreated his friends to select some other candidate. After he was nominated, an onslaught, unprecedented for ferocity and recklessness in political warfare, had seemed to render his election impossible, unless he would authorize some qualification of the alleged obnoxious doctrines of his speeches, particularly of his last Faneuil Hall speech. Mr. Sumner refused to retract, qualify, or explain. Ten lines from his pen — lines that a politician might have written without even the appearance of a change of sentiment — would have secured his election in January. No solicitation of friends or opponents could extort a line.

"A delegation of Hunkers applied to him for a few words to cover their retreat. In reply, he stated that he had no pledges to give, no explanations to make; he referred them to his published speeches for his position, and added, that he had not sought the office, but if it came to him it must find him an independent man. To another Democrat, who called on him on the same errand, he said, 'If by walking around my office I could secure the senatorship, I would not take a step.'

"In February he placed in the hands of General [now Vice-President] Wilson [then president of the state Senate] a letter authorizing that gentleman to withdraw his name, whenever, in his judgment, the good of the cause should require it." *

Besides a letter of acceptance sent to both Houses, Mr. Sumner, following the precedent set by John Quincy Adams in 1808, addressed the legislature directly. In that speech he said, "If I were to follow the customary course, I should receive this [certificate of election] in silence. But the protracted and unprecedented contest which ended in my election, the interest it awakened, the importance universally conceded to it, the ardor of opposition, and the constancy of support which it aroused, also the principles which more than ever among us it brought into discussion, seem to justify what my own feelings irresistibly prompt — a departure from this rule. . . .

"Your appointment finds me in a private station, with which I am entirely content. For the first time in my life I am called to political office. With none of the experience possessed by others to smooth the way of labor, I well might hesitate. But I am cheered by the generous confidence, which, throughout a lengthened contest, perse-

* Daily Commonwealth, April 25, 1851.

vered in sustaining me, and by the conviction that, amidst all seeming differences of party, the sentiments of which I am the known advocate, and which led to my original selection as candidate, are dear to the hearts of the people throughout this commonwealth. . . .

"Acknowledging the right of my country to the services of her sons wherever she chooses to place them, and with a heart full of gratitude that a sacred cause is permitted to triumph through me, I now accept the post of senator.

"I accept it as the servant of Massachusetts, mindful of the sentiments solemnly uttered by her successive legislatures, of the genius which inspires her history, and of the men, her perpetual pride and ornament, who breathed into her that breath of liberty which early made her an example to the States. In such service, the way, though new to my footsteps, is illumined by lights which cannot be missed. . . .

"Let me borrow, in conclusion, the language of another: 'I see my duty — that of standing up for the liberties of my country; and whatever difficulties and discouragements lie in my way, I dare not shrink from it; and I rely on that Being who has not left to us the choice of duties, that, whilst I conscientiously discharge mine, I shall not finally lose my reward.' These are words attributed to Washington in the early days of the American revolution. The rule of duty is the same for the lowly and the great; and I hope it may not seem presumptuous in one so humble as myself to adopt his determination, and to avow his confidence."

And so Massachusetts sent a MAN to represent her in the "high places of the field."

The same month Horace Mann wrote from his place in Washington, "My dear Sumner, *Laus Deo!* Good, better, best, better yet! By the necessity of the case, you are now to be a politician — an honest one. Scores have asked whether you would be true. I have underwritten to the amount of twenty reputations."

CHAPTER XV.

Lifting up and Casting down. — Thomas Sims a Fugitive Slave. — Returned to his "Master." — Theodore Parker. — Mr. Sumner's Opinion. — His First Remarks in the Senate. — Kossuth. — Land Bill. — Roads. — J. Fenimore Cooper. — Drayton and Sayres. — Anxiety of Mr. Sumner's Friends. — Fugitive Slave Bill. — Attempt to get a Hearing. — His Friends censure him. — Letter to Mr. Parker. — The great Opportunity improved.

We will go back a little way to the time when the voting for senator was yet going on in the legislature. Between the nineteenth and twentieth ballotings, — that is, between March 19 and April 20, 1851, — another scene, of far different character, was enacting in a United States commissioner's court, in the same city of Boston — different, yet strangely connected with the other in the State House.

In the one case the question was, which one of two freemen should be elevated to a high post of honor; in the other, whether a man, an American, should be sent back to slavery. What a jumble of ideas in a free, Christian land!

One American *was* exalted to office, another American *was* deemed to be a slave, the property of yet another American, and went down again into his prison-house.

Doubtless this example of the injustice and barbarity of slavery, right under the shadow of the State House, helped to nerve the friends of freedom to stand by Mr. Sumner.

Thomas Sims, poor fellow, had found his way to Boston in search of freedom, and for a time felt comparatively safe, close by the "Cradle of Liberty." He was seized under the false charge of having stolen a watch, and hurried off, after he had made a stout resistance, to the Court House, which was converted into a jail. While being taken from the carriage into the Court House, he uttered the broken cry, "I am in the hands of the kidnappers."

The jail was guarded by the city marshal and sixty members of the city police. A detachment of the military was also ordered out. Chains were placed around the building, and all citizens were strictly prohibited admission, except members of the press and the bar.

Before the commissioner, Sims was defended by Robert Rantoul, Jr., Charles G. Loring, and Samuel E. Sewall. The last gentleman, always an ardent friend of freedom, had specially interested himself in the case. On the 12th of April, Sims was adjudged to be the property of a man named Potter. In one week more he was back again in Savannah.

Being delivered to his "master," he was taken down State Street, under an escort of two or three hundred men, in violation of the laws of the State, on his way back to the house of bondage.

It was of this outrage that Theodore Parker, who was never silent when liberty was at stake, said at a public meeting, "Nine days he was on trial for more than his life, and never saw a judge, never saw a jury. He was sent forth into bondage from the city of Boston. You remember the chains that were put around the Court House, you remember the judges of Massachusetts stooping, crouching, creeping, crawling, under the chains of slavery, in order to get into their own court."

The truth of history compels us to add, that "the state and city authorities, the judiciary, the military, the merchants," and very many of the citizens, approved the surrender.

Some months before, Shadrach, a fugitive slave, had been rescued, and had escaped. The commercial interests of Boston seemed to require some offering to the slave power, and Sims was made to pass through the fire to appease the Southern Moloch.

Mr. Sumner was deeply interested in this infamous affair. April 19, a week after the rendition, he wrote to Mr. Parker from his office in Court Street. Mr. Parker had preached on the subject on Sunday, the 11th.

"May you live a thousand years, always preaching the truth of Fast day! That sermon is a noble effort. It stirred me to the bottom of my heart, at times softening me almost to tears, and then again filling me with rage. . . .

"You have placed the commissioner in an immortal pillory, to receive the hootings and rotten eggs of the advancing generations. . . .

"My appeal is to the people, and my hopes to create in Massachusetts such a public opinion as will render the law a dead letter. It is in vain to expect its repeal by Congress till the slave power is overthrown.

"It is, however, with a rare *dementia* that this power has staked itself on a position which is so offensive, and which cannot for any length of time be tenable. In enacting that law, it has given to the Free States a sphere of discussion which they would otherwise have missed."

And so Charles Sumner went to his seat at Washington, and Thomas Sims to a plantation in Georgia. But the lofty senator and the lowly slave were, after all, co-laborers in the cause of freedom — yes, and co-sufferers.

In December, 1851, Mr. Sumner took his place in the Senate; and it is an interesting fact, that the very day he went into the chamber, Henry Clay went out of it, never to return — a fact symbolical of the going out of the old era of compromise, and the coming in of a new era of principle.

Mr. Sumner's first speech in the Senate, December 10, was very short, but it was characteristic of the man. His heart embraced every man who, in whatever land, showed himself the self-sacrificing friend of our struggling humanity. When, then, a resolution was introduced by Mr. Seward extending to Louis Kossuth, the Hungarian patriot, a national welcome, it had in Mr. Sumner a warm advocate. "I see in him," said he, "more than in any other living man, the power which may be exerted by a single earnest, honest soul in a noble cause. . . . He seems at times the fiery sword of freedom, and then the trumpet of resurrection to the nations."

Mr. Sumner regarded slavery as now the one supreme question, but he could and did take a comprehensive survey of all subjects of national importance. And although senator from Massachusetts, he also knew that he was senator of the United States. Hence, when, in February, 1852, a bill came up affecting the interests of the land States in the West, — the Iowa Railroad Bill, — he strongly urged a grant of land to that State in aid of certain railroads. Hear what he had to say about roads: —

"It would be difficult to exaggerate the influence of roads as means of civilization. This at least may be said, where roads are not, civilization cannot be; and civilization advances as roads are extended. By roads religion and knowledge are diffused, — intercourse of all kinds is promoted, — producer, manufacturer, and consumer are all brought nearer together, — commerce is quickened, markets are created, — property, wherever touched by these lines, as by a magic rod is changed into new value; and the great current of travel, like that stream of classic fable, or one of the rivers of our own California, hurries in a channel of golden sand. The roads, together with the laws, of ancient Rome are now better remembered than her victories. The Flaminian and Appian Ways, once trod by such great destinies, still remain as beneficent representatives of ancient grandeur. Under God, the road and the schoolmaster are two chief agents of human improvement. The education begun by the schoolmaster is expanded, liberalized, and completed by intercourse with the world; and this intercourse finds new opportunities and inducements in every road that is built."

About the same time, Mr. Sumner, in response to an invitation to a proposed demonstration in memory of J. Fenimore Cooper, paid a just and graceful tribute to the great American novelist:

"As an author of clear and manly prose, as a portrayer to the life of scenes on land and sea, as a master of the keys to human feelings, and as a beneficent contributor to the general fund of happiness, he is remembered with delight. As a patriot who loved his country, who illustrated its history, who advanced its character abroad, and by his genius won for it the unwilling regard of foreign nations, he deserves a place in the hearts of the American people."

Some time after this, Mr. Sumner became interested in the case of two men, Drayton and Sayres, incarcerated at Washington for helping the escape of slaves. On the 14th of May, he submitted an opinion to the president upon his pardoning power, hoping to effect their release.

The case is thus stated by Mr. Sumner himself: —

"This case, from beginning to end, is a curious episode of anti-slavery history. The people of Washington were surprised, on the morning of April 16, 1848, at hearing that the 'Pearl,' a schooner from the North, had sailed down the Potomac with seventy-six slaves, who had hurried aboard in the vain hope of obtaining their freedom. The schooner was pursued and brought back to Washington, with her human cargo, and the liberators, Drayton, master, and Sayres, mate. As the latter were taken from the river-side to the jail, they were followed by a pro-slavery mob, estimated at from four to six thousand people, many armed with deadly weapons, amid wrathful cries of — 'Hang him!' 'Lynch him!' with all profanities and abominations of speech, and exposed to violence of all kinds, — the thrust of a dirk-knife coming within an inch of Drayton. The same mob besieged the jail, and, hearing that Hon. Joshua R. Giddings, the brave representative of Ohio, was there in consultation with the prisoners, demanded his immediate expulsion; and the jailer, to save bloodshed, insisted upon his departure. Nor was the prevailing rage confined to the jail. It extended to the office of the National Era, the anti-slavery paper, which was saved from destruction only through the courage and calmness of its admirable editor. The spirit of the mob entered both houses of

Congress, and the slave-masters raged, as was their wont.

"Meanwhile, Drayton and Sayres were indicted before the Criminal Court of the District of Columbia, for 'transporting slaves.' There were no less than one hundred and fifteen indictments against each of the prisoners, and the bail demanded of each was seventy-six thousand dollars. Hon. Horace Mann, a representative of Massachusetts, appeared for the defence. His speech on this occasion will be read with constant interest. The spirit of the mob without entered the court-room, betraying itself even in the conduct of the judge, while, standing near the devoted counsel for the defence, were men who cocked pistols and drew dirks in the mob that followed the prisoners to the jail. Of course the verdict was 'guilty,' and the sentence was according to the extreme requirement of a barbarous law.

"Drayton and Sayres lingered in prison more than four years, and during this long incarceration, they were the objects of much sympathy at the North. A petition to Congress in their behalf, signed by leading abolitionists, including the eloquent Wendell Phillips, was forwarded to Mr. Sumner for presentation to the Senate. On careful consideration, he was satisfied that such a petition, if presented, would excite the dominant power to insist more strongly than ever on the letter of the law, and he took the responsibility of withholding it. Meanwhile he visited the sufferers in prison, and appealed to President Fillmore for their pardon. In this application he was aided by that humane lady, Miss Dix. The president interposed doubts of his right to pardon in such a case, but expressed a desire for light on this point.

"At his invitation, Mr. Sumner laid before him a paper, which was referred to the attorney-general, Mr. Crittenden, who gave an opinion affirming the power of the president; adding, however, 'Whether the power shall be exercised in this instance is another and very different question.' This opinion bears date August 4, 1852, which, it will be observed, was some time after the presidential convention of the two great political parties. Shortly afterwards the pardon was granted.

"There was reason to believe that an attempt would be made to arrest the pardoned persons on warrants from the governor of Virginia. Anticipating this peril, Mr. Sumner, as soon as the pardon was signed, hurried to the jail in a carriage, and, taking them with him, put them in charge of a friend, who conveyed them that night to Baltimore, a distance of forty miles, where they arrived in season for the early morning trains north, and in a few hours were out of danger." *

About seven months had now elapsed since Mr. Sumner took his seat in Congress; and yet, with the exception of brief remarks on presenting a memorial from some Friends against the Fugitive Slave Bill, his voice had not been heard in defence of the great cause for which mainly he had been sent there. His friends in Massachusetts began to feel some measure of anxiety. Theodore Parker had written to him, more than a year before, "I hope you will be the senator *with a conscience.* I look to you to represent justice. I expect much of you. I expect heroism of the most heroic kind." Writing to Dr. S. G. Howe, Mr. Parker said, "Do you see what imminent

* Works of Charles Sumner. Boston: Lee & Shepard.

deadly peril poor Sumner is in? If he does not speak, then he is dead."

So potent in previous years had been the Southern spell, either by blandishments or menaces, to seal the lips of Northern men upon the subject of slavery, that it is scarcely strange that doubts even of Charles Sumner's courage and conscience began to arise; for he, too, had been approached, in the old way so well understood by Southern gentlemen, with soft and courteous words. But our Samson was not to be taken in the toils which had captured so many Northern men. He knew what their polished phrases meant.

He had counted the cost, and was all the while but watching his opportunity. At length, July 27, 1852, he broke silence. "I have a resolution," said he in his place, "which I desire to offer; and as it is not in order to debate it to-day, I give notice that I shall expect to call it up to-morrow, at an early moment in the morning hour, when I shall throw myself upon the indulgence of the Senate to be heard upon it.

"'*Resolved*, That the committee on the judiciary be instructed to consider the expediency of reporting a bill for the immediate repeal of the act of Congress, approved September 18, 1850, known as the Fugitive Slave Act.' "

The next day he asked permission to take up the resolution. " As a senator," he said, " under the responsibilities of my position, I have deemed it my duty to offer the resolution. I may seem to have postponed this duty to an inconvenient period of the session; but had I attempted it at an earlier day, I might have exposed myself to a charge of a different character. It might have been said, that, a new-comer, and inexperienced in this scene, without deliberation, hastily, rashly, recklessly, I pushed this question before the country. This is not the case now. I have taken time, and, in the exercise of my most careful discretion, at last ask the attention of the Senate."

And then he added, " Make such disposition of my resolution afterwards as to you shall seem best; visit upon me any degree of criticism, censure, or displeasure; but do not refuse me a hearing. 'Strike, but hear.' "

The Senate, by a vote of thirty-two against ten, refused to hear him. Those who voted in the affirmative were Messrs. Clarke, Davis, Dodge,

Foot, Hamlin, Seward, Shields, Upham, and Wade.

The slave power boasted, that, for that session at least, the Massachusetts abolitionist should not be heard.

But while his enemies boasted, his friends censured. Even now suspicion was not entirely removed. Surely Mr. Sumner might contrive some way to compel a hearing, if he wished to. So said many of his friends in Massachusetts. Even the Liberator allowed itself to indulge in an ungenerous fling at the silent senator. He must be under an overseer! Theodore Parker, too, who knew Mr. Sumner so well, was not satisfied, and so he wrote to him. To this the senator replied, August 11, —

"I will not argue the question of past delay. To all that can be said on that head, there is this explicit answer. With a heart full of devotion to our cause, in the exercise of my best discretion, and on the advice or with the concurrence of friends, I have waited. It may be that this was unwise, but it was honestly and sincerely adopted, with a view to serve the cause. Let this pass.

"You cannot desire a speech from me more

than I desire to make one. I came to the Senate on my late motion (July 27), prepared for the work, hoping to be allowed to go on, with the promise of leaders from all sides that I should have a hearing. I was cut off. No chance for courtesy. I must rely upon my rights.

"You tell me not to wait for the Civil Appropriation Bill. I know that it is hardly within the range of possibilities that any other bill should come forward, before this bill, to which my amendment can be attached. For ten days we have been on the Indian Appropriation Bill. With this the Fugitive Slave Bill is not germane.

"The Civil Appropriation Bill will probably pass the House to-day. It will come at once to the Senate, be referred to the Committee on Finance, be reported back by them with amendments. After the consideration of these amendments of the committee, *and not before*, my chance will come. *For this I am prepared, with a determination equal to your own.* All this delay is to me a source of grief and disappointment. But I know my heart; and I know that sincerely, singly, I have striven for the cause.

"You remember the picture in the 'Ancient Mariner' of the ship in the terrible calm? In such a calm is my ship at this moment; I cannot move it. But I claim the confidence of friends, for I know that I deserve it. . . . There is a time for all things."

Directly after he wrote again, "In my course I have thought little what people would say, whether Hunkers or Free Soilers, *but how I could most serve the cause.* This consciousness sustains me now, while I hear reports of distrust, and note the gibes of the press.

"*Nothing but death or deadly injustice, overthrowing all rule, can prevent me from speaking.* In waiting till I did, I was right."

It looks to us, at this time, as if Mr. Parker acted with a measure of officiousness, too much in the character of a conscience-keeper, when he thus seemed to dictate to Mr. Sumner his line of duty; though, perhaps, he used only the frank freedom of a friend.

But Mr. Sumner, on the spot, best understood his position, its difficulties and opportunities. After the 26th of August there was no more distrust.

We may here premise, that a chief artifice of

the Whigs and Democrats — both bidding for Southern patronage — was the cry, that they, standing by the compromise measures, constituted the national party, while all others were chargeable with sectionalism. Mr. Sumner determined to reverse the order, to prove that freedom was national, slavery sectional. But how could he get a hearing before a body which had just commanded silence? No thanks to the Senate. The Civil Diplomatic Appropriation Bill being under consideration, the following amendment was proposed by Mr. Hunter, of Virginia: —

"That, where the *ministerial officers of the United States have or shall incur extraordinary expenses* in executing the laws thereof, the payment of which is not specifically provided for, the President of the United States is authorized to allow the payment thereof, under the special taxation of the District or Circuit Court of the District in which the said services have been or shall be rendered, to be paid from the appropriation for defraying the expenses of the Judiciary."

The "extraordinary expenses" of course meant those incurred in the apprehension, trial, and rendition of fugitive slaves, under the recently enacted Fugitive Slave Bill.

His hour had come. Mr. Sumner immediately moved the following amendment to the amendment: —

"*Provided*, That no such allowance shall be authorized for any expenses incurred in executing the act of September 18, 1850, for the surrender of fugitives from service or labor; which said act is hereby repealed."

When it was known that Mr. Sumner intended to speak, several senators came to him, begging him to desist from his purpose. He replied, "God willing, I shall speak, and press the question to a vote, even if I am left alone."

He did speak, and for nearly four hours. It must have been a thrilling scene. There, before the speaker, were his fellow-senators, all of them bitter opponents, or timid friends, save a little handful of hated, yet despised abolitionists, a helpless minority. He was to speak upon a subject so "delicate," that barely to mention it was to throw the slaveholding members into spasms, — the one subject which alone, of all others, might not be brought into discussion. Whigs and Democrats had combined to compel him to silence; hitherto with success. But behold, he has the floor, and they must hear him.

Mr. Sumner knew that he was addressing more than the Senate. The whole country was his audience. And he rose to the greatness and solemnity of the occasion. Inspired by a profound sense of justice, sustained by a firm conviction that he was right, and by the certain belief in the final triumph of his cause, he knew that he had the advantage of his opponents. He knew that their consciences were on his side; and he looked them in the face without quailing. There was a voice which said to him, "Fear not, for they that be with us are more than they that be with them." He knew that in "dear old Massachusetts" and elsewhere, he had the warm sympathies of valued friends of humanity. His was the cause of God.

"Mr. President," he began, "here is a provision for extraordinary expenses incurred in executing the laws of the United States. Extraordinary expenses! Sir, beneath these specious words lurks the very subject on which, by a solemn vote of this body, I was refused a hearing. Here it is; no longer open to the charge of being an 'abstraction,' but actually presented for practical legislation; not introduced by me, but by the senator from Virginia (Mr. Hunter), on the recommendation of an important committee of the Senate; not brought forward weeks ago, when there was ample time for discussion, but only at this moment, without any reference to the late period of the session. The amendment which I offer proposes to remove one chief occasion of these extraordinary expenses. Beyond all controversy or cavil, it is strictly in order. And now, at last, among these final crowded days of our duties here, but at this earliest opportunity, I am to be heard — not as a favor, but as a right. The graceful usages of this body may be abandoned, but the established privileges of debate cannot be abridged. Parliamentary courtesy may be forgotten, but parliamentary law must prevail. The subject is broadly before the Senate. By the blessing of God it shall be discussed.

"With me, sir, there is no alternative. Painfully convinced of the unutterable wrong and woe of slavery, — profoundly believing that, according to the true spirit of the Constitution and the sentiments of the fathers, it can find no place under our national government, — that it is in every respect *sectional*, and in no respect *national*, — that it is always and everywhere creature and dependant of the *States*, and never anywhere creature or dependant of the *Nation*, and that the *Nation* can never, by legislative or other act, impart to it any support under the Constitution of the United States, — with these convictions I could not allow this session to reach its close without making or seizing an opportunity to declare myself openly against the usurpation, injustice, and cruelty of the late intolerable enactment for the recovery of fugitive slaves. Full well I know, sir, the difficulties of this discussion, arising from prejudices of opinion and from adverse conclusions, strong and sincere as my own. Full well I know that I am in a small minority, with few here to whom I can look for sympathy or support. Full well I know that I must utter things unwelcome to many in this body, which I cannot do without pain. Full well I know that the institution of slavery in our country, which I now proceed to consider, is as sensitive as it is powerful, possessing a power to shake the whole land, with a sensitiveness that shrinks and trembles at the touch. But while these things may properly prompt me to caution and reserve, they cannot change my duty or my determination to perform it. For this I willingly forget myself and all personal consequences. The favor and good-will of my fellow-citizens, of my brethren of the Senate, sir, grateful to me as they justly are, I am ready, if required, to sacrifice. Whatever I am or may be I freely offer to this cause.

"Party does not constrain me; nor is my independence lessened by any relations to the office which gives me a title to be heard on this floor. Here, sir, I speak proudly. By no effort, by no desire of my own, I find myself a senator of the United States. Never before have I held public office of any kind. With the ample opportunities of private life I was content. No tombstone for me could bear a fairer inscription than this: 'Here lies one who, without the honors or emoluments of public station, did something for his fellow-men.' From such simple aspirations I was taken away by the free choice of my native Commonwealth, and placed at this responsible post of duty, without personal obligations of any kind, beyond what was implied in my life and published words. . . .

"Rejoicing in my independence, and claiming nothing from party ties, I throw myself upon the candor and magnanimity of the Senate. I ask your attention; I trust not to abuse it. I may speak strongly, for I shall speak openly, and from the strength of my convictions. I may speak warmly, for I shall speak from the heart. But in no event can I forget the amenities which belong to debate, and which especially become this body. Slavery I must condemn with my whole soul; but here I need only borrow the language of slaveholders; nor would it accord with my habits or my sense of justice to exhibit them as the impersonation of the institution — Jefferson calls it the 'enormity' — which they cherish. Of them I do not speak; but without fear and without favor, as without impeachment of any person, I assail this wrong. Again, sir, I may err; but it will be with the fathers. I plant myself on the ancient ways of the republic, with its grandest names, its surest landmarks, and all its original altar-fires about me."

Referring to the effort to suppress free speech, Mr. Sumner said, "But, sir, this effort is impotent as tyrannical. Convictions of the heart cannot be repressed. Utterances of conscience must be heard. They break forth with irrepressible might. As well attempt to check the tides of Ocean, the currents of the Mississippi, or the rushing waters of Niagara. The discussion of slavery will proceed, wherever two or three are gathered together — by the fireside, on the highway, at the public meeting, in the church. The movement against slavery is from the Everlasting Arm. Even now it is gathering its forces, soon to be confessed everywhere. It may not be felt yet in the high places of office and power, but all who can put their ears humbly to the ground will hear and comprehend its incessant and advancing tread."

The argument proving the national character of freedom is thus condensed: "Considering that slavery is of such an offensive character that it can find sanction only in 'positive law,' and that it has no such 'positive' sanction in the Constitution, — that the Constitution, according to its preamble, was ordained to 'establish justice' and 'secure the blessings of liberty,' — that, in the convention which framed it, and also elsewhere at the time, it was declared not to sanction slavery, — that, according to the Declaration of Independence, and the Address of the Continental Congress, the nation was dedicated to 'liberty' and the 'rights of human nature,'—that, according to the principles of the common law, the Constitution must be interpreted openly, actively, and perpetually for freedom,—that, according to the decision of the Supreme Court, it acts upon slaves, *not as property*, but as persons,—that, at the first organization of the national government under Washington, slavery had no national favor, existed nowhere on the national territory, beneath the national flag, but was openly condemned, by nation, church, colleges, and literature of the time,—and finally, that according to an amendment of the Constitution, the national government can exercise only powers delegated to it, among which is none to support slavery,—considering these things, sir, it is impossible to avoid the single conclusion that slavery is in no respect a national institution, and that the Constitution nowhere upholds property in man."

Mr. Sumner thus characterized the Fugitive Slave Act of 1850: "Oppression by an individual is detestable; but oppression by law is worse. Hard and inscrutable, when the law, to which the citizen naturally looks for protection, becomes itself a standing peril. As the sword takes the place of the shield, despair settles down like a cloud. . . .

"With every attempt to administer the Slave Act, it constantly becomes more revolting, particularly in its influence on the agents it enlists. The spirit of the law passes into them, as the devils entered the swine. Upstart commissioners, mere mushrooms of courts, vie and re-vie with each other. Now by indecent speed, now by harshness of manner, now by denial of evidence, now by crippling the defence, and now by open, glaring wrong, they make the odious Act yet more odious. Clemency, grace, and justice die in its presence. All this is observed by the world. Not a case occurs which does not harrow the souls of good men, bringing tears of sympathy to the eyes, and those other noble tears which 'patriots shed over dying laws.'"

The heroism that shows itself in efforts to regain lost freedom is thus strikingly described: "Less by genius or eminent service than by suffering are the fugitive slaves of our country now commended. For them every sentiment of humanity is aroused.

> 'Who could refrain,
> That had a heart to love, and in that heart
> Courage to make his love known?'

Rude and ignorant they may be, but in their very efforts for freedom they claim kindred with all that is noble in the past. Romance has no stories of more thrilling interest. Classical antiquity has preserved no examples of adventure and trial more worthy of renown. They are among the heroes of our age. Among them are those whose names will be treasured in the annals of their race. By eloquent voice they have done much to make their wrongs known, and to secure the respect of the world. History will soon lend her avenging pen. Proscribed by you during life, they will proscribe you through all time. Sir, already judgment is beginning. A righteous public sentiment palsies your enactment."

The speech was followed by a debate, in which nineteen senators, from eighteen different States, took part; all in opposition to Mr. Sumner's amendment, except Mr. Chase, of Ohio, and Mr. Hale, of New Hampshire. Mr. Seward was absent. Senators from nine Free States were among the opponents. Three Southern senators indulged in personalities. Mr. Chase, afterwards the honored secretary of the treasury during the civil war, and yet later, chief justice of the Supreme Court of the United States, said, "In my judgment the speech of my friend from Massachusetts will mark AN ERA in American history." Henry Wilson, afterwards, for so many years, his co-agitator in the national Senate, and always his friend and able supporter, Wendell Phillips, Stephen C. Phillips, and many others, wrote to Mr. Sumner in a similar strain.

The vote which followed the debate tells the sad tale of a Senate sold to slavery. On Mr. Sumner's amendment: Yeas, 4; nays, 47. The four were Messrs. Chase, Hale, Wade, and Sumner.

But that small vote did not tell the whole story. *The truth had had a hearing.* Moreover, it had awakened the consciences, and touched the deeper, better feelings of some of the Southern auditors.

A letter written to Rev. Dr. Stebbins, about two months later, gives us a very interesting insight into Mr. Sumner's feelings at this time, and also shows the happy effect of his speech, even upon slaveholders: —

"NEWPORT, R. I., October 12, '52.

"MY DEAR SIR: I cannot receive the overflowing sympathy of your letter without a response. It has added to my happiness. The interest you express in that speech, and particularly in the latter part of it, emboldens me to write of it more freely than I have before.

"I went to the Senate determined to do my duty, but in my own way. Anxious for the cause, having it always in mind, I knew that I could not fail in loyalty, though I might err in judgment. All my instincts prompted delay. But meanwhile I was taunted and attacked at home. Had I been less conscious of the rectitude of my course, I might have sunk under these words. But I persevered in my own way.

"As I delivered the part to which you refer, I remember well the intent looks of the Senate, and particularly of Mr. King [president, *pro tem.*, of the Senate]. It was already dinner time, but all were silent and attentive, and Hale [John P. Hale, of N. H.] tells me that Mr. Underwood, of Kentucky, by his side, was in tears.

"From many leading Southern men I have received the strongest expressions of interest awakened in our cause, and a confession that they did not know before the strength of the argument on our side. Polk, of Tennessee, said to me, 'If you should make that speech in Tennessee, you would compel me to emancipate my niggers.' But enough of this. I have been tempted to it by the generosity of your letter.

"Thankfully and truly yours,

"CHARLES SUMNER."

CHAPTER XVI.

Return to Massachusetts. — Warm Welcome. — Speech at Lowell. — Free Soil Party. — Superintendents of Armories. — Convention to revise the Constitution of Massachusetts. — Colored Militia. — The Representative System. — Nebraska and Kansas. — Stephen A. Douglas. — Mr. Sumner's Speech. — Final Protest.

MR. SUMNER, on his return to Massachusetts, at the close of the session, was warmly welcomed by the friends of freedom. He had done his duty well, under circumstances of the most trying character. Where others had failed, he had not. At the State Convention of the Free Soil party, held in Lowell, September 15, 1852, presided over by Stephen C. Phillips, of Salem, Mr. Sumner was received with much enthusiasm.

"After an absence," he said, "of many months, I have now come home to breathe anew the invigorating Northern air, to tread again the free soil of our native Massachusetts, and to enjoy the sympathy of friends and fellow-citizens. But, while glad in your greetings, thus bounteously lavished, I cannot accept them for myself. I do not deserve them. They belong to the cause which we all have at heart, and which binds us together. . . . I have done nothing but my duty."

Farther on he said, "At the present time in our country, there exists a deep, controlling, conscientious feeling against slavery. . . . The rising public opinion cannot flow in the old political channels. It is impeded, choked, and dammed back. But if not *through* the old parties, then *over* the old parties, this irresistible current *shall* find its way. It cannot be permanently stopped. If the old parties will not become its organs, they must become its victims. The party of Freedom will certainly prevail. It may be by entering into and possessing one of the old parties, filling it with our own strong life; or it may be by drawing to itself the good and true from both, who are unwilling to continue in a political combination when it ceases to represent their convictions; but, in one way or the other, its ultimate triumph is sure.

"At this moment we are in a minority. At the

last popular election in Massachusetts there were twenty-eight thousand Free Soilers, forty-three thousand Democrats, and sixty-four thousand Whigs. But this is no reason for discouragement. According to recent estimates, the population of the whole world amounts to about eight hundred millions. Of these, only two hundred and sixty millions are Christians, while the remaining five hundred and forty millions are mainly Mahometans, Brahmins, and idolaters. Because the Christians are in this minority, that is no reason for renouncing Christianity, and for surrendering to the false religions; nor do we doubt that Christianity will yet prevail over the whole earth, as the waters cover the sea. The friends of freedom in Massachusetts are likewise in a minority; but they will not, therefore, renounce freedom, nor surrender to the political Mahometans, Brahmins, and idolaters of Baltimore; nor can they doubt that their cause, like Christianity, will yet prevail."

Then, referring to the candidates of the party, he added, "With such a cause and such candidates, no man can be disheartened. The tempest may blow, — but ours is a life-boat, not to be harmed by wind or wave. The Genius of Liberty sits at the helm. I hear her voice of cheer saying, 'Whoso sails with me comes to shore.'"

On his return to the Senate, next year, Mr. Sumner made some remarks in favor of employing civil instead of military superintendents of armories. Here his peace principles came out — another, though slight, example of his remarkable consistency. "I do affirm confidently," he said, "that the genius of our institutions favors civil life rather than military life,— and that, in harmony with this, it is our duty, whenever the public interests will permit, to limit and restrict the sphere of military influence. This is not a military monarchy, where the soldier is supreme, but a republic, where the soldier yields to the civilian. . . .

"The idea which has fallen from so many senators, that the superintendent of an armory ought to be a military man, . . . seems to me to be as illogical as the jocular fallacy of Dr. Johnson, that he 'who drives fat oxen should himself be fat.'"

Mr. Sumner was a member of the convention which met in 1853 to revise and amend the constitution of Massachusetts. He was an able and influential member. Among other resolutions which he advocated was the following: "That in the organization of the volunteer military companies of the Commonwealth there shall be *no distinction of color or race.*"

He also spoke on the representative system and its proper basis, and on bills of rights — their history and policy.

On the former topic he said, "This is an invention of modern times. In antiquity there were republics and democracies, but there was no representative system. Rulers were chosen by the people, as in many commonwealths; senators were designated by the king or by the censors, as in Rome; ambassadors or legates were sent to a federal council, as to the Assembly of the Amphictyons; but in no ancient state was any body of men ever constituted by the people to represent them in the administration of their internal affairs. In Athens, the people met in public assembly, and directly acted for themselves on all questions, foreign or domestic. This was possible there, as the state was small, and the Assembly seldom exceeded five thousand citizens, — a large town-meeting, or mass-meeting, we might call it, — not inaptly termed 'that fierce democratie' of Athens."

After alluding to the representative system as it exists in England, Mr. Sumner said, that "to our country belongs the honor of first giving to the world the idea of a system which, discarding corporate representation [as in England], founded itself absolutely on equality." The American system, as distinguished from the English, is the applying the rule of three to representation — a representation not according to property, not according to territory, not according to any corporate rights, but of persons, according to their respective numbers. "It gives to the great principle of human equality a new expansion and application. It makes all men, in the enjoyment of the electoral franchise, whatever their diversities of intelligence, education, or wealth, or wheresoever they may be within the borders of the commonwealth, whether in small town or populous city, absolutely equal at the ballot-box."

"I cannot doubt that the district system, whereby the representative power will be distributed in just proportion, according to the rule of three, among the voters of the Commonwealth, is the true system, destined at no distant day to prevail."

In this connection Mr. Sumner said, "No lawgiver or statesman can disregard either history or abstract reason. He must contemplate both. He will faithfully study the Past, and will recognize its treasures and traditions; but, with equal fidelity, he will set his face towards the Future, where all institutions will at last be in harmony with truth."

Mr. Sumner's return to his seat in 1853 was signalized by a new and more audacious stage in the pro-slavery movement. Disappointed in California, the South was looking about for the means of extending the area of slavery even into regions from which it had been forever excluded by solemn compact. Thus originated the great struggle about Kansas and Nebraska. New States were soon to be formed out of the Territory of Nebraska, lying north of thirty-six degrees thirty minutes north latitude. The slave power coveted this fertile region — this garden of Naboth.

A Northern man, a native of free New England, Stephen A. Douglas, senator from Illinois, was the chief instrument in the perpetration of the great crime which soon followed. He submitted a bill, dividing the Territory into two, Nebraska and Kansas, and declaring the prohibition of slavery contained in the Missouri Compromise of 1820 "inconsistent with the principles of non-intervention by Congress with slavery in the States and Territories, as recognized by the legislation of 1850, commonly called the Compromise Measures."

According to this bill, Congress was not to legislate slavery into, nor exclude it from, any Territory or State, but to leave the people thereof perfectly free to form and regulate their domestic institutions in their own way, subject only to the Constitution of the United States. This was just what was wanted by the South — a chance to carry slavery into all the new Territories.

Mr. Sumner spoke most earnestly against the repeal of the Missouri prohibition of slavery, taking for his motto, "Cursed be he that removeth his neighbor's landmark, *and all the people shall say, Amen.*" The last words were emphasized by Mr. Sumner in the printed speech, indicating his remarkable, unwavering faith in the triumph of Right.

These were his opening words: —

"I approach this discussion with awe. The mighty question, with untold issues, oppresses me. Like a portentous cloud surcharged with irresistible storm and ruin, it seems to fill the whole heavens, making me painfully conscious how unequal to the occasion I am — how unequal, also, is all that I can say to all that I feel.

"The question for your consideration . . . concerns an immense region, larger than the original thirteen States, vying in extent with all the existing Free States, — stretching over prairie, field, and forest, — interlaced by silver streams, skirted by protecting mountains, and constituting the heart of the North American continent — only a little smaller, let me add, than three great European countries combined, — Italy, Spain, and France, — each of which, in succession, has dominated over the globe. This territory has been likened, on this floor, to the garden of God. . . . The bill now before us proposes to organize and equip two new territorial establishments, with governors, secretaries, legislatures, councils, legislators, judges, marshals, and the whole machinery of civil society. Such a measure at any time would deserve the most careful attention. But at the present moment it justly excites peculiar interest, from the effort made . . . to open this immense region to slavery."

Mr. Sumner arraigned this bill on two grounds: "First, in the name of public faith, as an infraction of solemn obligations. . . . Secondly, in the name of freedom, as an unjustifiable departure from the original anti-slavery policy of our fathers." He showed that Southern members urged the compromise of 1820, and that *it passed both Houses without a division.* It was as much a Southern as a Northern measure. It was approved by John C. Calhoun and other Southern members of Monroe's cabinet. Mr. Sumner would have the South keep the compact.

To the argument that this proposition was a measure of peace, he replied, "Peace depends on mutual confidence. It can never rest secure on broken faith and injustice;" and he added, "Amidst all seeming discouragements, the great omens are with us. Art, literature, poetry, religion, everything which elevates man, are all on our side. The plough, the steam engine, the telegraph, the book, every human improvement, every generous word anywhere, every true pulsation of every heart which is not a mere muscle and nothing else, gives new encouragement to the warfare with slavery. The discussion will proceed. . . . No political Joshua now, with miraculous power, can stop the sun in its course through the heavens. It is even now rejoicing, like a strong man, to run its race, and *will yet send its beams into the most distant plantations, melting the chains of every slave.*" And this, nearly ten years before emancipation, when slavery seemed bent on yet new conquests!

To the objection that the movement against slavery was dangerous to the Union, Mr. Sumner replied, that in freedom only true union could exist, and that in the abolition of slavery the North and the South would hereafter be bound more closely together. In this connection he quoted from Shakespeare the remarkable dialogue between Brutus and Cassius, in which Brutus might be considered as representing the North, Cassius the South: —

> " *Cas.* Urge me no more; I shall forget myself.
> Have mind upon your health; tempt me no farther.
> . . . .
> *Brut.* Hear me, for I will speak.
> Must I give way and room to your rash choler?
> . . . . . .

Cas. O ye gods! ye gods! must I endure all this?
Brut. All this? Ay, more; fret till your proud heart break;
Go, show your slaves how choleric you are,
And make your bondmen tremble. Must I budge?
Must I observe you? Must I stand and crouch
Under your testy humor?

. . . . . .

Cas. Do not presume too much upon my love;
I may do that I shall be sorry for.
Brut. You have done that you should be sorry for.
There is no terror, Cassius, in your threats;
For I am armed so strong in honesty,
That they pass by me as the idle wind,
Which I respect not.

. . . . .

Cas. A friend should bear his friend's infirmities,
But Brutus makes mine greater than they are.
Brut. I do not, TILL YOU PRACTISE THEM ON ME.
Cas. You love me not.
Brut. I do not like your faults."

All which ends at last in united heart and hand. So would it be if slavery should disappear.

Three months later, May 25, 1854, Mr. Sumner uttered his last protest against the infamous bill, and against slavery in Nebraska and Kansas. It was at the final passage. At midnight, Mr. Sumner offered numerous remonstrances against the bill from different parts of the country, chiefly from New England, and then spoke briefly, but most eloquently. Among other things, he said, —

"In passing such a bill as is now threatened, you scatter, from this dark midnight hour, no seeds of harmony and good-will, but, broadcast through the land, dragon's teeth, which haply may not spring up in direful crops of armed men, yet, I am assured, sir, will fructify in civil strife and feud. From the depths of my soul, as loyal citizen and as senator, I plead, remonstrate, protest against the passage of this bill. I struggle against it as against death; but, as in death itself corruption puts on incorruption, and this mortal body puts on immortality, so from the sting of this hour I find assurance of *that triumph by which freedom will be restored to her immortal birthright in the Republic.*

"Sir, the bill you are about to pass is at once the worst and the best on which Congress ever acted. Yes, sir, WORST and BEST at the same time.

"It is the worst bill, inasmuch as it is a present victory of slavery. In a Christian land, and in an age of civilization, a time-honored statute of freedom is struck down, opening the way to all the countless woes and wrongs of human bondage. Among the crimes of history, another is soon to be recorded, which no tears can blot out, and which in better days will be read with universal shame. . . . There is another side, to which I gladly turn. Sir, it is the best bill on which Congress ever acted, *for it annuls all past compromises with slavery, and makes any future compromises impossible.* Thus it puts Freedom and Slavery face to face, and bids them grapple. Who can doubt the result? It opens wide the door of the Future, when, at last, there will really be a North, and the slave power will be broken, — when their wretched despotism will cease to dominate over our government, no longer impressing itself upon everything at home and abroad. . . . Then, sir, standing at the very grave of Freedom in Nebraska and Kansas, I lift myself to the vision of that happy resurrection by which freedom will be assured, not only in these Territories, but everywhere under the national government. More clearly than ever before, I now penetrate that great Future when slavery must disappear. Proudly I discern the flag of my country, as it ripples in every breeze, at last, in reality as in name, the Flag of Freedom, — undoubted, pure, and irresistible. Am I not right, then, in calling this bill the best on which Congress ever acted?

"Sorrowfully I bend before the wrong you commit. Joyfully I welcome the promise of the Future."

It was with reference to this iniquitous bill that Horace Mann wrote to Mr. Sumner, —

"I cannot describe my feelings to you on the Nebraska Bill. I seem like one who is dragged by fiery devils or Douglases — it don't matter which — into Tophet, from which, for the next five hundred years, I see no escape. It is a case of desperation. It so encompasses me about, that nothing but the power and wisdom of God seems capable of reaching outside of it. Have you any hope?"

CHAPTER XVII.

Anthony Burns. — Meeting in Faneuil Hall. — Dr. Howe. — Wendell Phillips. — Theodore Parker. — The Court House assailed. — A Man killed. — The Military called out. — The Examination. — Attempt to purchase Burns. — The Trial proceeds. — Mr. Ellis and Mr. Dana. — Sims surrendered to his "Master." — Scene in State Street. — Mr. Sumner's Speech. — Remonstrances against the Fugitive Slave Act. — Mr. Sumner's Life in Danger. — Lines by Mr. Whittier.

WHILE Mr. Sumner was thus thundering at the slave power in the Senate, the slave power was busy in Boston in carrying out one part of its horrible programme.

Anthony Burns, a fugitive from Virginia, had been in the employ of Mr. Pitts, a colored citizen of Boston, about three weeks, when, one evening — May 24, 1854 — just after closing the shop, he was arrested on a warrant from the United States

Commissioner. He was taken to an upper room in the Court House, — now become the United States slave-pen, — where he was kept for the night under a strong guard of officers. "He seemed stunned and stupefied by fear."

The next day, the 25th, he was brought before the commissioner for trial. Richard H. Dana, Jr., Charles M. Ellis, and Robert Morris volunteered to be his counsel. At their solicitation, the case was adjourned to Saturday.

The excitement was now intense throughout the city and the state, both among the abolitionists and their enemies. On Friday evening an immense concourse of people filled Faneuil Hall, at the call of leading abolitionists. Among the officers were such men as William B. Spooner, Francis Jackson, Samuel G. Howe, Timothy Gilbert, F. W. Bird, Rev. Mr. Grimes, and T. W. Higginson.

Dr. Howe said, "Nothing so well becomes Faneuil Hall as the most determined resistance to a bloody and overshadowing despotism. It is the will of God that every man should be free; we will as God wills — God's will be done. No man's freedom is safe unless all men are free."

Wendell Phillips said, "I am against squatter sovereignty in Nebraska, and against kidnapper's sovereignty in Boston. . . . When Burns comes up for trial, get a sight at him, and don't lose sight of him. There is nothing like the mute eloquence of a suffering man to urge to duty; be there, and I will trust the result."

Theodore Parker proposed that, when the meeting adjourn, it do so to meet in Court Square the next morning at nine o'clock. "It was in the people's power so to block up every avenue that the man could not be carried off."

Mr. Parker and Mr. Phillips counselled no attempt at a rescue till the next day.

But, it being reported that a company of colored persons were attempting Burns's rescue in Court Square, most of the audience made their way to that place. The Court House was being vigorously assaulted, and a door was battered down, while the cry arose, "Rescue him!" "Bring him out!" During the mêlée a man named Batchelder, who had volunteered in behalf of the Fugitive Slave Act, was killed.

The police being found unequal to the emergency, the authorities ordered out two companies of artillery, who arrived at midnight.

The next morning, two corps of United States Marines were quartered within the walls of the Court House. Three city companies received orders from the major general of the State militia to be in readiness.

Saturday morning the examination was resumed. The prisoner was brought in under strong guard. His counsel urged further delay, which was granted.

Meanwhile the friends of Burns sought his liberation by purchase, and twelve hundred dollars, the price demanded by Suttle, were placed in the hands of Rev. Mr. Grimes, pastor of the Second Colored Baptist Church. So confident were they of success, that on Sunday morning a carriage was at the door of the Court House, to take Burns away. But it was decided to detain him till the next day. Suttle afterwards refused to sell.

Sunday was an anxious day in Boston. Theodore Parker, in Music Hall, said, "I understand there are one hundred and eighty-four marines lodged in the Court House, every man of them furnished with a musket and a bayonet, with his side-arms and twenty-four ball cartridges. . . .

Look at Boston to-day. There are no *chains* around your Court House — there are *ropes* around it. A hundred and eighty-four United States soldiers are there. They are, I am told, mostly foreigners — the scum of the earth."

On Monday, the 29th, the trial was renewed. Mr. Ellis made the opening argument. Addressing the commissioner, he said, —

"Sir, you sit here judge and jury betwixt that man and slavery. Without a commission, without any accountability, without any right of challenge, you sit to render a judgment, which, if against him, no tribunal can review and no court reverse."

Referring to the claimants, he said, "I wish to look the men in the eye who dare to come here, with pistols in their pockets, to ask us to meet a case with our opposing counsel armed, hemmed in with armed men, entering court with muskets at our breasts, trying a case under the muzzles of their guns. I choose to ask these men, face to face, by what show of right they speak of law and justice."

On Wednesday, Mr. Dana made his argument in the defence. It is worthy of note that Joshua

R. Giddings, member of Congress from Ohio, an indomitable champion of freedom, was among the spectators.

Mr. Dana made a sarcastic reference to the remarkable peace enjoyed in Boston since the arrest of Burns, because of the posse of specials, gathered from the purlieus of the city by the marshal: —

"Why, sir, people have not felt it necessary to lock their doors at night; the brothels are tenanted only by women; fighting-dogs and racing-horses have been unemployed, and Ann Street and its alleys and cellars show signs of a coming millennium."

Alluding to the statement made by Brent, a witness from Virginia, that Burns had expressed a willingness to return with Suttle, Mr. Dana said, —

"If he was willing to go back, why did they not send to Pitts's shop, and tell the prisoner that Colonel Suttle was at the Revere House, and would give him an opportunity to return? No, sir, they lurked about the thievish corners of the streets, and measured his height and his scars, to see if they answered to the record, and seized him by fraud and violence, six men of them, and hurried him into bonds and imprisonment. Some one hundred hired men, armed, keep him in this room, where once Story sat in judgment — now a slave-pen. One hundred and fifty bayonets of the regulars, and fifteen hundred of the militia, keep him without. If all that we see about us is necessary to keep a man who is willing to go back, pray, sir, what shall we see when they shall get hold of a man who is not willing to go back?"

In conclusion, he said to the commissioner, "You recognized, sir, in the beginning, the presumption of freedom. Hold to it now, sir, as to the sheet-anchor of your peace of mind as well as of his safety. If you commit a mistake in favor of the man, a pecuniary value, not great, is put at hazard. If against him, a free man is made a slave forever. If you have, on the evidence or on the law, the doubt of a reasoning and reasonable mind, an intelligent misgiving, then, sir, I implore you, in view of the cruel character of this law, in view of the dreadful consequences of a mistake, send him not away, with that tormenting doubt in your mind. It may turn to a torturing certainty."

"The eyes of many millions are upon you, sir. You are to do an act which will hold its place in the history of America, in the history of the progress of the human race. May your judgment be for liberty, and not for slavery; for happiness, and not for wretchedness; for hope and not for despair; and may be the blessing of him that is ready to perish may come upon you."

The commissioner decided that Burns was the slave of Suttle, and should be given up to his "master."

It was now June 2, ten days since the arrest. Burns was to be taken, that day, on board the steamer Jane Taylor. "The police cleared the square, and guarded the entrances. Early in the morning, a detachment of United States artillery marched up State Street with a field-piece from the Navy Yard, which was planted in Court Square. Several companies of the State militia were in readiness."

From different offices in the vicinity of the Court House there were exhibited "signs of woe." Among the most conspicuous mourners at the tragic scene was John A. Andrew, afterwards the "war governor" of Massachusetts, always an ardent friend of Charles Sumner. The windows of his office were festooned in black.

After ten o'clock in the morning, the stores on State Street were closed, and all business suspended. The excitement was intense. The streets in the vicinity were crowded with people, thousands having come from neighboring towns, all anxious to witness the last act of the tragedy. From the Court House away down State Street, a passage for the officers of *justice* with their unfortunate victim, was guarded by troops.

At length the melancholy procession began. It passed down the street towards Long Wharf. A rescue was impossible. Among the throng who gazed upon the innocent victim, and upon the armed men who were there to prevent his escape, there prevailed, for the most part, the silence of a smothered indignation — an indignation which, from that hour, with very many, was to take the shape of active and deadly opposition to slavery. Mr. Sumner's powerful words in Congress were feeble in comparison with the mute eloquence of that horrid scene.

What Mr. Sumner thought of it may be

learned from a speech, about three months after its occurrence, before the Republican State Convention at Worcester.

"Contemporaneously with the final triumph of this outrage at Washington, another dismal tragedy was enacted at Boston. In those streets where he had walked as freeman, Anthony Burns was seized as slave, under the base pretext that he was a criminal, imprisoned in the Court House, which was turned for the time into fortress and barracoon, guarded by heartless hirelings, whose chief idea of liberty was license to wrong, escorted by intrusive soldiers of the United States, watched by a prostituted militia, and finally given up to a slave-hunter by the decree of a petty magistrate, who did not hesitate to take upon his soul the awful responsibility of dooming a fellow-man, in whom he could find no fault, to a fate worse than death.

"How all this was accomplished I need not now relate. Suffice it to say, that, in doing this deed of woe and shame, the liberties of all our citizens, white as well as black, were put in jeopardy; the mayor of Boston was converted to a tool, the governor of the Commonwealth to a cipher, the laws, the precious sentiments, the religion, the pride and glory of Massachusetts, were trampled in the dust, and you and I and all of us fell down, while the slave power flourished over us."

This case, says Mr. Greeley, "probably excited more feeling than that of any other alleged fugitive, in that it attained unusual publicity, and took place in New England after the North had begun to feel the first throbs of the profound agitation excited by the repudiation of the Missouri Compromise."

In Washington it awakened the deepest feeling, and intensified the hostility to Mr. Sumner. The death of Batchelder was falsely attributed to his speech of the 24th. Pro-slavery papers in Washington published the most insulting and inflammatory articles against him, and his life was in imminent peril. His friends advised him to leave the city; but he would not abandon his post, nor arm himself, nor cease his daily walk to and from the Capitol.

Letters came in from different parts of the country, especially from New England, expressing profound sympathy or proffering protection.

Mr. Sumner was grateful for the former, but invariably declined the latter. He knew no fear. He was doing his duty. God was his defence.

Massachusetts had sent a man back to slavery. Yet not Massachusetts. The act did not represent her real spirit. That soon appeared in an aroused and indignant public sentiment. During the very month in which Burns was returned to slavery, a petition, with twenty-nine hundred signatures, was forwarded to Congress, praying for the repeal of the Fugitive Slave Bill.

Speaking on the petition, Mr. Sumner said, with reference to himself, as having vehemently opposed this bill, "For all that I have thus uttered I have no regret or apology, but rather joy and satisfaction. Glad I am in having said it; glad I am now in the opportunity *of affirming it all anew.*"

He further said, "It is true that the Slave Act was with difficulty executed, and that one of its servants perished in the madness. On these grounds the senator from Tennessee charges Boston with fanaticism. I express no opinion on the conduct of individuals; but I do say, that the fanaticism which the senator condemns is not new in Boston. It is the same which opposed the execution of the Stamp Act, and finally secured its repeal. It is the same which repealed the Tea Tax. It is the fanaticism which finally triumphed on Bunker Hill. The senator says that Boston is filled with traitors. That charge is not new. Boston of old was the home of Hancock and Adams. Her traitors now are those who are truly animated by the spirit of the American Revolution. In condemning them, in condemning Massachusetts, in condemning these remonstrants, you simply give proper conclusion to the utterance on this floor, that the Declaration of Independence is a 'self-evident lie.'"

This was June 26, twenty-four days after the rendition of Burns. On the 28th Mr. Sumner replied to his assailants; for his speech on the petition had been assailed with brutal and vulgar violence. Better for them had they let him alone. They roused a lion.

"I think," said he, referring to Mr. Butler, from South Carolina, and Mr. Mason, from Virginia, who had been particularly virulent and abusive, — "I think that I am not the only person on this floor, who, listening to these two self-confident champions of that peculiar fanaticism of the South, was reminded of the striking words of Jefferson, picturing the influence of slavery, when he says, —

"'The whole commerce between master and slave is a perpetual exercise of the most boisterous passions, — the most unremitting despotism on the one part, and degrading submission on the other. Our children see this, and learn to imitate it; for man is an imitative animal. . . . The parent storms. The child looks on, catches the lineaments of wrath, puts on the same airs in the circle of smaller slaves, gives a loose rein to the worst of passions, and, thus nursed, educated, and duly exercised in tyranny, cannot but be stamped by it with odious peculiarities. *The man must be a prodigy who can retain his manners and morals undepraved by such circumstances.*'

"Nobody, who witnessed the senator from South Carolina or the senator from Virginia in this debate, will place either of them among the prodigies described by Jefferson. As they spoke, the Senate Chamber must have seemed to them, in the characteristic fantasy of the moment, a plantation well-stocked with slaves, over which the lash of the overseer had free swing.

"Sir, it gives me no pleasure to say these things. It is not according to my nature. Bear witness that I do it only in just self-defence against the unprecedented assaults and provocations of this debate. In doing it I desire to warn certain senators, that if, by any ardor of menace, or by any tyrannical frown, they expect to shake my fixed resolve, they expect a vain thing."

Verily, Massachusetts was not now exposing herself to the humiliating rebuke which a slave-holding representative, twenty-eight years before, administered to a member of the House from that state, who had said of slavery, that "*while* it subsists, *where* it subsists, its duties are presupposed and sanctioned by religion." A new era had come. Courage had succeeded to cringing, conscience to complaisance. So was it with Massachusetts.

But with the South, her better days were passed. She was the slave of slavery. She was afraid of the light. She could not endure arguments. Her defence of herself was abuse and the bludgeon. Surely so terrible a disease called for a sharp remedy. A true Daniel had now come to judgment.

Mr. Sumner's reply was thorough and unanswerable. And this made it the more offensive to Southern ears. It was therefore seriously proposed among Southern members to expel him from the Senate. One member said he was a fit candidate for jail, another for a strait-jacket. "He was assailed," said Mr. Giddings, referring to the speeches of June 26 and 28, "by the whole slave power in the Senate, and for a time he was the constant theme of their vituperation. The maddened waves rolled and dashed against him for two or three days, until eventually he obtained the floor himself. Then he arose and threw back the dashing surges with a power of inimitable eloquence utterly indescribable. . . . There he stood towering above the infamous characters who had attempted to silence him, while I sat and listened with rapturous emotion."

As the hatred, on the one hand, was bitter, so, on the other, the congratulations of his friends, the friends of freedom and free speech, came in to Mr. Sumner from every quarter. His boldness toned up the public conscience, and gave new strength and courage to every friend of freedom.

Not discomfited by the raging storm, Mr. Sumner returned to the onset against the Fugitive Slave Bill a month later, July 31. It was in this wise. Mr. Seward having "reported a bill for the relief of a poor and aged woman, whose husband had died of wounds received in the war of 1812, Mr. Adams, of Mississippi, moved, as an amendment, another bill for the relief of Mrs. Batchelder, widow of a person killed in Boston, while aiding as a volunteer in the enforcement of the Fugitive Slave Act." The amendment being adopted, Mr. Sumner introduced the following amendment: "*Provided*, That the Act of Congress, approved September 18, 1850, for the surrender of fugitives from service or labor, be, and the same is hereby, repealed." An exciting debate ensued, and the Senate refused leave to introduce the bill — ten to thirty-five.

It was with reference to this debate that Mr. Whittier, an ardent and intimate friend of Mr. Sumner, wrote the following lines: —

"Thou knowest my heart, dear friend, and well canst guess,
That, even though silent, I have not the less
Rejoiced to see thy actual life agree
With the large future which I shaped for thee,
When, years ago, beside the summer sea,

White in the moon, we saw the long waves fall
Baffled and broken from the rocky wall,
That to the menace of the brawling flood
Opposed alone its massive quietude,
Calm as a fate, with not a leaf nor vine
Nor birch-spray trembling in the still moonshine,
Crowning it like God's peace. I sometimes think
That night-scene by the sea prophetical
(For Nature speaks in symbols and in signs,
And through her pictures human fate divines), —
That rock, wherefrom we saw the billows sink
In murmuring rout, uprising clear and tall
In the white light of heaven, the type of one
Who, momently by Error's host assailed,
Stands strong as Truth, in greaves of granite mailed,
And, tranquil-fronted, listening over all
The tumult, hears the angels say, Well done!"

CHAPTER XVIII.

Rise of the Republican Party. — Great Changes. — Freedom gaining Ground. — Republican Convention. — Mr. Sumner's Speech. — Duties of Massachusetts. — The Supreme Court and the Fugitive Slave Act. — Judges. — Letter to Agricultural Society. — Mercantile Library Association. — "Position and Duties of the Merchant." — Granville Sharp. — Seamen's Wages. — Fugitive Slave Bill.

THE party of Freedom, which had successively borne the names of Liberty Party and Free Soil Party, now assumed that of REPUBLICAN. Its first convention, under this new designation, was held at Worcester, September 7, 1854.

Ten years had wrought a mighty change. The slave power was still in the ascendant, and resolved, by whatever means, to retain its supremacy. It had humiliated the North, and dragged away in triumph from its towns and cities numerous fugitives. It still domineered in the National Congress. It held all the National offices. It controlled the army, the navy, and the judiciary.

But its excessive fury had at last aroused the slumbering North. Freedom had compelled a hearing in the National Council. Champions of her cause had at length appeared who could not be cajoled or intimidated. Slavery, though haughty and defiant, was filled with new alarm.

Under such circumstances, the first Republican Convention came together. Its members were inspired with strong hopes. A great future was before the party of Freedom.

Mr. Sumner was invited to be present, and was welcomed with unbounded joy. He had "fought with wild beasts" at Washington, and won the gratitude of all the friends of Freedom.

Addressing the Convention, he said, —

"After months of constant, anxious service in another place, away from Massachusetts, I am permitted to stand among you again, my fellow-citizens, and to draw satisfaction and strength from your generous presence. Life is full of change and contrast. From Slave Soil I have come to Free Soil. From the tainted breath of Slavery I have passed into the bracing air of Freedom. And the heated antagonism of debate, shooting forth its fiery cinders, is changed into this brimming, overflowing welcome, while I seem to lean on the great heart of our beloved Commonwealth, as it palpitates audibly in this crowded assembly.

"Let me say at once, frankly and sincerely, that I am not here to receive applause or to give occasion for tokens of public regard, but simply to unite with fellow-citizens in new vows of duty. And yet I would not be thought insensible to the good-will now swelling from so many honest bosoms. It touches me more than I can tell."

He then proceeded to show what were "the duties of Massachusetts at the present crisis."

"Our duties in National and State affairs are identical, — in the one case to put the National Government, in all its departments, and in the other case, the State Government, in all its departments, openly, actively, and perpetually, on the side of Freedom."

Speaking of the Slave Oligarchy, he said, "Lord Chatham once exclaimed, that the time had been, when he was content to bring France to her knees; now he would not stop till he had laid her on her back. Nor can we be content with less in our warfare. We must not stop till we have laid the Slave Power on its back."

Referring to the decision of the Supreme Court of the United States, affirming the constitutionality of the Fugitive Slave Act, and to the alleged consequent duty of absolute submission, Mr. Sumner said,—

"For myself, let me say, that I hold judges, and especially the Supreme Court, in much respect; but I am too familiar with the history of judicial proceedings to regard them with any superstitious reverence. Judges are but men, and in all ages have shown a full share of human frailty.

"Alas! alas! the worst crimes of history have been perpetrated under their sanction. The blood of martyrs and of patriots, crying from the ground, summons them to judgment.

"It was a judicial tribunal which condemned Socrates to drink the fatal hemlock, and which pushed the Saviour barefoot over the pavements of Jerusalem, bending beneath his cross.

"It was a judicial tribunal which, against the testimony and entreaties of her father, surrendered the fair Virginia *as a slave*,—which arrested the teachings of the great Apostle to the Gentiles, and sent him in bonds from Judea to Rome,—which, in the name of the old religion, persecuted the saints and fathers of the Christian Church, and adjudged them to a martyr's death, in all its most dreadful forms,—and afterwards, in the name of the new religion, enforced the tortures of the Inquisition, amidst the shrieks and agonies of its victims, while it compelled Galileo to declare, in solemn denial of the great truth he had disclosed, that the earth did not move round the sun.

"Ay, sir, it was a judicial tribunal in England which . . . lighted the fires of persecution at Oxford and Smithfield, over the cinders of Latimer, Ridley, and John Rogers,—which, after elaborate argument, upheld the fatal tyranny of ship-money against the patriot resistance of Hampden,—which, in defiance of justice and humanity, sent Sidney and Russell to the block —which persistently enforced the laws of Conformity that our Puritan fathers persistently refused to obey, and afterwards, with Jeffries on the bench, crowned the pages of English history with massacre and murder, even with the blood of innocent women.

"Ay, sir, it was a judicial tribunal in our own country, surrounded by all the forms of law, which hung witches at Salem, — which affirmed the constitutionality of the Stamp Act, while it admonished jurors and people to obey, — and which now, in our day, lends its sanction to the unutterable atrocity of the Fugitive Slave Act."

Mr. Sumner believed that he was bound to obey the Constitution *as he understood it*, and not as he did *not* understand it! He believed the Fugitive Slave Act to be unconstitutional, and therefore he did not regard it as binding upon him. It was against the divine law, and he would obey God rather than man. He would disobey the human law, and take the consequences, whatever they might be. "The good citizen, at all personal hazard, will refuse to obey it."

On the 25th of the same month, Mr. Sumner sent a characteristic letter to the Norfolk Agricultural Society, giving his reasons for not accepting an invitation to attend: —

"From the mother earth we may derive many

lessons, and I doubt not they will spring up abundantly in the footprints of the Society. *There is one which comes to my mind at this moment, and which is of perpetual force.*

"The good farmer obeys the natural laws, nor does he impotently attempt to set up any behest of man against the ordinances of God, determining day and night, summer and winter, sunshine and rain. The good citizen will imitate the good farmer, nor will he impotently attempt to set up any statutes of man against the ordinances of God, which determine good and evil, right and wrong, justice and injustice." An ingenious argument against the Fugitive Slave Act.

On November 13, he addressed the Mercantile Library Association of Boston on the "Position and Duties of the Merchant, as illustrated in the Life of Granville Sharp."

This oration marks a great change in public opinion on the subject of slavery. When, seven years before, he addressed the Association, he called his lecture "an attempt to expose slavery before a promiscuous audience, at a time when the subject was *too delicate to be treated directly.*" Then he spoke of "*white* slavery in the Barbary

States." Now he could speak directly of negro slavery in the United States, and be "well received." He could even rebuke merchants of Boston who had not only aided, but, in some cases, instigated the arrest and rendition of Sims and Burns.

Granville Sharp, a London merchant, born in 1735, was held up as a model business man, and, above all, as a *man;* a man who carried his conscience into trade, but never made a trade of conscience; who was more than a successful merchant, a philanthropist of the purest character, a special foe to slavery, "heralding by many years the labors of Clarkson and Wilberforce." He boldly assailed the slave-trade, and slavery itself. He labored to prove that slavery could not exist under the British Constitution. Cases of slaves arrested in England by foreign masters had awakened his sympathies. Though often balked, he never rested till the Chief Justice of England at length declared, that the moment a slave touched British soil he became free.

"Imitating him," said Mr. Sumner, in conclusion, "commerce would thrive none the less, but goodness more. Business would not be checked, but it would cease to be pursued as the 'one idea' of life. Wealth would still abound; but there would be also that solid virtue, never to be moved from truth. . . .

"The hardness of heart engendered by the accursed greed of gain, and by the madness of worldly ambition, would be overcome; the perverted practice, that *policy is the best honesty*, would be reversed; and merchants would be recalled, gently, but irresistibly, to the great practical duties of this age, and thus win the palm of true honesty, which trade alone can never bestow.

> 'Who is the honest man?
> He that doth still and strongly good pursue,
> To God, his neighbor, and himself, most true.'"

Thus, on all occasions, addressing young men, merchants, scholars, politicians, in the lyceum, at literary festivals, in conventions of the people, in the Senate, everywhere that he could get the ear of his fellow-men, Mr. Sumner held up the same high standard of right and truth, the authority of conscience, the will of God.

Returning to Congress, he introduced a bill, February 12, 1855, "to secure wages to seamen in case of wreck." "The measure now proposed," he said, "is of direct importance to the one hundred and fifty thousand seamen constituting the mercantile marine of the United States. It also concerns the million of men constituting the mercantile marine of the civilized world, any of whom, in the vicissitudes of the sea, may find themselves in American bottoms. I commend it as a measure of enlightened philanthropy, and also of simple justice."

His motion to refer it to the Committee on Commerce was agreed to. Southern as well as Northern senators could do justice to seamen, in making secure their hard-earned wages; but not yet did the former heed the warning, "Woe unto him that useth his neighbor's service *without* wages, *and giveth him not for his work.*"

On the 23d of the same month, another opportunity was given Mr. Sumner to demand the repeal of the Fugitive Slave Bill. It was on a motion of Mr. Toucey, of Connecticut, (!) to remove "cases arising from trespasses and damages under the Fugitive Slave Act," from the State Courts to the Circuit Court of the United

States. The purpose of the mover, "a Northern man with Southern principles," was to give more efficiency to the Fugitive Slave Act.

On this Mr. Sumner said, —

"On a former occasion, as slavery was about to clutch one of its triumphs, I rose to make my final opposition at midnight. It is now the same hour. Slavery is pressing again for its accustomed victory, which I undertake again for the moment to arrest. It is hardly an accidental conjunction which constantly brings slavery and midnight together. . . .

"I do not adequately expose this bill, when I say it is a sacrifice to slavery. It is a sacrifice to slavery in its most odious form. Bad as slavery is, it is not so bad as hunting slaves. There is seeming apology for slavery at home, in States where it prevails, founded on difficulties in the position of the master, and the relations of personal attachment it sometimes excites; but every apology fails when you seek again to enslave the fugitive whom the master cannot detain by duress or kindness, and who, by courage and intelligence, under guidance of the North Star, can achieve a happy freedom. Sir, there is a wide difference between slave-holder and slave-hunter.

"But the bill before you is to aid in the chase of slaves. . . . Not from Slave Soil, but from Free Soil, comes this effort. A senator from the North, a senator from New England, lends himself to the work, and with unnatural zeal helps to bind still stronger the fetter of the slave."

To the inquiry of Mr. Rusk, of Texas, where slavery was mentioned in the bill, Mr. Sumner ingeniously replied, "I might ask the senator to point out any place in the Constitution of the United States where 'slavery' is mentioned."

After earnest denunciation of the Fugitive Slave Bill, he moved its *repeal*, with the following result: ayes 9, nays 30. The nine were Messrs. Brainerd, Chase, Cooper, Fessenden, Gillette, Seward, Sumner, Wade, and Wilson.

And so ended one more effort for freedom.

CHAPTER XIX.

Lecture before the Mercantile Library Association. — " The Anti-Slavery Enterprise. " — Opposition to Truth. — The first to welcome Truth. — Mr. Hayes. — Dignity of the Cause of Freedom. — — A work for Every One. — Meeting at Faneuil Hall. — The Rip Van Winkle Party. — The Know Nothing Party.

" HANCOCK STREET, 23d November, 1856.

" MY DEAR SIR: An unkindly current of air is often more penetrating than an arrow. From such a shaft I suffered on the night of my address to the Mercantile Library Association, more than a week ago, and no care or skill has been efficacious to relieve me."

This forms part of a letter of excuse from Mr. Sumner for not delivering a lecture — the first of a course organized in Boston for the discussion of slavery. Mr. Sumner was silenced. A " current of air " had effected what the acts and threats of slaveholders had failed to do. But kindly Nature ere long relented, and released him from her bonds. He returned to his seat in the Senate.

The following spring, in 1855, Mr. Sumner gave the lecture referred to above — "The Anti-Slavery Enterprise: Its Necessity, Practicability, and Dignity." It awakened so much interest, that its repetition was requested in Boston, and in many places in New York. Its successive delivery in Metropolitan Hall and Niblo's Theatre, New York, and in Brooklyn, forms an era in the anti-slavery cause. Said the New York Tribune, "That a lecture should be repeated in New York is a rare occurrence. That a lecture on anti-slavery should be repeated in New York, even before a few despised fanatics, is an unparalleled occurrence. But that an anti-slavery lecture should be repeated, night after night, to successive multitudes, each more enthusiastic than the last, marks the epoch of a revolution in popular feeling; it is an era in the history of Liberty."

In the beginning of this speech, which was three hours long, Mr. Sumner briefly sketched the rapid progress of anti-slavery sentiment. Referring to the opposition which it had met with, he said, "Thus, in all ages, is truth encountered. At first persecuted, gagged, silenced, crucified, she cries out from the prison, the rack, the stake, the cross, till at last her voice is heard. And when that voice is really heard, whether in martyr cries, or in earthquake tones of civil convulsion, or in the calmness of ordinary speech, such as I now employ, or in that still, small utterance inaudible to the common ear, then is the beginning of victory! 'Give me where to stand, and I will move the world,' said Archimedes; and truth asks no more than did the master of geometry.

"Viewed in this aspect, the present occasion rises above any ordinary course of lectures or series of political meetings. It is the inauguration of Freedom. From this time forward, her voice of warning and command cannot be silenced."

Speaking of the objection to the anti-slavery enterprise, that it "lacked the authority of names eminent in Church and State," Mr. Sumner said, "If this be so, the more is the pity on their account; for our cause is needful to them more than they are needful to our cause. Alas! it is only according to example that it should be so. It is not the eminent in Church and State, the rich and powerful, the favorites of fortune and of place, who most promptly welcome Truth, when she heralds change in the existing order of things. It is others in poorer condition who open hospitable hearts to the unattended stranger. This is a sad story, beginning with the Saviour, whose disciples were fishermen, and ending only in our day."

"There is now in Boston a simple citizen whose example may be a lesson to Commissioners, Marshals, Magistrates, while it fills all with the beauty of a generous act. I refer to Mr. Hayes, who resigned his place in the city police, rather than take part in the pack of the Slave-hunter. He is now the doorkeeper of the public edifice honored this winter by the triumphant lectures on slavery. Better be a doorkeeper in the house of the Lord than a dweller in the tents of the ungodly. Has he not chosen well? Little think those now doing the work of slavery, that the time is near when all this will be dishonor and sadness. For myself, long ago my mind was made up. Nothing will I have to do with it. How can I help to make a slave? The idea alone is painful. To do this thing would plant in my soul a remorse which no time could remove or mitigate. His chains would clank in my ears. His cries would strike upon my heart. His voice would be my terrible accuser. Mr. President, may no such voice fall on your soul or mine!"

Of the dignity of the enterprise he thus discoursed: —

"It concerns the cause of human freedom, which from earliest days has been the darling of History. By all the memories of the past, by all the stories of childhood and the studies of youth, by every example of magnanimous virtue, by every aspiration of the good and true, by the fame of martyrs swelling through all time, by the renown of patriots whose lives are landmarks of progress, by the praise lavished upon our fathers, you are summoned to this work. . . . Who can doubt that our cause is nobler than that of our fathers? *for is it not more exalted to struggle for the freedom of others than for our own?*"

Speaking of the practicability of the enterprise, he said there was a place for every man. "Providence is felt through individuals; the dropping of water wears away the rock; and no man can be too humble or poor for this work, while to all the happy in genius, fortune, or fame, it makes a special appeal. Here is room for the strength of Luther and the sweetness of Melancthon; for the wisdom of age and the ardor of youth; for the judgment of the statesman and the eloquence of the orator; for the grace of the scholar and the inspiration of the poet; for the learning of the professor and the skill of the lawyer; for the exhortation of the preacher and the persuasion of the press; for the various energy of man and the abounding sympathy of woman."

At a Republican rally in Faneuil Hall, November 2, 1855, on the eve of an election, Mr. Sumner spoke for two hours and a quarter, showing that the Republican party alone represented the principles of Freedom and the Constitution. His speech began with these stirring words: —

"Are you for Freedom, or are you for Slavery? This is the question which you are to answer at the coming election. Above all other questions, national or local, it lifts itself directly in the path of every voter. There it is. It cannot be avoided. It cannot be banished away. It cannot be silenced. Forever sounding in our ears, it has a mood for every hour, — stirring us at times as with the blast of a trumpet, then visiting us in solemn tones, like the bell which calls to prayer, and then again awaking us to unmistakable duty, like the same bell, when at midnight it summons all to stay the raging conflagration."

Tried by this test, the Democratic and Whig parties were utterly wanting; so also was the Know Nothing or Anti-foreign party. "Men do not gather grapes from thorns, nor figs from thistles; nor do they expect patriotism from Benedict Arnold." The Democratic party sustained "the tyrannies and perfidies of the slave oligarchy." The Whig party was thus handsomely disposed of: —

"According to familiar rule, handed down from distant antiquity, we are to say nothing but good of the dead. How, then, shall I speak of the late powerful Whig party, by whose giant contests the whole country was once upheaved, but which has now ceased to exist, except as the shadow of a name? Here in Massachusetts, a few who do not yet know that it is dead have met together and professed the old allegiance. They are the Rip Van Winkles of our politics. This respectable character, falling asleep in the mountains, drowsed undisturbed throughout the war of the revolution, and then, returning to his native village, ignorant of all that had passed, made haste to declare himself 'a loyal subject of the king, God bless him!' But our Whigs are less tolerant and urbane than this awakened sleeper. In petulant and irrational assumption they are like the unfortunate judge, who, being aroused from slumber on the bench by a sudden crash of thunder, exclaimed, 'Mr. Crier, stop the noise in court!' The thunder would not be hushed; nor will the voice of Freedom, now reverberating throughout the land."

Speaking of the so-called American party, Mr. Sumner uttered a plea for our foreign population. It should not be politically proscribed. Roman Catholics should "give some assurance of their purpose . . . to become useful, loyal, and permanent members of our community." With this explanation he would extend generous welcome to foreigners. "The history of our country, in its humblest as well as most exalted spheres, testifies to the merits of foreigners. Their strong arms have helped furrow our broad territory with canals, and stretch in every direction the iron rail. They fill our workshops, navigate our ships, and even till our fields. . . . At the bar and in the high places of commerce you find them; enter the retreats of learning, and there you find them, shedding upon our country the glory of science.

"A party, then, which, beginning in secrecy, interferes with religious belief, and founds a discrimination on the accident of birth, is not the party for us."

And so Mr. Sumner proved the necessity of the Republican party. "'Where liberty is, there is my country,' was the sentiment of that great apostle of freedom, Benjamin Franklin. . . . In a similar strain, I would say, 'Where liberty is, there is my party.'"

That party has gained for itself a most honorable name. Under God, it abolished slavery, it saved the nation. Its more recent history we pass by in silence.

CHAPTER XX.

Growing arrogance of the Slave Power. — Nebraska and Kansas. — Violence in Washington. — Mr. Sumner's Speech, "The Crime against Kansas." — Question of Admitting Kansas as a State. — Douglas's Bill. — Letters to Theodore Parker. — Mr. Seward's Bill. — A Great Debate. — The Monster Swindle. — Emigration to Kansas. — Border Ruffians. — A Usurping Legislature. — Slave Legislation. — Senator Butler and South Carolina.

We have now reached a period when the slavery question was fast hastening to a dreadful crisis. The Nebraska Bill had revealed in unmistakable colors the daring and desperate character of the slave power. Kansas had become the theatre of a deadly strife. "The border ruffian policy," says Vice-President Wilson, "which was filling that Territory with alarm and bloodshed, had its representatives in Washington, walking its streets, hanging around its hotels, and stalking through the Capitol. To the extreme arrogance of embittered and aggressive words were added the menace and actual infliction of personal violence. Indeed, the course of these men assumed the form of a reckless and relentless audacity never before exhibited. Members of Congress went armed in the streets, and sat with loaded revolvers in their desks." It should be added, that Mr. Sumner always went unarmed.

Under such peculiar circumstances it was, that Mr. Sumner delivered, on May 19 and 20, 1856, his speech entitled *The Crime Against Kansas; The Apologies for the Crime; The True Remedy.*

By the Nebraska Bill, passed in 1854, the Missouri Compromise of 1820, prohibiting slavery north of 36° 30′ north latitude, was violated, and the vast region known as Kansas and Nebraska, as also Minnesota, Washington, and Oregon Territories, were opened to slavery.

By this bill it was left to each Territory whether to introduce or exclude slavery.

The question now immediately pending was the admission of Kansas, as a State, into the Union. The pro-slavery party were of course resolved, if possible, to have it come in as a Slave State. For this purpose Mr. Douglas introduced a bill, March 17, 1856, "to authorize the people of the Territory of Kansas to form a Constitution and State Government, preparatory to their admission into the Union, when they have the requisite population."

Beneath the seeming fairness of this bill there lurked an infamous plot. It was designed, by delay, to so manipulate the voting power in the Territory, under the direction of the president, an agent of slavery, that a slave constitution should be adopted, and Kansas present herself for admission to the Union as a Slave State.

A letter from Mr. Sumner to Theodore Parker, under date of March 26, 1856, shows the plan adopted by the friends of freedom in Congress, in opposition to the pro-slavery plot: —

"I am glad you are to open on Kansas. Let me suggest to press the admission of Kansas *at once* with her present constitution. *This is the policy we have adopted*, and it will crowd Douglas and Cass infinitely. This proposition is something practical; and on this we must fight the presidential election. . . .

"Seward will make a grand speech. I shall follow as soon as possible, *and use plain words.*

"O! this enormity is not really understood. The more I think of it, the more its wickedness glares."

Two days before his speech (May 17), Mr. Sumner wrote to the same friend, "Alas! alas! the tyranny over us is complete. Will the people submit? When you read this I shall be saying — in the Senate — they will not! Would that I had your strength. But I shall pronounce the most thorough Philippic ever uttered in a legislative body."

According to the policy referred to above, Mr. Seward submitted, by way of substitute, another bill, providing for immediate action: "A Bill for the Admission of the State of Kansas into the Union," with a free constitution.

Thereupon ensued the great debate, in which Mr. Sumner took so prominent a part, using "*plain words.*" He reviewed the whole history of the conspiracy for extending slavery into regions solemnly consecrated to freedom. The Nebraska Bill he called "a swindle" — "a swindle of the North by the South" — "a swindle of the whole country" — "a swindle of popular sovereignty" — "a swindle of a great cause" — "a swindle of God-given, inalienable rights. Turn it over, look at it on all sides, and it is everywhere a swindle; and if the word I now employ has not the authority of classical usage, it has, on this occasion, the indubitable authority of fitness. No other word will adequately express the mingled meanness and wickedness of the cheat."

From this original monster swindle, other swindles were to issue. The region being opened to slavery, "it was confidently anticipated, that, by the activity of" secret slavery emigration societies, "slavery might be introduced into Kansas, quietly, but surely, without arousing conflict — that the crocodile egg might be stealthily dropped in the sunburnt soil, there to be hatched, unobserved, until it sent forth its reptile monster."

But, unfortunately for this plot, emigration was open from the Free States, and the South soon had cause to fear a decided failure. Large numbers of people flocked to Kansas, for the double purpose of finding a home and saving the Territory to freedom. There sprang up a conflict which reddened the soil with blood, and revealed in many ways the desperate character of the slave power. Shall Kansas be the home of Freedom, or the den of Slavery? That became the all-absorbing question through anxious years.

"Popular sovereignty," the vaunted glory of the Nebraska Bill, designed to carry slavery into that Territory, was discovered to be full of danger to the South. Northern emigrants outnumbered those from the South. Now, then, that very feature of the bill must be trampled under foot by its own progenitors. The people of Kansas must be robbed of the rights solemnly — no, falsely — guaranteed to them. They were not to be allowed to decide against slavery. This outrage was attempted in five separate invasions of Kansas by armed bands, in one case numbering eighteen hundred men, from Missouri, and by other acts of perfidy instigated or sanctioned at Washington. By controlling the ballot-box, these invaders elected a slavery delegate to Congress in 1854.

"The first ballot-box," says General Pomeroy, "that was opened upon our virgin soil was closed to us by overpowering numbers and impending force. . . . They came upon us, not in the guise of voters, to steal away our franchise, but boldly and openly, to snatch it with a strong hand. They came directly from their own homes, and in compact and organized bands, with arms in hand and provisions for the expedition, marched to our polls, and, when their work was done, returned whence they came."

"This infliction," says Mr. Sumner, "was a significant prelude to the grand invasion of the 30th March, 1855, at the election of the first territorial legislature under the organic law, when an armed multitude from Missouri entered the Territory in larger numbers than General Taylor commanded at Buena Vista, or than General Jackson within his lines at New Orleans — much larger than our fathers rallied on Bunker Hill.

"On they came as an army with banners, organized in companies, with officers, munitions, tents, and provisions, as though marching upon a foreign foe, and breathing loud-mouthed threats that they would carry their purpose, if need were, by the bowie-knife and the revolver. . . . Arrived at their several destinations on the night before the election, the invaders pitched their tents, placed their sentries, and waited for the coming day."

"They came," says General Pomeroy, "with drums beating and flags flying, and their leaders were of the most prominent men in the State" [Missouri.]

Accordingly, in flagrant contempt of their own bill, the free people of Kansas had imposed upon them a pro-slavery legislature. "Thus was conquered the Sebastopol of that Territory."

One year after the first invasion, another, the most formidable of all, "burst upon the heads of the devoted people" of Kansas. An army of eighteen hundred men, "with seven pieces of cannon, *belonging to the United States*," threatened the town of Lawrence. Though compelled at last to "a mean retreat," they committed shameful excesses, including several murders. All this was to punish the unreasonable people of Kansas for refusing to submit to foreign and lawless dictation.

"From the beginning the spirit of evil hung upon the skirts of this interesting Territory, harrowing its peace, disturbing its prosperity, and keeping its inhabitants under the painful alarms of war. All security of person, property, and labor was overthrown, . . . a wrong which is small only by the side of the giant wrong, for the consummation of which all this is done. . . . As every point in a wide-spread horizon radiates from a common centre, so everything said or done in this vast circle of crime radiates from the *One Idea*, that Kansas, at all hazards, must be made a Slave State."

"To accomplish this result, three things are attempted: *first*, by outrages of all kinds to drive the friends of freedom out of the Territory; *secondly*, to deter others from coming; and, *thirdly*, to obtain complete control of the government."

The usurping legislature formally recognized slavery in a law of thirteen sections. "In three sections only is the penalty of death denounced no less than forty-eight different times against the heinous offence . . . of interfering with . . . property in flesh. Thus is Liberty sacrificed to Slavery, and *Death summoned to sit at the gates as guardian of the Wrong*."

"Mark, three different legislative enactments constituted part of this work," so as "*to defy all effort at change through ordinary forms of law.*"

"*First*, according to one act, all who deny, by

spoken or written word, the 'right of persons to hold slaves in this Territory,' are denounced as felons, to be punished by imprisonment at hard labor for a term not less than two years — it may be for life. . . . *Secondly*, by another act, no person can practise as an attorney, unless he shall obtain a license from the territorial courts, which, of course, a tyrannical discretion will be free to deny; and, after obtaining such license, he is constrained to take an oath 'to support and sustain' . . . the Territorial Act and the Fugitive Slave Bill. . . . And *thirdly*, by another act, all persons 'conscientiously opposed to the holding slaves,' or 'who do not admit the right to hold slaves in this Territory,' are excluded from the jury on every question, civil or criminal, arising out of arrested slave property."

To insure the enforcement of these infamous statutes, the President of the United States appointed proper instruments, in the shape of governor, chief justice, judges, secretary, attorney, and marshal. The legislature imposed a crowd of officers upon the people, whom they had no voice in appointing.

"The final, inexorable work remained to be done." To guard against the possibility of any change at a future election, two different acts were passed: the first excluding from the elective franchise all who would not take the oath to support the Fugitive Slave Bill; the second entitling all other persons to vote who tendered a tax of one dollar to the sheriff on the day of election; thus disfranchising all opposed to slavery, and at the same time opening the door to the votes of the invaders.

"Thus was the crime consummated. Slavery stands erect, clanking its chains on the Territory of Kansas, surrounded by a code of death, and trampling upon all cherished liberties, whether of speech, the press, the bar, the trial by jury, or the electoral franchise. And, sir, all this is done, not merely to introduce a wrong which is itself a denial of all rights, and in dread of which mothers have taken the lives of their offspring, . . . but it is taken for the sake of political power, in order to bring two new slaveholding senators upon this floor, and thus to fortify in the national government the desperate chances of a waning oligarchy. As the gallant ship, voyaging on pleasant summer seas, is assailed by a pirate crew, and plundered of its doubloons and dollars, so is this beautiful Territory now assailed in peace and prosperity, and robbed of its political power for the sake of slavery. Even now the black flag of the land pirates from Missouri waves at the mast-head. In their laws you hear the pirate yell, and see the flash of the pirate knife; while, incredible to relate, the President,* gathering the slave power at his back, testifies a pirate sympathy.

"Emerging from all the blackness of this crime, where we seem to have been lost as in a savage wood, and turning our backs upon it, as upon devastation and death, from which, while others have suffered, we have escaped, I come, now, to the apologies which the crime has found. . . . Great crimes of history have never been without apologies. The massacre of St. Bartholomew, which you now instinctively condemn, was, at the time, applauded in high quarters, and even commemorated by a papal medal, which may still be procured at Rome, — as the crime against Kansas, which is hardly less conspicuous in dreadful eminence, has been shielded on this floor by extenuating words, and even by a presidential

* Franklin Pierce.

message, which, like the pap... be forgotten in considering th... men."

For all these evils Mr. Sumner recommended what he styled "the remedy of justice and peace, proposed by the senator from New York, and embodied in his bill. . . . This is sustained by the prayer of the people of the Territory, setting forth a constitution formed by spontaneous movement, in which all there had opportunity to participate, without distinction of party. . . . In offering this proposition, the senator from New York has entitled himself to the gratitude of the country. Throughout a life of unsurpassed industry, and of eminent ability, he has done much for freedom which the world will not let die; but than this he has done nothing more opportune, and he has uttered no words more effective than this speech, so masterly and ingenious, by which he vindicated it."

During the delivery of this speech, Mr. Butler, of South Carolina, interrupted the speaker no less than thirty-five times. Mr. Sumner thus paid his respects to him:—

"With regret I come again upon the senator

..d, who, omnipresent in this
..s with rage at the simple sug-
..ansas has applied for admission as a State, and, with incoherent phrase, discharges the loose expectoration of his speech, now upon her representative, and then upon her people. There was no extravagance of the ancient parliamentary debate which he did not repeat; nor was there any possible deviation from truth which he did not make — with so much of passion, I gladly add, as to save him from the suspicion of intentional aberration. But the senator touches nothing which he does not disfigure — with error, sometimes of principle, sometimes of fact. He shows an incapacity for accuracy, whether in stating the Constitution or in stating the law, whether in details of statistics or diversions of scholarship. He cannot ope his mouth, but out there flies a blunder. . . .

"But it is against the people of Kansas that the sensibilities of the senator are particularly roused. Coming, as he announces, 'from a State,' — ay, sir, from South Carolina, — he turns with lordly disgust from this newly-formed community, which he will not recognize as even 'a member of the body politic.' Pray, sir, by what title does he indulge in this egotism? Has he read the history of the 'State' which he represents? He cannot, surely, forget its shameful imbecility from slavery, confessed throughout the Revolution, followed by its more shameful assumption for slavery since. He cannot forget its wretched persistence in the slave-trade, as the very apple of its eye, and the condition of its participation in the Union. He cannot forget its constitution, which is republican only in name, confirming power in the hands of the few, and founding the qualifications of its legislators on 'a settled freehold estate of five hundred acres of land, *and* ten negroes.'"

Mr. Sumner concludes with these impressive words:

"In just regard for free labor, which you would blast by deadly contact with slave labor, — in Christian sympathy with the slave, whom you would task and sell, — in stern condemnation of the crime consummated on that beautiful soil, — in rescue of fellow-citizens, now subjugated to tyrannical usurpation, — in dutiful respect for the early fathers, whose aspirations are ignobly thwarted,

— in the name of the Constitution outraged, of the laws trampled down, of justice banished, of humanity degraded, of peace destroyed, of freedom crushed to earth, — and in the name of the heavenly Father, whose service is perfect freedom, I make this last appeal."

Such was this famous speech, — "a grand and terrible philippic, worthy of the grand occasion; the severe and awful truth, which the sharp agony of the national crisis demanded." *

* J. G. Whittier.

CHAPTER XXI.

Effect of Mr. Sumner's Kansas Speech. — Mr. Sumner assaulted. — Preston S. Brooks. — Scene in the House. — Retirement of Brooks. — Southern Sympathy. — Northern Indignation. — Meetings in Massachusetts. — Faneuil Hall. — Peleg W. Chandler. — Josiah Quincy. — Wendell Phillips. — Ralph Waldo Emerson. — Horace Mann. — Courier and Enquirer. — Mr. Sumner's Mother.

IN the Senate, and in the country at large, the speech of Mr. Sumner produced a profound impression, both upon the foes and friends of slavery. The former rejoiced, the latter were exasperated. Those especially "whose course had been subjected to this terrible arraignment were excited to madness; and summary vengeance was agreed upon as the only remedy that would meet the exigency of the hour." The speech could not be answered; the speaker must be silenced. Such is always the last argument of guilt.

The select agent of the slave power to carry out their fell purpose was Preston S. Brooks, a representative from South Carolina, and nephew of Senator Butler. After the adjournment of the Senate, on the 22d of May, two days after the speech, Mr. Sumner remained at his desk engaged in writing. While so engaged, Brooks, whom he did not know, approached him and said, "I have read your speech twice over, carefully. It is a libel on South Carolina, and Mr. Butler, who is a relative of mine."

While these words were passing from his lips, he commenced a series of blows with a bludgeon upon the senator's head, by which the latter was stunned, disabled, and smitten down, bleeding and insensible, on the floor of the chamber. From that floor he was taken by friends, borne to the ante-room, where his wounds were dressed, and then he was carried by Mr. Wilson, assisted by Captain Darling, doorkeeper of the House, faint and bleeding, to his lodgings.

"The injuries of Mr. Sumner were serious, and became the subject of constant anxiety to his friends. It was four years before he was pronounced convalescent." * He never entirely recovered from the effect of the assault, which was, doubtless, the remote cause of his death, eighteen years after.

"Mr. Sumner, though confessedly the superior of his assailant in stature and physical strength, sitting and cramped beneath his writing-desk, over which he was bending, with pen in hand, taken unawares and at disadvantage, and his assailant raining blows upon his unprotected head, fairly represented Freedom and Slavery as they stood at that time confronting each other. Freedom, though instrinsically stronger than its antagonist, was yet practically weaker. . . .

"In the evening of the day of the assault, the Republican senators met at the house of Mr. Seward. In a lean minority, — only one fifth of the Senate, — they knew that they were at the mercy of the majority, which was dominated by the incensed and inexorable leaders of the slave power. Always bitter and implacable, they were now still more determined and audacious. Always zealous, their zeal was more inflamed by

* Wilson.

the fresh fuel these proceedings would add. What new victims would be required, who they should be, and whom their appetite for vengeance, whetted by this taste of blood, would select, they knew not. Not unlikely some who gathered there, like the disciples of John the Baptist, after their master had fallen a victim to a tyrant's power, felt that, though the night was dark and the future was forbidding, it was no time to despair or to remit effort. Nor would they, without remonstrance, submit to such an invasion of their personal and political rights. It was agreed that Mr. Wilson should call the attention of the Senate to the subject the next day, and, unless some member of the dominant party should move a committee of investigation, Mr. Seward should make such motion.

"On the assembling of the Senate, amid deep excitement, crowds filling every available space in the Chamber and all its approaches, Mr. Wilson rose, and having narrated briefly the facts of the transaction, said, 'Sir, to assail a member of the Senate out of this Chamber 'for words spoken in debate' is a grave offence, not only against the rights of a senator, but the constitutional privileges of this House; but, sir, to come into this Chamber and assault a member in his seat, until he falls exhausted and senseless on this floor, is an offence requiring the prompt and decisive action of the Senate. Senators, I have called your attention to this transaction. I submit no motion. I leave it to older senators, whose character, whose position in this body and before the country, eminently fit them for the task of devising measures to redress the wrongs of a member of this body, and to vindicate the honor and dignity of the Senate.'

"As no Democratic senator proposed any action, Mr. Seward offered a resolution for a committee of five members, to be appointed by the president, to inquire into the assault and to report the facts, together with their opinion thereon. On motion of Mr. Mason, the resolution was so amended as to provide that the committee should be chosen by the Senate; and Pearce of Maryland, Cass of Michigan, Dodge of Wisconsin, Allen of Rhode Island, and Geyer of Missouri, were selected. The committee was chosen wholly from the Democratic party, and contained no one friendly to Mr. Sumner. The same day, Lewis

D. Campbell introduced a resolution into the House of Representatives reciting the particulars of the assault, and proposing a select committee of five to report such action as might be proper for the vindication of the House. After a brief debate, the resolution was adopted, and Campbell of Ohio, Pennington of New Jersey, Spinner of New York, Cobb of Georgia, and Greenwood of Arkansas, were appointed. . . .

"The Senate committee reported want of jurisdiction, because, it contended, 'authority devolves solely upon the House, of which he is a member;' and the Senate itself took no further action.

"The House committee entered at once upon the investigation, and proceeded to examine the witnesses of the transaction. Visiting Mr. Sumner at his room, they took his deposition from his sick bed. He made substantially the same statement as that already given, mentioning the additional fact that, on coming to consciousness, 'he saw Mr. Douglas and Mr. Toombs standing in the Senate, and Mr. Slidell in the anteroom, from which the latter 'retreated at once.'

"This statement becoming known, these senators felt called upon to make explanations of their knowledge of the affair, and of the course they had adopted in relation to it. Mr. Slidell, referring to the fact that he was conversing with other senators, among whom was Mr. Douglas, when a messenger rushed in with the intelligence that somebody was beating Mr. Sumner, contemptuously said, 'We heard this remark without any particular emotion. For my part, I confess I felt none. I am not disposed to participate in broils of any kind. I remained very quietly in my seat. The other gentleman did the same. We did not move.'

"He stated that, a few minutes afterwards, he went into the Senate Chamber, and was told that Mr. Sumner was lying in a state of insensibility. Returning to the anteroom, and attempting to pass out, he saw the wounded man as he was carried into the anteroom, 'his face covered with blood, and evidently faint and weak.' 'I am not,' said Mr. Slidell, 'particularly fond of scenes of any sort. I have no associations or relations of any kind with Mr. Sumner. I have not spoken to him for two years. I did not think it necessary to express any sympathy or make any advances towards him.' Slidell closed his remarks by saying he was free from any participation, connection, or counsel in the matter.

"Douglas, too, deemed it his duty to make some explanation. He said that when the messenger passed through the room, and said somebody was beating Mr. Sumner, 'I rose immediately to my feet. My first impulse was to come into the Senate Chamber and help to put an end to the affray if I could. But it occurred to my mind in an instant that my relations to Mr. Sumner were such that if I came into the hall my motives would be misconstrued, perhaps, and I sat down again.'

"He stated that a few moments afterwards he went into the Senate Chamber, and saw the crowd gathering about Mr. Sumner, who was prostrate on the floor. He closed his remarks by stating he did not know that he was in the Capitol, that he did not know that any man thought of attacking him, and that he had not the slightest suspicion of what was to happen.

"Mr. Toombs said, 'As for rendering Mr. Sumner any assistance, I did not do it.' It was also given in evidence that Mr. Keitt was present at the assault, not only consenting to the action of his colleague, but with violent demonstrations and profane expressions warning off all who would interfere to save the victim from his assailant." *

On the other hand, the friends of freedom displayed a tender and courageous sympathy for the suffering senator, and a righteous indignation at the outrage committed.

Mr. Wilson, a long-tried and steadfast friend, was among the first to hasten to the side of his stricken colleague, and to render him every brotherly attention. Afterwards, in his place, he nobly represented Massachusetts in his denunciation of the attack as "brutal, murderous, and cowardly."

The House committee brought in two reports; the majority recommending the expulsion of Brooks, and expressing disapprobation of Edmonson and Keitt; the minority pleading want of jurisdiction.

Here also Massachusetts vindicated her right to utter her sentiments on the floor of Congress, and defended her representative in the other Chamber from his assailants, whether they employed tongue or bludgeon. Mr. Burlingame was particularly bold and eloquent. Of Mr. Sumner's

* Wilson.

speech he said, 'It was severe, because it was launched against tyranny. It was severe, as Chatham was severe, when he defended the feeble colonies against the giant oppression of the mother country. It was made in the face of a hostile Senate. It was continued through the greater portion of two days; and yet, during that time, the speaker was not once called to order. This fact is conclusive as to the personal and parliamentary decorum of his speech. He had provocation enough. His State had been called 'hypocritical.' He himself had been called 'a puppy,' 'a fool,' 'a fanatic,' and 'a dishonest man.' No man knew better than he did the proprieties of the place, for he had always observed them. No man knew better than he did parliamentary law, because he had made it the study of his life. No man saw more clearly than he did the flaming sword of the Constitution turning every way, guarding all the avenues of the Senate. But he was not thinking of these things; he was not thinking then of the privileges of the Senate, nor of the guarantees of the Constitution. He was there to denounce tyranny and crime; and he did it. He was there to speak for the rights of an empire, and he did it bravely and grandly."

"The House," says Mr. Wilson, "censured Keitt, but failed to condemn Edmonson. Keitt resigned. One hundred and twenty-one members voted to expel Brooks, and ninety-five voted against expulsion. Having failed to expel, — a two-thirds vote being necessary, — a vote of censure was adopted by a large majority.

"After these votes were declared, Mr. Brooks addressed the House in a speech of mingled assumption, insolence, and self-conceit. While disclaiming all intention to insult Congress, the Senate, or the State of Massachusetts, he seemed to be utterly oblivious that there had been any infringement of law or the rights of others; it being simply, he said, 'a personal affair, for which I am personally responsible.' With infinite effrontery he affirmed, 'I went to work very deliberately, as I am charged, — and this is admitted, — and speculated somewhat as to whether I should employ a horsewhip or a cowhide; but knowing that the senator was my superior in strength, it occurred to me that he might wrest it from my hand, and then (for I never attempt anything I do not perform) I might have been compelled to do that which I would have regretted the balance of my natural life.' What that contingency he so coolly admitted was, every reader can conjecture.

"With still greater assurance and self-assertion, he claimed, as a matter of credit for his forbearance, that he had not plunged the nation into civil war, as if he had held the destinies of the Republic in his hands. 'In my heart of hearts,' he said, 'such a menacing line of conduct I believe would end in subverting this government and drenching this hall in blood. No act of mine, on my personal account, shall inaugurate revolution; but when you, Mr. Speaker, return to your own home, and hear the people of the great North — and they are a great people — speak of me as a bad man, you will do me the justice to say that a blow struck by me at this time would be followed by a revolution; and this I know.'

"Concluding his speech, he announced the resignation of his seat, and walked out of the House."

One of the saddest features of this affair was the general, in most cases the enthusiastic, approval accorded to Brooks by the Southern people. The men applauded him, fair women smiled upon him. Not only the young "chivalry," but grave and reverend heads, professors of science, teachers of youth, and preachers of righteousness, joined in the general jubilation. There were, of course, individual exceptions; but the proofs of an all but universal satisfaction with the bloody deed are too numerous and strong to be controverted. The South indorsed the act, and made it its own. South Carolina placed the crown upon the head of her censured representative, by returning him immediately to Congress, with the bludgeon in his hand. Brooks was the hero of the hour; though later, he confessed that he was heart-sick of the gifts and honors heaped upon him as the prince of bullies.

Jefferson Davis, to an invitation to attend a public dinner in honor of Brooks, was not slow to reply, "I have only to express to you my sympathy with the feeling which prompts the sons of Carolina to welcome the return of a brother who has been the subject of vilification, misrepresentation, and persecution, because he resented a libellous assault upon the representative of their mother."

The students and officers of the University of Virginia voted a cane to their hero, — their diploma, — expressing their sense of his superior attainments in the noble science of assault and battery. Never was a seat of learning prostituted to a more ignoble use.

In view of these facts, which might be greatly multiplied, what proof we have of the power of prejudice, especially of the blinding, demoralizing influence of slavery! But we gladly turn from such exhibitions of human folly and frenzy.

All through the Free North there sprang up instantly a feeling which stood in marked and most favorable contrast with these Southern demonstrations. Slavery and freedom were more and more revealing their opposite characters. Where the latter prevailed, the people, regardless of political differences, rushed together to express their profound sense of a great wrong done to Liberty. Massachusetts, as most directly assailed, was the most deeply moved. But everywhere, every man felt that in the attack upon Mr. Sumner, he himself had been personally smitten. Where was free speech, where was liberty of any kind, if such deeds of violence could be allowed?

The most important result of this atrocity was

the deeper impression now made upon the minds of all anti-slavery men, or that now for the first time awakened among men hitherto indifferent or hostile to the movement for freedom — that slavery was the crowning shame and curse of the country. It was slavery that had beaten to the ground a representative of the people — a defender of liberty; and slavery must fall.

"When," said his colleague, Mr. Wilson, "I lifted his bleeding body from the floor, and laid him upon a lounge, and then washed his blood from my hands, I swore eternal vengeance to slavery, and consecrated my life anew to the cause of human freedom." And such was the feeling in ten thousand hearts, all over the North.

At a public meeting in Faneuil Hall, Hon. Peleg W. Chandler said, — and his words were but an expression of the universal feeling, — "It is precisely because I have been and am now his personal friend, and it is precisely because I have been and now am his political opponent, that I am here to-night. . . . Yet personal feelings are of little or no consequence in this outrage. It is a blow not merely at Massachusetts, a blow not merely at the name and fame of our common country,—it is a blow at constitutional liberty all the world over; it is a stab at the cause of universal freedom. Whatever may be done in this matter, however, one thing is certain, one thing is sure. The blood of this Northern man now stains the Senate floor, and let me tell you that not all the water of the Potomac can wash it out. Forever, forever and aye, that stain will plead in silence for liberty wherever man is enslaved, for humanity all over the world, for truth and for justice, now and forever."

The Hon. Josiah Quincy, then in the eighty-fifth year of his age, said, in a meeting at Quincy,—

"The blow struck upon the head of Charles Sumner did not fall upon him alone. It was a blow purposely aimed at the North. It was a blow struck at the very Tree of Liberty. It speaks to us in words not to be mistaken. It says to us that Northern men shall not be heard in the halls of Congress, except at the point of the bowie-knife, the bludgeon, and revolver.

"The bludgeon, heretofore only brandished, has at last been brought down. Charles Sumner needs not our sympathy; if he dies, his name will be immortal—his name will be enrolled with the names of Warren, Sidney, and Russell; if he lives, he is destined to be the light of the nation."

At another meeting in Boston, Wendell Phillips spoke with even more than his wonted eloquence.

"Nobody," he said, "needs now to read this speech of Charles Sumner to learn whether it is good. We measure the amount of the charge by the length of the rebound. When the spear, driven to the quick, makes the devil start up in his own likeness, we may be sure it is the spear of Ithuriel. That is my way of measuring the speech which has produced this glorious result. O, yes, glorious! for the world will yet cover every one of those scars with laurels. Sir, he *must* not die! We need him yet, as the vanguard leader of the hosts of Liberty. Nay, he shall yet come forth from that sick chamber, and every gallant heart in the Commonwealth be ready to kiss his very footsteps."

Referring to what some had regarded as coarseness in one of Mr. Sumner's comparisons,

Mr. Phillips said, "In utter scorn of the sickly taste, of the effeminate scholarship that starts back in delicate horror at a bold illustration, I dare to say there is no animal God has condescended to make, that man may not venture to name. And if any ground of complaint is supposable in regard to this comparison, which shocks the delicacy of some men and some presses, it is the animal, not Mr. Douglas, that has reason to complain. . . . I place the foot of my uttermost contempt on those members of the press in Boston that have anything to say in criticism of his language, while he lies there prostrate and speechless — our champion, beaten to the ground for the noblest word Massachusetts ever spoke in the Senate."

Ralph Waldo Emerson, in a speech at Concord, said, "Well, sir, this noble head, so comely and so wise, must be a target for a pair of bullies to beat with clubs! The murderer's brand shall stamp their foreheads, wherever they may wander in the earth.

"But I wish, sir, that the high respects of this meeting shall be expressed to Mr. Sumner. . . . I wish that he may know the shudder of terror that ran through all this community on the first tidings of this brutal attack. Let him hear that every man of worth in New England loves his virtues, — that every mother thinks of him as the protector of families, — that every friend of freedom thinks him the friend of freedom."

Horace Mann, his early and devoted friend, wrote to Mr. Sumner, "We are wounded in your wounds, and bleed in your bleeding." Writing later, he said, "It is impossible to tell how much we have felt for you — sorrow, admiration, hope, affection for you; grief, indignation, contempt, abhorrence for the malefactor. Mrs. Mann read one account of the outrage, and could never read another. She said she felt the concussion of the blows all through her brain."

The legislature of Massachusetts passed a series of resolves concerning the assault, describing it as "brutal and cowardly in itself, a gross breach of parliamentary privilege, a ruthless attack upon the liberty of speech, an outrage of the decencies of civilized life, and an indignity to the Commonwealth of Massachusetts."

They demanded of the national Congress "a prompt and strict investigation" of the affair, and the expulsion of Brooks and any other member concerned with him in the assault.

Beyond Massachusetts, everywhere but at the South, a similar feeling was manifested. Governor Clark, of New York, wrote to Mr. Sumner, expressing his abhorrence of the assault, and his personal sympathy with the sufferer.

In New York an "immense meeting, and unprecedented in character," declared the conduct of Brooks to have been "brutal, murderous, and cowardly."

An editorial in the Courier and Enquirer, of New York, admirably summed up the moral result of the act of Brooks: —

"The fact is incontestable, that when the Massachusetts senator again crosses the threshhold of that Senate Chamber, slavery will have to confront the most formidable foe it ever had to face before the public eye. He will come with every muscle braced and every sinew strung by the sense of measureless personal wrong; but, infinitely more than that, he will come armed with the indignation and shielded by the moral support of the whole North. Hitherto he has figured but in one character — the assailant of slavery; henceforth he will be also the accredited assertor and champion of the most sacred right of freedom of speech, and as such will command tenfold greater consideration. His antagonists have affected to despise him before, and to treat him with scorn. The day for that has passed. The public man, who has once been the occasion of such an outburst of sympathy and good-will as has within the last week sprung from the mouth of millions upon millions of his countrymen, is no longer a man to be disdained. He has henceforth position, power, and security beyond any of his adversaries." A true prophecy, in due time to be fulfilled to the letter.

The expressions of regard and sympathy which came to Mr. Sumner from so many quarters must have been peculiarly grateful to his heart. He received them as proofs both of personal friendship and of interest in the cause in which his life had been imperilled. But there were other testimonials, which, though he was grateful for the sentiment which prompted them, he felt constrained instantly to decline. One was the payment by the State of the expense of his illness, which was recommended by the governor to the legislature; the other "a massive and elaborate silver vase, bearing upon its summit a figure representing Charles Sumner holding his Kansas Speech in his right hand," with other elegant artistic designs.

As soon as Mr. Sumner learned that these were in progress, he courteously, but firmly, refused them, expressing his wish that the money designed to be thus appropriated might be applied for the benefit of Kansas.

Throughout this terrible scene there was one heart upon which fell a burden of anxiety and grief peculiarly its own. It was the heart of the mother. She was then living in Boston, at the age of seventy-one, a widow, and already bereaved of several children. The tidings which flew over the wires that her noble son, who had spoken so truly and bravely, was a dreadful sufferer from blows which might prove fatal, must have pierced her heart as with a sword. Ah, how she wished to fly to him, that she might watch over him as only a mother can, and tell him how much she loved him, how proud she was of him; or if, as her fears might suggest, he should not recover, that a mother's hand might perform the last sad offices. What anxious hours were hers between the first news of his being smitten and the better tidings that he would not die.

We are glad to know, from the testimony of her pastor, that she bore the great trial with Christian patience, worthy the mother of such a son. And besides the supports of religion, she had this strong consolation, that he had suffered because of his fidelity to his convictions in the cause of humanity.

As to the son, in those moments when murderous strokes were raining upon him, how must his mind have flown to that mother — sadder, no doubt, for her sake, than for his own.

Thank God, it was to be his privilege, in after years, to be with that fond mother when "heart and flesh were failing" her.

CHAPTER XXII.

Mr. Sumner's Health. — Rest necessary. — Return to Boston. — Welcome Reception. — His Tribute to Henry Wilson. — Reception given to Brooks. — Re-election of Mr. Sumner. — Six Years' Changes. — Letter of Acceptance. — Letter to a Friend. — Sails for Europe. — Letter. — Return. — To Europe again. — Meets De Tocqueville. — Brown-Sequard. — Saved by "Fire." — Letter. — Cured. — Returns to the Senate. — Changes.

MR. SUMNER has disappeared from the Senate, but he has not finished his course. He has yet other battles to fight, other triumphs to win. And his long silence of four suffering years shall plead eloquently for the cause which he has so much at heart.

Mr. Sumner hoped that, after a few weeks of absence, he would be able to resume his seat in the Senate. But the injuries he had received proved to be far too serious to allow a speedy return. Fever ensued, followed by extreme exhaustion, and "for three days he was in a critical situation." The case was a "formidable" one. It was weeks before the wounds were closed. Pains in the head came on in paroxysms. Then ensued "a feeling of oppressive weight or pressure on the brain, as of 'a fifty-six pound weight' upon his head. At the same time he lost flesh and strength, his appetite was irregular, and his nights wakeful. Every step he took seemed to produce a shock upon his brain. His walk was irregular and uncertain, and after slight efforts he would lose almost entire control of the lower extremities." Such was the report of Dr. Perry.

It was certain that an entire suspension of mental labor was necessary. There must be perfect rest, with the most careful medical treatment. Several months were spent in this way, chiefly at Philadelphia and Cape May.

In November, nearly six months after he was struck, Mr. Sumner was so far recovered that he was able to return to his home in Boston. The public reception then given him was most hearty and enthusiastic. Everybody came out to greet him. As his carriage passed through the streets, he was cheered by sympathizing multitudes, while the ladies "showered their bouquets upon him from sidewalks and windows."

Mr. Sumner was able to speak but a few words. Addressing the governor, he said, —

"I thank you for this welcome. I thank, also, the distinguished gentlemen who have honored this occasion by their presence. I thank, too, these swelling multitudes who contribute to me the strength and succor of their sympathies; and my soul overflows especially to the young men of Boston, out of whose hearts, as from an exuberant fountain, this broad-spreading hospitality took its rise."

In that part of his address which he had not strength to deliver, but which afterwards appeared in the journals, Mr. Sumner spoke of his feelings under an enforced absence from Washington: —

"More than five months have passed since I was disabled from the performance of my public duties. During this weary period I have been constrained to repeat daily the lesson of renunciation — confined at first to my bed, and then only slowly regaining the power even to walk. But, beyond the constant, irrepressible grief which must well up in the breast of every patriot, as he discerns the present condition of his country, my chief sorrow has been caused by the necessity to which I was doomed, of renouncing all part in the contest for human rights, which, beginning in Congress, has since enveloped the whole land. . . . From day to day and week to week I vainly sought that health which we value most when lost, and which perpetually eluded my pursuit. For health I strove, for health I prayed. With uncertain steps I sought it at the sea-shore, and I sought it on the mountain-top.

> Two voices are there: one is of the sea,
> One of the mountains; each a mighty voice:
> In both from age to age thou didst rejoice;
> They were thy chosen music, Liberty!'

I listened to the admonitions of medical skill, as I courted all the bracing influences of nature, while time passed without the accustomed healing on its wings."

In the course of his remarks, Mr. Sumner paid a deserved tribute to the worth of his "able, generous, and faithful colleague, Henry Wilson."

"Together we labored in mutual trust, honorably leaning upon each other. By my disability he was left sole representative of Massachusetts on the floor of the Senate, throughout months of heated contest, involving her good name and most cherished sentiments. All who watched the current of debate, even as imperfectly as I did in my retirement, know with what readiness, courage, and power he acted, — showing himself, by extraordinary energies, equal to the extraordinary occasion. But it is my especial happiness to recognize his unfailing sympathies for myself, and his manly assumption of all the responsibilities of the hour."

In conclusion, Mr. Sumner said, —

"With thanks for this welcome, accept also my new vows of duty. In all simplicity let me say that I seek nothing but the triumph of truth. To this I offer my best efforts, careless of office or honor. Show me that I am wrong, and I stop at once; but in the complete conviction of right, I shall persevere against all temptations, against all odds, against all perils, against all threats, — knowing well, that whatever may be my fate, the Right will surely prevail. Terrestrial place is determined by celestial observation. Only by watching the stars can the mariner safely pursue his course; and it is only by obeying those lofty principles which are above men and human passion, that we can make our way safely through the duties of life. In such obedience I hope to live, while, as a servant of Massachusetts, I avoid no labor, shrink from no exposure, and complain of no hardship."

When Brooks returned to his native city, he was warmly welcomed. But how marked the contrast with the present reception! Brooks was lauded and caressed as the hero of slavery, for a deed of mingled cruelty and cowardice; Mr. Sumner, as the champion of freedom, for brave words spoken in behalf of an oppressed community — the one as the assailant, the other as the martyr, of liberty. Mr. Sumner had no subsequent occasion to be "heart-sick" of the honors heaped upon him.

Among those who gave welcome to Mr. Sumner, none rejoiced like the aged mother, as with tears and smiles she embraced once more her son, given to her, as it were, from the dead. With what motherly pride she looked out from her window to see the crowds assembled to do him honor, and heard the loud cheers that went up in praise of his righteous conduct!

To give joy to a mother's heart by an honorable and useful career, though in a sphere humbler than the great senator's, is worth the serious endeavor of any young man. To be regardless of a mother's feelings, in a life of vice and dissipation, proves the absence of all true nobility of character.

In Boston and vicinity Mr. Sumner spent several months under medical treatment, compelled to pass much of the time in bed. But still his health seemed to improve, so that his physician could say, "Time and repose will do the rest."

His term of office had now expired, but Massachusetts would not dismiss him from her service. Who could take the place of Charles Sumner? For six years he had maintained the honor of the old Commonwealth and the cause of freedom, amidst contempt, abuse, menace, and peril of life, with an ability, an eloquence, a fidelity, a purity of purpose, and a conscientious regard to truth and justice, unsurpassed in senatorial history. And had he not suffered as the representative of Massachusetts? Every heart cried out for his re-election, and when the vote was counted, January 9, 1857, he had received three hundred and thirty-three out of three hundred and forty-five votes in the House, and the entire vote of the Senate.

Six years before, he was elected by a bare majority of two votes; now he is returned by a "spontaneous unanimity." Then he was in the vigor of his young manhood; now he is an invalid, too feeble to take his seat, and compelled even to leave his country in search of strength. But whether silent in his seat, prostrate upon his bed, or a wanderer in foreign lands, he is the Commonwealth's chosen champion. His vacant seat will tell a daily story of wrong and outrage, and thus utter its eloquent condemnation of a system founded in and defended by violence. Such a man can never be silent.

In Mr. Sumner's letter of acceptance he said, "This renewed trust I accept with gratitude, enhanced by the peculiar circumstances under which it is bestowed. But far beyond any personal gratification is the delight of knowing, by this sign, that the people of Massachusetts, forgetting ancient party hates, have at last come together in fraternal support of a sacred cause, compared with which the fate of any public servant is of small account."

In February, 1857, towards the close of the session, he returned to Washington, and was again in his seat; but, March 1, he wrote to a friend, "I have sat in my seat only on one day. After a short time the torment to my system became great, and a cloud began to gather over my brain. I tottered out, and took to my bed. I long to speak, but I cannot. Sorrowfully I resign myself to my condition. . . .

"What I can say must stand adjourned to another day. Nobody can regret this so much as myself, and my unhappiness will be increased if I have not your sympathy in this delay.

"I may die; but if I live, a word shall be spoken in the Senate which shall tear slavery open from its chops to its heels. . . .

"Till then, patience."

Warned by his medical advisers to seek rest abroad, Mr. Sumner set sail for Europe on March 7, 1857. From on board the steamship he spoke "a last word for Kansas," in a letter to Mr. Redpath. "With a farewell to my country, as I seek a foreign land, hoping for health long deferred, I give my last thoughts to suffering Kansas, not without devout prayers that the ruffian usurpation which now treads her down may be peaceably overthrown, and that she may be lifted into the enjoyment of freedom and repose."

While absent, he made his restoration to health his daily care. He received the best medical advice, to which he faithfully submitted. He travelled, as strength would allow, in France, Switzerland, England, and Scotland. He had the pleasure of feeling that he was really improving, though amid frequent relapses. From Heidelberg, September 11, he wrote to a friend in an encouraging strain: —

"Weeks have now passed since I have seen a letter or newspaper from home. During this time I have been travelling away from news, and am now famished. On arrival at Antwerp I trust to find letters at last.

"I have been ransacking Switzerland; I have visited most of its lakes, and crossed several of its mountains, mule-back. My strength has not allowed me to venture upon any of those foot expeditions, the charm of Swiss travel, by which you reach places out of the way; but I have seen much, and have gained health constantly.

"I have crossed the Alps by the St. Gothard, and then recrossed by the Great St. Bernard, passing a night with the monks and dogs. I have spent a day at the foot of Mont Blanc, and another on the wonderful Lake Leman. I have been in the Pyrenees, in the Alps, in the Channel Islands. You will next hear of me in the Highlands of Scotland.

"I see our politics now in distant perspective, and I am more than ever satisfied that our course is right. It is slavery which degrades our country, and prevents its example from being all-conquering. In fighting our battle at home, we fight the battle of Freedom everywhere. Be assured, I shall return, not only with renewed strength, but with renewed determination to give myself to our great cause."

Against the advice of eminent physicians, Mr. Sumner resolved to attempt the resumption of his official duties. In December, 1857, he was once more in his seat.

But a trial of his strength convinced him that he was yet far from being well. His disease had, indeed, assumed new and alarming features. Once more he must quit the Senate Chamber to seek rest and medical help abroad. In May, 1858, he crossed the Atlantic.

In Paris he had the sympathy of noble men, among whom was De Tocqueville. "*Nous nous sommes occupés de vous beaucoup dernièrement,*" said this great man to Mr. Sumner, who replied, "*Ah, monsieur, je me suis occupé de vous toute ma vie.*" *

But above all it was his good providence to meet the most skilful physician of the age — Brown-Sequard. At last he had found a healer. But at what a cost of pain, even to agony, was a cure to come! He was to be saved by "fire."

We cannot do better here than give some extracts from a lecture, — one of a course at the Lowell Institute, in Boston, — by Brown-Sequard, just after Mr. Sumner's death, as reported in the Daily Journal. The subject for the evening was "Nervous Diseases," and the lecturer took advantage of the opportunity thus presented him

* "We have had you upon our minds a great deal of late.' "Ah, sir, I have had you in my mind all my life."

of adding a word in honor of the memory of his patient and friend, and paid one of the truest and most delicate compliments to his name that has yet been given. He was very deeply affected, even to tears, in which many of the audience joined. He began as follows: —

"In this, my fifth lecture here, I have to beg your forgiveness for being moved. Since 1857 the great man who has left us has been under my care, and been also my very dear friend. I sympathized in every one of the generous impulses which have aided in raising him to such a high place of influence in his country, and therefore it is very easy for you to understand that I am now hardly able to say more about his greatness, and the blow which our country and you, in this transition, have suffered. In a moment, when I am a little more in control of my nerves, I will have to say something else about him — something which I never mentioned in his life. I knew that the modesty, by far greater in him than anybody knew to exist, would have been wounded if I had spoken as I will when I am more free in my thought and in the articulation of my voice."

He then proceeded, for a few moments, in the

consideration of the subject of his lecture, which was in regard to the nervous system. He continued: —

"When Mr. Sumner first came under my care, he was suffering from a derangement of some fibres of the nerves. As you all know, he had received a blow upon the head. His spine, as he was sitting, was bent in two places. His bent spine had produced the effects of a sprain; and when I saw him in Paris he had recovered altogether from the first effects of the blow. He had then two troubles: one was, that he could not make use of his brain at all. He could not read a newspaper or write a letter. He was in a fearful state. It seemed to him as if his head would explode, as if there was some great force in it pushing the parts away from each other. Indeed, his emotions were fearful to me. Often, in conversation, if anything was said calling for any degree of deep thought, he suffered intensely immediately, so that we had to be extremely careful with him. He had another trouble, of the same nature as regards external appearances, but occupying another portion of the spine, and causing other symptoms. It was a sprain at the level of the last dorsal vertebra. The irritation there was intense, and any motion was extremely hard. When he walked, he had to push forward his right foot and then his left, holding on all the while to his back with both hands to relieve the pain. It had been thought that he was paralyzed as to his lower limbs; it had been thought that he had a disease of the brain, and that was regarded as being the cause of the paralysis of the lower limbs. Fortunately the discovery made with regard to the vaso-motor nerves led me at once to find that he had no disease of the brain and no paralysis. He had only an irritation of the vaso-motor nerves, at their exit from the spine. When I asked him if he was conscious of any weakness in his limbs, he said, 'Certainly not; I only cannot walk on account of the pain.' What was to to be done then was to apply counter-irritation on these two sprains; the only point which has led me to speak of this. I told him the best plan of treatment would consist in the application of moxa, the most painful application to the skin. I asked him if he would not take chloroform to dull the pain or remove it altogether. I shall always remember his impressive assent when I had said that. He said, 'Doctor, if you can say positively that I shall derive just as much benefit if I take chloroform as if I do not, then I will take chloroform; but if there is to be any degree whatever of greater amelioration in case I don't take chloroform, then I shall not take it.' I didn't have the courage to deceive him. I told him there would be more good if he didn't take chloroform. So I had to submit him to the martyrdom of the greatest suffering that can be inflicted by medical practice, and burned him. I thought that, after the torture of the first time, he would then resort to chloroform; but for five times after, in accordance with his own determination, the operation was performed without it. I never saw a patient before that would submit to such a thing. The only explanation for his conduct was this: at that time he was much abused. Report had reached him that some of his countrymen at home considered that he was amusing himself in Paris, pretending to be ill; and he wanted to return as quickly as possible. A few days, therefore, were of great importance to him; so he passed through all that terrible and most intense suffering, the greatest I have ever had the misfortune to inflict, be it upon man or animal. I have mentioned it on this account, only to show what kind of a man he was. And I will only add that I have seen him always since to be ready to submit to anything for the sake of what he thought was right, and in other spheres you all know that such was his character about everything."

At this point the speaker was completely overcome by his emotion, and, begging permission to defer the remainder of his lecture to another time, he hastily withdrew from the stage.

Another account adds, that when Mr. Sumner called on Brown-Sequard, he asked what kind of remedy would be used, to which the doctor replied, "Fire." The patient instantly accepted the harsh remedy, and when the next day was proposed as the time for its first application, he insisted upon that very afternoon.

Here was more than physical courage — here was moral bravery of the highest kind; for with Mr. Sumner, a cure was not merely the sweet renewal of health, but the certainty of putting on again his armor in the defence of a cause dearer to him than life. He was eager for the conflict.

After a time Mr. Sumner left Paris for the South of France, still undergoing daily the most severe treatment. From a letter to a friend, written September 11, 1858, we learn how he now spent his time, and what were his feelings.

"Look at the map of Europe, and you will find, nestling in the mountains of Savoy, between Switzerland and France, the little village of Aix, generally known as Aix-les-Bains, from the baths which give it fame. There I am now. The country about is most beautiful, the people simple and kind.

"My life is devoted to health. I wish that I could say that I am not still an invalid; yet, except when attacked by the pain on my chest, I am now comfortable, and enjoy my baths, my walks, and the repose and incognito which I find here.

"I begin the day with *douches*, hot and cold, and, when thoroughly exhausted, am wrapped in sheet and blanket, and conveyed to my hotel, and laid on my bed. After my walk, I find myself obliged again to take to my bed for two hours before dinner. But this whole treatment is in pleasant contrast with the protracted suffering from fire which made the summer a torment. And yet I fear that I must return to that treatment.

"It is with a pang unspeakable that I find myself thus arrested in the labors of life, and in the duties of my position. This is harder to bear than the fire. I do not hear of friends engaged in active service . . . without a feeling of envy."

Returning to Paris, Brown-Sequard gave him the joyful information that the cure was complete.

Hope long, long and most painfully deferred, is at last realized. Through four tedious years of suspense and pain, he has looked forward to this hour; and now it has come.

He hears the call of duty from across the waters, and when Congress opens, December, 1859, he takes up his work, in the exulting consciousness that this time it shall not drop from his hands.

But where are the men who had compelled him to lay down that work, and because it was so faithfully done? Two of the most prominent actors, the most audacious, arrogant, insulting, and, for the time being, seemingly most potential,

— Brooks and Butler, — were in their graves in less than a year after the assault, Brooks having experienced a sudden and most agonizing death. The contrast is impressive.

CHAPTER XXIII.

Excited State of Feeling. — Letters to Mr. Claflin. — John Brown. — His Demeanor; his Execution; his previous Interview with Mr. Sumner. — John Brown in Congress. — Kidnapping. — Petitions against Slavery tabled. — Letter from Horace Mann. — Speech, "Barbarism of Slavery." — Allusion to Brooks. — Reply of Mr. Chesnut. — Mr. Sumner's Life in Danger.

At the time of Mr. Sumner's return to the Senate,* the country was in a state of intense excitement. John Brown had just made his bold attack upon slavery, and was on the eve of his execution.

The Fugitive Slave Bill had provoked several of the Free States to pass Personal Liberty Bills, for the protection of their citizens from Southern

* The Senate was still strongly Democratic, and of the extreme pro-slavery stamp, though the Republican minority now numbered twenty-four. That minority was soon to be an overwhelming majority.

domination, which, in turn, had roused the pro-slavery party to madness. Secession was beginning to show itself. A presidential canvass was just at hand, involving a direct issue between freedom and slavery.

Under these circumstances, when the air was filled with alarms, and many were putting forward plans for peace, Mr. Sumner wrote to a friend as follows:—

"WASHINGTON, January, '60.

"MY DEAR CLAFLIN: Massachusetts has now an important post. The greatest difficulty is to be true to herself and her own noble history.

"In the name of Liberty I supplicate you not to let her take any backward steps—*not an inch, not a hair's breadth!*

"It is now too late for any fancied advantage from such conduct. It only remains that she do nothing by which liberty suffers, or by which her principles are recanted. Remember well that not a word from the legislature can have the least influence in averting the impending result; that the only security is the firmness which nothing can shake.

"Let the timid cry, but let Massachusetts stand stiff—God bless her!

"We are on the eve of great events, and this

month will try men's souls. But our duty is clear as noonday, and bright as the sun.

"Ever sincerely yours,

"CHARLES SUMNER."

John Brown had now found his way into Congress, — for his "soul" was "marching on," — in the Harper's Ferry Investigation, in the Senate, on the question of imprisoning a citizen for refusing to testify in the case. This was March 12, 1860.

The investigation arose from the famous enterprise of the "Hero of Osawatomie," who, October 17, 1859, with a force of twenty-two men, captured the United States Arsenal at Harper's Ferry. His object was to set in motion a plan which he had formed for the general liberation of the slaves. It was charged upon him that he intended to provoke insurrection, but he solemnly denied having any such purpose; and his word was as good as an oath. He hoped to effect a peaceful exodus of the slaves without rebellion or bloodshed. What he had already done in Missouri, in a small way, when he "took slaves without the snapping of a gun on either side" to Canada, he said he wished now to accomplish on a grander scale.

On his trial — for he was soon overpowered — he said, with noble simplicity, that he had only carried out the principles of the New Testament, "which taught him that all things 'whatsoever I would that men should do unto me, I should do even so to them.'"

To us his scheme seems a mad one, but there can be no doubt of his entire conscientiousness. He was a man of heroic nature, a devout Christian of the old Puritan style, a perfectly unselfish philanthropist. His very enemies were powerfully impressed by the nobleness of his demeanor in the court-room, in the jail, and at his execution. The letters which he wrote to his family and to his friends, after his sentence to death, show a sweet tenderness of spirit and a courageous and peaceful trust in God.

In prison he was cheerful to the very last, and an eye-witness testifies that on the day of his execution, December 2, 1859, he walked out of the jail "with a radiant countenance, and the step of a conqueror." "His face was even joyous, and it has been remarked that probably his was the lightest heart in Charlestown that day. A black woman, with a little child in her arms, stood by the door. He stopped a moment, and, stopping, kissed the child affectionately. Another black woman, with a child, as he passed along, exclaimed, 'God bless you, old man! I wish I could help you; but I can't.' He looked at her with a tear in his eye." *

Compare this man, so gentle and heroic, the friend of the poor and oppressed even unto death, with the border ruffians of Missouri, whom we have seen, in defiance of all law and all justice, attempting to set up slavery in Kansas. If we cannot approve John Brown's plan of liberation, we can admire his magnanimous spirit and his generous purpose; while, in the other case, both the men and their scheme deserve only unmingled condemnation.

In the case before the Senate, Mr. Sumner contended that that body had not the power to compel testimony, under pains and penalties, except in cases involving self-defence.

"This," said he, "is a fearful prerogative; and permit me to say, that, in assuming it, you liken yourselves to the Jesuits, at the period of their most hateful supremacy, when it was said that

* The American Conflict, by Horace Greeley.

their power was a sword whose handle was at Rome, and whose point was in the most distant places. You take into your hands a sword whose handle will be in this Chamber, to be clutched by a mere partisan majority, and whose point will be in every corner of the republic."

Ah, why did not these senators, who were so anxious for *justice* to be done, summon witnesses to testify about the raids into Kansas, and the attack upon Lawrence? But it was when Slavery, not Liberty, was in danger, that these republicans of the South were aroused.

Mr. Sumner must have felt a peculiar interest in the case before the Senate, for he had met John Brown in Boston while there suffering from his injuries received from Brooks. Perhaps that meeting had some connection with the present case. Rev. James Freeman Clarke mentions that, calling at that time on Mr. Sumner at his home in Hancock Street, he found him resting in an easy-chair, and with him three gentlemen. One was Captain Brown. "They were speaking of the assault by Preston Brooks, and Mr. Sumner remarked, 'The coat I had on at the time is in that closet. Its collar is stiff with blood. You can see it if you please, captain.' Brown arose, went to the closet, slowly opened the door, carefully took down the coat, and looked at it for a few moments with the reverence that a Roman Catholic regards the relic of a saint. Perhaps the sight caused him to feel a still deeper horror of slavery, and to take a stronger resolution of attacking it in its strongholds. So the blood of the martyrs is the seed of the church."

A few days later, Mr. Sumner spoke again upon a similar subject — "An attempt to kidnap a citizen, under order of the Senate." It was an attempt to bring Mr. Sanborn, of Concord, Mass., to Washington, as a witness in the Harper's Ferry affair. Mr. Sumner denied the right to do so, and declared the attempt to be kidnapping. Two days later, he presented twelve different petitions against slavery, containing fifteen hundred and eighty-nine names. The Senate, still in bondage to the slave power, laid them on the table.

A few months after the assault upon Mr. Sumner, his friend Horace Mann wrote to him, "Seek the noblest revenge, which is strength" —

strength to resume the contest with slavery. One opportunity to deal a heavy blow at that system he had improved; another had come.

The session was far advanced into June. Mr. Sumner had been testing his strength for another vigorous encounter. His revenge was sure — not personal — his noble nature disdained that, — but the revenge of saying again, in his place, all that was in his heart for the cause of human rights.

When last he had spoken at any length, it was on the subject of admitting Kansas as a Free State. That was four years ago, May 19 and 20, 1856. During his absence the question had remained unsettled, and now, on the 4th of June, 1860, he takes up the theme where he had left it. Then he spoke on the "Crime against Kansas;" now he dwells on the "Barbarism of Slavery."

He does so for the best of reasons. He had seen that merely dwelling on particular examples of the injustice of slavery had not brought the desired result. The Nebraska "swindle" had been exposed, the crime against Kansas had been laid bare; and still the swindle remained, and

Kansas was refused her rights. The South was growing more rapacious. What should be done?

Mr. Sumner's logical mind saw no hope but in laying the axe at the root of the tree. He would strike at slavery itself, the bitter root whence had sprung that harvest of woes which the nation was reaping. He would carry, not "the war into Africa, but Africa into the war." He would kill the monster whose arms were strangling the nation.

"The Barbarism of Slavery" — the most appropriate theme, because the most radical. And thus did Mr. Sumner enter upon his speech: —

"Mr. President: Undertaking now, after a silence of more than four years, to address the Senate on this important subject, I should suppress the emotions natural to such an occasion if I did not declare, on the threshold, my gratitude to that Supreme Being through whose benign care I am enabled, after much suffering and many changes, once again to resume my duties here, and to speak for the cause so near my heart.

"To the honored Commonwealth whose representative I am, and also to my immediate associates in this body, with whom I enjoy the fellowship which is found in thinking alike concerning the Republic, I owe thanks, which I seize the moment to express, for indulgence extended to me throughout the protracted seclusion enjoined by medical skill; and I trust that it will not be thought unbecoming in me to put on record here, as an apology for leaving my seat so long vacant, without making way, by resignation, for a successor, that I acted under the illusion of an invalid, whose hopes for restoration to natural health continued against oft-recurring disappointment.

"When last I entered into this debate, it became my duty to expose the crime against Kansas, and to insist upon the immediate admission of that Territory as a State of this Union, with a constitution forbidding slavery. Time has passed, but the question remains. Resuming the discussion precisely where I left it, I am happy to avow that rule of moderation which, it is said, may venture to fix the boundaries of wisdom itself.

"I have no personal griefs to utter; only a vulgar egotism could intrude such into this Chamber. I have no personal wrongs to avenge; only a brutish nature could attempt to wield that vengeance which belongs to the Lord. The years that have intervened and the graves that have opened since I spoke have their voices, which I cannot fail to hear.

"Besides, what am I, what is any man among the living or among the dead, compared with the question before us? It is this alone which I shall discuss, and I begin the argument with that easy victory which is found in charity."

Mr. Sumner proceeded to say that in his former speech he had left untouched the most important part of the argument — "that found in the Character of Slavery."

"This," he added, "is no time for soft words or excuses. They may turn away wrath; but what is the wrath of man? This is no time to abandon any advantage in the argument. Senators sometimes announce that they resist slavery on political grounds only, and remind us that they say nothing of the moral question. This is wrong. Slavery must be resisted not only on political grounds, but on all other grounds, whether social, economical, or moral. Ours is no holiday contest; nor is it any strife of rival factions, of White and Red Roses, of theatric Neri and

Bianchi; but it is a solemn battle between right and wrong, between good and evil. Such a battle cannot be fought with rose-water. There is austere work to be done, and freedom cannot consent to fling away any of her weapons."

Mr. Sumner assailed slavery as guilty of a five-fold wrong: its claiming property in man,—its abrogation of marriage,—its abrogation of the parental relation,—its closing the gates of knowledge,—its appropriation of all the toil of its victims.

With reference to the first, he said,—

"Under what ordinance of Nature or of Nature's God is one human being stamped an owner, and another stamped a thing? God is no respecter of persons. . . . God is the Father of the human family, and we are all his children. Where, then, is the sanction of the pretension by which a brother lays violent hands upon a brother? To ask these questions is humiliating; but it is clear there can be but one response. . . . On all grounds of reason, and waiving all questions of 'positive' statute, the Vermont judge was nobly right, when, rejecting the claim of a slave-master, he said, 'No, not until you show a bill of sale from the Almighty.'"

The closing words are these: —

"Thus, sir, speaking for freedom in Kansas, I have spoken for freedom everywhere, and for civilization; and as the less is contained in the greater, so are all arts, all sciences, all economies, all refinements, all charities, all delights of life, embodied in this cause. You may reject it, but it will be only for to-day. The sacred animosity of freedom and slavery can end only with the triumph of freedom."

His terrible arraignment of slavery was received with "profound and ominous silence" — the silence which precedes the storm.

The slave party in the Senate, taught a lesson by the universal horror — save at the South — which followed the assault upon Mr. Sumner after his former speech, now determined upon a different policy. They affected to regard the present speech as only worthy of contempt, all the while feeling the barbed arrows of truth rankling in their bosoms.

Mr. Chesnut, of South Carolina, was their mouthpiece, and vented his spleen in some very choice expressions: "After ranging over Europe, crawling through the back doors to whine at the feet of British aristocracy, craving pity, and reaping a rich harvest of contempt, the slanderer of States and men reappears in the Senate. We had hoped to be relieved from the outpourings of such vulgar malice. . . . In this I am disappointed. . . .

"It has been left for this day, for this country, for the abolitionists of Massachusetts, to deify the incarnation of malice, mendacity, and cowardice. . . . We do not intend to contribute, by any conduct on our part, to increase the devotees at the shrine of this new idol. We know what is expected and what is desired. We are not inclined again to send forth the recipient of punishment howling through the world, yelping fresh cries of slander and malice. These are the reasons which I feel it due to myself and others to give to the Senate and the country, why we have quietly listened to what has been said, and why we can take *no other notice of the matter*."

Why did not the senator from South Carolina undertake to disprove the statements made by Mr. Sumner?

But what it was decided not to do in the Senate Chamber, was attempted outside of it. Mr. Sumner's life was in peril; and because he refused to take any personal precautions, some friends, without his knowledge, kept guard over his house, and escorted him to and from the Capitol.

At the North, the speech was regarded by some as very truthful, indeed, but very imprudent.

By multitudes it was read with delight, not because Southern wickedness was exposed, but because the truth had been spoken. The veil that concealed the cancer had been torn away; now there was hope of a cure. It was a hideous spectacle, but abhorrence would rouse to action.

This speech doubtless hastened the crisis, and helped to bring on the war. That was, however, no fault of the speaker, unless the Saviour was at fault when he said, "I bring not peace, but a sword." The sword of truth is the necessary precursor of true and lasting peace.

The nation had tried compromises long enough. Now was Justice lifting up her voice, to try her power, where every other remedy had only aggravated the disease, and left the patient nigher to death.

Thank God, a man had arisen to speak the truth, without fear or favor. To-day the nation lives, in the new strength of universal liberty.

CHAPTER XXIV.

Fanaticism of the Slave Power. — Jefferson Davis's Resolutions in the Senate. — Democratic National Convention in Charleston. — Bell and Everett. — Republicans and Abraham Lincoln. — Mr. Lincoln's Views. — Mr. Sumner at the Cooper Institute. — "Republican Party." — West India Emancipation. — Mr. Sumner. — "Presidential Candidates and the Issues." — "Mrs. Toodles." — Mr. Lincoln elected. — The Rebellion at the Door. — President Buchanan's Cure-all. — South Carolina. — Ordinance of Secession. — Fort Sumter. — Sixth Massachusetts Regiment at Baltimore. — Speech of Mr. Sumner to Major Devens's Company, at New York.

Events are rapidly ripening for a great crisis. The country is in violent agitation. The future wears a lowering aspect.

It is plain that the slave power is bent on employing the most extreme measure for strengthening its position. The union of the States is of little account in comparison with slavery. That must be maintained at all hazards.

In the Senate, only a few days before Mr. Sumner's last speech, Jefferson Davis carried through a series of resolutions, one of which directly affirmed " the constitutional right of any citizen of the United States to take his slave property into the common Territories, and there hold and enjoy the same while the territorial condition continues."

This was a great advance on Mr. Douglas's plan of " popular sovereignty," so called, which left it optional with a Territory to admit or reject slavery. The South wanted more. A slave-owner must be allowed to take his slaves into any Territory, whether the majority of the inhabitants willed it or not. Slavery must have the national patronage and protection.

This, of course, would divide the Democratic, which was also a pro-slavery, party, as the Northern wing were not ready to adopt so ultra a measure. But the South cared not for that. If the Democratic party would not follow their lead, they would break with it.

Accordingly, when the Democratic National Convention met in Charleston, S. C., in April, 1860, to nominate a President and Vice-President, a division ensued. The Convention broke up in confusion. The party of the majority adjourned to Baltimore, June 18; that of the minority, comprising men of the most extreme Southern doctrines, adjourned to Richmond, and afterwards to Baltimore. The former nominated Stephen A. Douglas for President; the latter, John C. Breckinridge.

Thus the South was withdrawing more and more within itself, even then having in view a Southern Confederacy.

In the mean time, another party, composed mainly of old-fashioned Whigs, adopting only the Constitution as its platform, and declining to take any open stand either for or against slavery, had nominated John Bell for President, and Edward Everett for Vice-President. Though professedly non-committal, it was really pro-slavery. Not to be against slavery, was to be for it. Neutrality was no longer possible.

There was certainly need of another nomination for the Presidency, to represent the party of Freedom. The Republicans had just selected ABRAHAM LINCOLN as their standard-bearer.

Mr. Lincoln, in his own admirable way, which showed genius as well as philanthropy and patriotism, had clearly defined his position.

Mr. Douglas's so-styled "Popular Sovereignty" was thus defined: "*If any one man choose to enslave another, no third man shall be allowed to object!*"

The three parties represented, respectively, by Breckinridge, Douglas, and Bell, were assailed with a quotation from Scripture, and an ingenious commentary thereon: "'*A house divided against itself cannot stand.*' I believe this government cannot permanently endure, half slave and half free. I do not expect the Union to be dissolved — I do not expect the house to fall — but I do expect that it will cease to be divided. It will become all one thing or all the other." This was another way of putting Mr. Seward's "irrepressible conflict."

And thus the parties stood in the spring of 1860 — three for Slavery, one for Freedom; three for Barbarism, one for Civilization; "all one thing, or all the other."

Mr. Sumner entered with all his heart into the presidential contest. He hailed the advent of a new era — the *whole house* dedicated to Freedom.

In the month of July, about a month after his speech in the Senate, he spoke at the Cooper Institute, New York, on "The Republican Party: its Origin, Necessity, and Purpose."

This great speech was another blow "at the root" — at slavery itself. It was full of hope. "All good omens," he said, "are ours. The work cannot stop. Quickened by the triumph now so near, with a Republican president in power, State after State, quitting the condition of a Territory, and spurning slavery, will be welcomed into our Plural Unit, and, joining hands together, will become a belt of fire girt about the Slave States, within which slavery must die, — or, happier still, joining hands together, they will become to the Slave States a zone of Freedom, radiant, like the ancient *cestus* of Beauty, with transforming power."

Mr. Sumner would be content with nothing short of universal emancipation. His view of such a measure may be learned from a letter to a public meeting convened to celebrate emancipation in the British West Indies: —

"Nothing shows the desperate mendacity of the partisans of slavery more than the unfounded persistence with which they call this act 'a failure.' If it be a failure, then is virtue a failure, then is justice a failure, then is humanity a failure, then is God himself a failure; for virtue, justice, humanity, and God himself, are all represented in this act.

"The true policy of this world is found in justice. Nothing is truer than that injustice, besides its essential wickedness, is folly also. The unjust man is a fool."

At a Republican State Convention, at Worcester, August 29, 1860, Mr. Sumner discussed the presidential candidates and the issues.

He spoke of the candidates, with the single exception of Mr. Lincoln, as "differing superficially among themselves, but all concurring in friendship for slavery, and in withstanding its prohibition anywhere. . . . The whole trio are no better than Mrs. Malaprop's idea of Cerberus, 'three gentlemen at once,' and must be encountered together."

Describing the Bell party, he said,—

"Its plan, so far as known, is this: You will

remember that, by the Constitution of the United States, in the event of failure to elect by the people, the House of Representatives is empowered to choose a president out of the three highest candidates for that office.

"Now, assuming, first, that the Republican candidate will not be elected by the people, — and, secondly, assuming that there will be no election by the House, — this party, turning next to the vice-presidency, assumes, thirdly, that Mr. Everett will be one of the two highest candidates for the vice-presidency, and, fourthly, that Mr. Everett will be elected by the Senate vice-president, and then will become president, like John Tyler and Millard Fillmore, — not through the death of a president, but through a double failure by the people and by the House.

"Such is the calculation by which this band of professed Conservatives seek repose for the country.

"Permit me to say that it is equalled only by the extravagance of Mrs. Toodles, in the farce. Her passion was auctions, where she purchased ancient articles of furniture, under the idea that they might some day be useful.

"Once, to the amazement of her husband, she brought home a brass door-plate with the name of Thompson spelled with a p. 'But what is this for?' he demanded. 'Why,' said Mrs. Toodles, with logic worthy of the Bell party, 'though we have been married many years without children, it is possible, my dear, that we may have a child; that child may be a daughter, and may live to the age of maturity, and she *may* marry a man of the name of Thompson spelled with a p. Then how handy it would be to have this door-plate in the house!'

"I doubt whether any person really familiar with affairs can consider this nomination for the vice-presidency of more practical value than Mrs. Toodles's brass door-plate, with the name of Thompson spelled with a p, picked up at an auction.

"But then, in a certain most difficult contingency, at the end of a long train of contingencies, how handy it must be to have it in the house!"

In speaking of the Breckinridge party, he said,—

"I confess myself perplexed between abhorrence for its dogma and respect for its frankness. . . . There is something even in criminal boldness which we are disposed to admire. We like an open foe, who scorns to hide in deceit, and meets us in daylight. . . . And yet this very frankness reveals an insensibility to reason and humanity, which, when recognized, must add to our abhorrence."

The Douglas party he described as "last in character, — for who can respect what we know to be a deceit? The statesman founds himself on principles; sometimes it is his office to frame expedients; but popular sovereignty, as now put forward, is not a principle — O, no! not even an expedient; it is nothing but a device, a pretext, an evasion, a dodge, a trick, in order to avoid the commanding question, whether slavery shall be prohibited in the Territories."

"To protect this 'villany' [slavery], . . . the right of the people to govern themselves is invoked, — forgetful that this divine right can give no authority to enslave others, that even the people are not omnipotent, and that never do they rise so high as when, recognizing the everlasting laws of Right, they bend to the behests of Justice.

"Far different is the position of Mr. Lincoln, who has openly said, 'If I were in Congress, and a vote should come up on a question whether slavery should be prohibited in a new Territory, in spite of the Dred Scott decision, I would vote that it should. That is what I would do.'"

Early in November it was known that Mr. Lincoln had a majority of electoral votes. This at once decided the action of the South. They had gone into the canvass with the dishonorable intention of abiding by the result if it should be in favor of their candidate — Mr. Breckinridge; otherwise to rebel.

And this was what they wanted a plausible pretext for doing. The South was, therefore, rejoiced that Mr. Lincoln was elected. Now they could say, The abolitionists have obtained control of the government, and we cannot and will not submit to them.

Rebellion was at the door.

President Buchanan, in his Message, December 3, spoke of the disturbed and threatening condition of the country. He had hard words for the North, soft ones for the South. "How easy," said he, "would it be for the American people to settle the slavery question forever, and to restore peace and harmony to this distracted country!" How so? By yielding everything to the South. That was the meaning of his long tirade against Northern anti-slavery movements.

Blear-eyed man! how poorly he read the signs of the times! how little he comprehended the deep questions that were agitating and rending the country! How easy to put down the earthquake!

On December 20, South Carolina passed her ordinance of secession. Other States speedily followed. The president said there was nothing he could now do to avert the storm.

A gracious Providence, on March 4, 1861, put a strong, faithful pilot at the helm. He thought something could be done. He declared his purpose to maintain the authority of the government over the whole country.

There had been proposed all sorts of preventives for the impending storm — plans of conciliation, concession, compromise. In vain! The South was in earnest.

On the 12th of April, 1861, the signal gun was

fired. Fort Sumter was attacked by rebel guns. The war was begun, and by the South.

Three days after, April 15, President Lincoln, true to his word, issued a proclamation for seventy-five thousand men to suppress the insurrection.

The Sixth Massachusetts Regiment, in quick response, was in Baltimore on the 19th, on its way to Washington. Attacked by secessionists, four of their number were killed, and thirty-six wounded. The first blood was shed.

Mr. Sumner was in Baltimore the day before, and narrowly escaped a mob, which was in search of him.

On the 20th, at New York, he met the Third Battalion of Massachusetts Rifles, under Major Devens, on their route to Fort Henry, and addressed them in stirring words: —

"I cannot see before me so large a number of the sons of Massachusetts, already moving to the scene of trial, without feeling anew the loss we have just encountered: I allude to the death, at Baltimore, of devoted fellow-citizens, who had sprung forward so promptly at the call of country. As I heard that they had fallen, my soul was touched. And yet, when I thought of the cause for which they met death, I said to myself, that, for the sake of Massachusetts, ay, and for their own sake, I would not have it otherwise. They have died well, for they died at the post of duty, and so dying have become an example and a name in history, while Massachusetts, that sent them forth, adds new memories to a day already famous in her calendar, and links the present with the past."

"It was on the 19th of April that they died, and their blood was the first offering of patriotism in the great cause that snatched them from the avocations of peace."

CHAPTER XXV.

Defeat at Bull Run. — Mr. Sumner at Worcester. — "Emancipation our best Weapon." — Speech at New York. — "The Rebellion; its Origin and Mainspring." — One Way of Safety. — Speech against returning Fugitive Slaves from the Federal Lines. — Eulogy on Colonel Baker. — "The Trent." — Mason and Slidell; their Capture. — Mr. Sumner urges their Surrender. — Neutral Rights.

THE war went on with varying fortunes. Some border States were divided, being largely favorable to the South without actually joining the rebel Confederacy, and several additional Slave States went over to the enemy. The defeat of the Federal forces at Bull Run, July 21, was a great shock to the North, but it accomplished the important purpose of revealing the real magnitude of the task of subduing the South.

In October, 1861, at the Republican State Convention at Worcester, while affairs were in a condition of mingled hope and fear, Mr. Sumner boldly announced this proposition — Emancipation our best weapon. He saw that slavery was at once the strength and weakness of the enemy, and he would invoke the war power of the government to abolish it. The right, he said, was unquestionable. The necessity was urgent.

"It is often said that war will make an end of slavery. This is probable. But it is surer still that the overthrow of slavery will make an end of the war.

"If I am correct in this averment, which I believe beyond question, then do reason, justice, and policy unite, each and all, in declaring that the war must be brought to bear directly on the grand conspirator and omnipresent enemy.

"Not to do so is to take upon ourselves all the weakness of slavery, while we leave to the rebels its boasted resources of military strength.

"Not to do so is to squander life and treasure in a vain masquerade of battle, without practical result.

"Not to do so is blindly to neglect the plainest dictates of economy, humanity, and common sense, — and, alas! simply to let slip the dogs of war on a mad chase over the land, never to stop until spent with fatigue or sated with slaughter.

"Believe me, fellow-citizens, I know all imagined difficulties and unquestioned responsibilities. But, if you are in earnest, the difficulties will at once disappear, and the responsibilities are such as you will gladly bear. This is not the first time that a knot hard to untie was cut by the sword; and we all know that danger flees before the brave man. Believe that you can, and you can. The will only is needed. Courage now is the highest prudence.

"It is not necessary even, borrowing a familiar phrase, to carry the war into Africa. It will be enough if we carry Africa into the war, in any form, any quantity, any way. The moment this is done, rebellion will begin its bad luck, and the Union become secure forever."

Though this speech was received with great applause when delivered, the public mind was divided as to the expediency of immediate emancipation. Then, as many times since, Mr. Sumner was thought by not a few to be premature and unpractical; but then, ere long, as well as since, his most advanced and objectionable propositions were subsequently adopted. The nation was compelled to adopt emancipation as necessary to success.

The next month he urged the same proposition, with new arguments and illustrations, at an immense meeting in New York. His theme was, The Rebellion; its Origin and Mainspring.

He called slavery "the ruling idea" of the rebellion. "It is slavery that marshals these hosts and breathes into their embattled ranks its own barbarous fire. It is slavery that stamps its character alike upon officers and men. It is slavery that inspires all, from general to trumpeter. It is slavery that speaks in the word of command, and sounds in the morning drum-beat. It is slavery that digs trenches and builds hostile forts. It is slavery that pitches its wicked tents, and stations its sentries over against the national Capitol. It is slavery that sharpens the bayonet and runs the bullet, — that points the cannon, and scatters the shell, blazing, bursting with death. Wherever the rebellion shows itself, whatever form it takes, whatever thing it does, whatever it meditates, it is moved by slavery; nay, the rebellion is slavery itself, incarnate, living, acting, raging, robbing, murdering, according to the essential law of its being.

"Nor is this all. The rebellion is not only ruled by slavery, but, owing to the peculiar condition of the Slave States, it is, for the moment, according to their instinctive boast, actually re-enforced by this institution.

"As the fields of the South are cultivated by slaves, . . . the white freemen are at liberty to play the part of rebels. The slaves toil at home, while the masters work at rebellion; and thus, by singular fatality, is this doomed race, without taking up arms, actually engaged in feeding, supporting, succoring, and invigorating those battling for their enslavement.

"But how shall the rebellion be crushed? . . . You will strike where the blow is most felt; nor will you miss the precious opportunity. The enemy is before you; nay, he comes out in ostentatious challenge, and his name is Slavery. You can vindicate the Union only by his prostration. Slavery is the very Goliath of the rebellion, armed with coat of mail, with helmet of brass upon the head, greaves of brass upon the legs, a target of brass between the shoulders, and with the staff of his spear like a weaver's beam. But a stone from a simple sling will make the giant fall upon his face to the earth.

"Amid all surrounding perils there is one only which I dread. It is the peril from some new surrender to slavery, some fresh recognition of its power, some present dalliance with its intolerable pretensions.

"Worse than any defeat, or even the flight of an army, would be this abandonment of principle. From all such peril, good Lord, deliver us!

"And there is *one way of safety*, clear as sunlight, pleasant as the paths of peace. Over its broad and open gate is written, JUSTICE. In that little word is victory. Do justice, and you will be twice victors; for so you will subdue the rebel master, while you elevate the slave.

"Do justice frankly, generously, nobly, and you will find strength instead of weakness, while all seeming responsibility disappears in obedience to God's eternal law. Do justice, though the heavens fall. But they will not fall. Every act of justice becomes a new pillar of the Universe, or it may be a new link of that

> 'golden, everlasting chain,
> Whose strong embrace holds heaven, and earth, and main.'"

The opinion that safety was through emancipation was gaining ground every day. The inhuman practice of some of our generals in refusing to receive fugitive slaves within their camps, and in thrusting them out of their lines, awakened general indignation.

Mr. Sumner brought up the subject in the Senate, December 2, 1861, and said with reference to one general, "I take the liberty of saying — and I wish that my words may reach his distant headquarters — that every fugitive slave he surrenders will hereafter rise in judgment against him with a shame which no possible victory can remove."

On the 11th of that month, Mr. Sumner delivered, in the Senate, a most eloquent eulogy upon Colonel Baker, late a senator from Oregon.

In the unfortunate engagement at Ball's Bluff, October 21, 1861, Colonel Baker was sent by his superior officer to encounter a far stronger rebel force. He was a most brave as well as skilful commander, and did all that mortal could do in so unequal a contest. But he was overpowered by numbers, and fell, shot through the head.

In his eulogy, Mr. Sumner said of him, —

"In the Senate he took at once the post of orator. His voice was not full and sonorous, but sharp and clear. It was penetrating rather than commanding, and yet, when touched by his ardent nature, became sympathetic and even musical. Countenance, body, and gesture, all shared the unconscious inspiration of his voice, and he went on, master of his audience, master also of himself. All his faculties were completely at command. Ideas, illustrations, words, seemed to come unbidden and range in harmonious forms — as in the walls of ancient Thebes each stone took its proper place of its own accord, moved only by the music of a lyre.

"His fame as a speaker was so familiar even before he appeared among us, that it was sometimes supposed he might lack those solid powers without which the oratorical faculty itself exercises only a transient influence.

"But his speech on this floor in reply to a slaveholding conspirator, now an open rebel, showed that his matter was as good as his manner, and that, while master of fence, he was also master of ordnance. His oratory was graceful, sharp, and flashing, like a cimeter; but his argument was powerful and sweeping, like a battery.

"Another speech showed him in a different character. It was his instant reply to the Kentucky senator — John C. Breckinridge — not then expelled from this body.

"The occasion was peculiar. A senator, with treason in his heart, if not on his lips, had just sat down. Our lamented senator, who had entered the Chamber direct from his camp, rose at once to reply. He began simply and calmly; but, as he proceeded, the fervid soul broke forth in words of surprising power. On the former occasion he presented the well-ripened fruits of study; but now he spoke with the spontaneous utterance of his natural eloquence, meeting the polished traitor at every point with weapons keener and brighter than his own.

"But the question is painfully asked, 'Who was author of this tragedy, now filling the Senate Chamber, as already it has filled the country, with mourning?' There is a strong desire to hold somebody responsible, where so many perished unprofitably. But we need not appoint committees, or study testimony, to know precisely who took this precious life.

"That great criminal is easily detected, — still erect and defiant, without concealment or disguise. The guns, the balls, and the men that fired them, are of little importance. It is the power behind all, saying, 'The State, it is I,' that took this precious life; *and this power is slavery.* The nine balls that slew our departed brother came from slavery. Every gaping wound of his slashed bosom testifies against slavery. The brain so rudely shattered has its own voice, and the tongue so suddenly silenced in death speaks now with more than living eloquence. To hold others responsible is to hold the dwarf agent and dismiss the giant principal. Nor shall we do great service, if, merely criticising some local blunder, we leave untouched that fatal forbearance through which the weakness of the rebellion is changed into strength, and the strength of our armies is changed into weakness.

"May our grief to-day be no hollow pageant, nor expend itself in this funeral pomp! It must become a motive and impulse to patriotic action.

"But patriotism itself, that commanding charity, embracing so many other charities, is only a name, and nothing else, unless we resolve, calmly, plainly, solemnly, that slavery, the barbarous enemy of our country, the irreconcilable foe of our Union, the violator of our Constitution, the disturber of our peace, the vampire of our national life, sucking its best blood, the assassin of our children, and the murderer of our dead senator, shall be struck down.

"And the way is easy. The just avenger is at hand, with weapon of celestial temper. Let it be drawn. Until this is done, the patriot, discerning clearly the secret of our weakness, can only say, sorrowfully, —

> 'bleed, bleed, poor country!
> Great tyranny, lay thou thy basis sure,
> For goodness dares not check thee.'" *

It must not be supposed that Mr. Sumner stood alone as an early champion of emancipation, as an act of justice and a military necessity. President Lincoln doubtless believed in it even then. The question of time probably made the chief difference between them.

* Macbeth, Act iv., Scene iii.

But it was well that Mr. Sumner was thus pronounced in his opinion, and that he reiterated it in different places with so much earnestness. The subject was kept distinct before the public eye, and sank deep into the public heart; and thus the way was made clear for emancipation when it came, and for a final adjustment of the whole question of our duty to the colored race. The public conscience and judgment were educated.

In December, 1861, there came up in the Senate a case which awakened intense interest in this country and in England. At one time it threatened war between the two countries. It was the case of the *Trent*, a British steamship, running between Havana and England.

Early in the rebellion, two Confederate envoys, James M. Mason, of Virginia, and John Slidell, of Louisiana, were accredited, the first to Great Britain, the second to France, in the hope of "arraying the two great nations against the United States, and enlisting them openly in support of" the Confederate government.

"These two old men," said Mr. Sumner, in the Senate, January 9, 1861, "with their two younger associates, stole from Charleston (October 12, 1861) on board a rebel steamer, and, under cover of darkness and storm, running the surrounding blockade, and avoiding the neutral cruisers, succeeded in reaching the neutral island of Cuba, where, with open display, and the knowledge of the British consul, they embarked on board the British mail-packet Trent, bound for St. Thomas, where they were to embark for England. . . .

"While on their way, the pretended ambassadors were arrested (on the 8th of November) by Captain Wilkes, of the United States steamer San Jacinto, . . . who, on this occasion, acted without instructions from his government."

They were brought to the United States, and confined in Fort Warren, near Boston.

This event caused great joy throughout the North. Everybody smiled at the arrest of the rebel mischief-makers, so suddenly and unexpectedly brought to grief. Everybody hoped they might long enjoy the hospitalities of their prison-home. The Secretary of the Navy fully justified the capture.

But it soon appeared that there was another

side to the question. The British government was greatly incensed at the act of Captain Wilkes. It was gross "outrage" to a British craft to fire a shell across her bow, and abstract four of her passengers. The unconditional surrender of the captured party was required, as a proper atonement for the "insult." France concurred in the demand as a just one. War was threatened in case of a refusal.

We were in a dilemma. The thought of releasing the two conspirators, whom we held so nicely in our grasp, and sending them forth again on their treasonable mission, was far from agreeable; it was positively humiliating. It must not be.

But what if a war with England should be added to the one we were now staggering under! The President and his cabinet took the matter into grave consideration.

While the case was yet pending, and it was believed that our government favored the surrender of the men, the subject came before the Senate. Mr. Hale strongly opposed the surrender as "a fatal act." Mr. Sumner took the opposite ground, in a speech which reviewed the whole question of international law, and the practice of the United States and Great Britain, relative to the case. He declared that "British precedents and practice" *might* justify the act of Captain Wilkes, and that these had probably led him "into his mistake."

But on the other hand, he said, "The seizure of the rebel emissaries on board *a neutral ship* cannot be justified, according to *declared American principles and practice.* There is no single point where the seizure is not questionable." There was "the constant, uniform, unhesitating practice of his own country on the ocean, conceding always the greatest immunities to neutral ships, unless sailing to blockaded ports, refusing to consider despatches contraband of war, refusing to consider persons other than soldiers or officers as contraband of war, and protesting always against an adjudication of personal rights by summary judgment of the quarter-deck."

The vessel should have been taken into port to undergo a judicial trial. It was not allowable that a navy officer should substitute himself for such tribunal.

The government took this view of the case,

and set the prisoners at liberty. Thus war was happily averted.

Mr. Sumner was the more earnest for such a settlement, as opening the way for great "reforms in maritime law," so that war might be "despoiled of its most vexatious prerogatives, while innocent neutrals are exempt from its torments." He would have "privateering," with "contraband of war," and the "right of search," abandoned. "Commercial blockade" should disappear, "to complete the triumph of neutral rights."

"Such a change, just in proportion to its accomplishment, will be a blessing to mankind, inconceivable in grandeur. The statutes of the sea, thus refined and elevated, will be agents of peace instead of agents of war. Ships and cargoes will pass unchallenged from shore to shore, and those terrible belligerent rights, under which the commerce of the world has so long suffered, will cease from troubling. . . .

"Meanwhile through all present excitement, amidst all trials, beneath all threatening clouds, it only remains for us to uphold the perpetual policy of the republic, and to stand fast on the ancient ways."

This speech, so thoroughly American in its spirit, and yet exhibiting so catholic and beneficent a statesmanship, tended greatly to elevate Mr. Sumner in the public esteem. Even those who had depreciated him as a man of "one idea" were convinced of their mistake.

The public generally, in spite of their prejudices, readily acquiesced in the peaceful solution of a vexed and perilous question, and the government was left free to give its undivided energies to the suppression of the rebellion.

CHAPTER XXVI.

Recognition of Hayti and Liberia. — Confiscation of Rebel Property. — Proclamation of Emancipation. — Mr. Sumner in Faneuil Hall. — "Bridge of Gold." — Aid of the Slaves necessary to Success. — Providential Judgments. — Changed Character of the War. — Mr. Sumner's Re-election. — Contrast. — Privateers. — Our Foreign Relations. — Recognition of a Slave Republic denounced.

So long as slavery ruled in the national councils, the governments of Hayti and Liberia could obtain no recognition at Washington. Southern members of Congress had denounced such a proposition as nothing less than "treason," and as sure, if carried out, "to convulse the Union."

But with the inauguration of the Republican party in Washington, a new era came in. President Lincoln, in his Message, December, 1861, recommended the long-neglected duty. "If," said he, "any good reason exists why we should longer persevere in withholding our recognition of the independence and sovereignty of Hayti and Liberia, I am unable to discern it."

Mr. Sumner was equally "unable," and in a speech in the Senate, April 23, 1862, he strongly urged the measure, as an act of justice to those nations, and as beneficial to our own commerce.

Dark-hued ambassadors from Hayti and Liberia have appeared in Washington, but as yet the heavens have not fallen. They have taken their places beside the representatives of the most powerful nations of the world, and have received both civil and social recognition. Thus one more great advance is made in the interests of humanity.

As the war advanced, Mr. Sumner continually urged the necessity of weakening the rebellion by the confiscation of rebel property, and the freeing of slaves as far as it could be done. He would have *indemnity for the past, and security for the future.*

He argued that "municipal law under the Constitution, and the rights of war under international law," authorized the government to deal with the rebels as "criminals and enemies."

It was now far into the second year of the war. The contest had been attended with many disasters. The rebellion had proved to be difficult to master. A new method must be tried.

On the 22d of September, 1862, President Lincoln put forth a proclamation of *partial* emancipation, declaring that, on the first day of January, 1863, all persons held as slaves within any State, or designated part of a State, then in rebellion, should be forever free. This was followed, January 1, 1863, by an absolute proclamation of freedom.

Soon after the first proclamation, Mr. Sumner, at a meeting in Faneuil Hall, presided over by Hon. William Claflin, defended the measure. "Thank God," said he, "for what is already done, and let us all take heart as we go forward to uphold this great edict! For myself I accept the proclamation without note or comment. . . .

"Fellow-citizens, a year has passed since I addressed you; but, during this time, what events for warning and encouragement! Amidst vicissitudes of war, the cause of human freedom has steadily and grandly advanced,—not, perhaps, as you could desire, yet it is the only cause which has not failed. Slavery and the Black Laws all abolished in the national capital; slavery interdicted in all the national territory; Hayti and Liberia recognized as independent republics in the family of nations; the slave-trade placed under the ban of a new treaty with Great Britain; all persons in the military and naval service prohibited from returning slaves or sitting in judgment on the claims of a master; the slaves of rebels emancipated by coming within our lines; a tender of compensation for the abolition of slavery: such are some of Freedom's triumphs in the recent Congress. Amidst all doubts and uncertainties of the present hour, let us think of these things and be comforted. I cannot forget, that, when I last spoke to you, I urged the liberation of the slaves of rebels . . . and I further suggested, if need were, *a bridge of gold for the retreating fiend.** And now all that I proposed is embodied in the legislation of the country, as the supreme law of the land."

* President Lincoln, according to a resolution recommended by him to Congress, March 6, 1862, and passed April 2, issued a proc-

In another part of the speech he said: —

"Wherever I turn in this war I find the African ready to be our saviour.

"If you ask for strategy, I know nothing better than that of the slave Robert Small, who brought the rebel steamer Planter, with its armament, out of Charleston, and surrendered it to our commodore as prize of war.

"If you ask for successful courage, I know nothing better than that of the African Tillman, who rose upon a rebel prize crew, and, overcoming them, carried the ship into New York.

"If you ask for heroism, you will find it in that nameless African on board the Pawnee, who, while passing shell from the magazine, lost both his legs by a ball, but, still holding a shell, cried out, 'Pass up the shell — never mind me; my time is up.'

"If you ask for fidelity, you will find it in that slave, also without a name, who pointed out the

lamation, April 10, offering pecuniary compensation to any State that would adopt gradual emancipation. This was the "bridge of gold;" but no State ever set foot upon it.

At the beginning of the next session, another, and the last plan of like character, was proposed, but failed to pass.

road of safety to the harassed, retreating army of the Potomac.

"And if you ask for evidence of desire for freedom, you will find it in the little slave-girl, journeying North, whom Banks took up on his cannon.

"But . . . it is not enough to show that slaves can render important assistance, by labor, by information, or by arms. . . . The case is stronger still. *Without the aid of the slaves this war cannot be ended successfully.*

"If the instincts of patriotism did not prompt this support [of the proclamation], I should find a sufficient motive in the duty which we all owe to the Supreme Ruler, God Almighty, whose visitations upon our country are now so fearful.

"Not rashly would I make myself the interpreter of His will; and yet I am not blind. According to a venerable maxim of jurisprudence, 'Whoso would have equity must do equity;' and God plainly requires equity at our hands. We cannot expect success while setting at nought this requirement, proclaimed in His divine character, in the dictates of reason, and in the examples of history, — proclaimed also in the events of this protracted war.

"Terrible judgments have fallen upon the country: plagues have been let loose, rivers have been turned into blood, and there is a great cry throughout the land, for there is not a house where there is not one dead; and at each judgment we seem to hear that terrible voice which sounded in the ears of Pharaoh: 'Thus saith the Lord God of the Hebrews, Let my people go, that they may serve me.'

"I know not how others are touched, but I cannot listen to the frequent tidings of calamity descending upon our arms, of a noble soldier lost to his country, of a bereavement at the family hearth, of a youthful son brought home dead to his mother, without catching the warning, 'Let my people go!' Nay, every wound, every sorrow, every hardship that we are compelled to bear in taxation, in want, in derangement of business, has a voice crying, 'Let my people go!'

"And now, thank God, the word is spoken! — greater word was seldom spoken. Emancipation has begun, and our country is already elevated and glorified. The war has not changed in *object*, but it has changed in *character*. Its object now, as at the beginning, is simply to put down the rebellion; but its character is derived from the new force at length enlisted, stamping itself upon all that is done, and absorbing the whole war to itself."

"We have been trying to do without justice," said Ralph Waldo Emerson, at the beginning of the war. Justice at last had its opportunity.

The time had now arrived for the election of a senator for Massachusetts, Mr. Sumner's second term having expired.

In consequence of his early and earnest advocacy of emancipation, there were many who sought to prejudice the public mind against him, with a view to defeat his re-election. But in vain.

January 15, 1863, he received an almost unanimous vote in the Senate and the House. Massachusetts was true to herself.

How great the contrast between Mr. Sumner's first election and first appearance in Congress, and the present! Then he came in by a majority of two, now by almost a unanimity; and in the Senate, he then stood almost alone, excluded from committees, denied parliamentary courtesies and the common social civilities, and brutally assaulted. Now the slave power was dethroned, its leaders in the government gone, Congress anti-slavery, himself chairman of the most important committee in the Senate, and an acknowledged leader. All in twelve years.

In the conduct of the war Mr. Sumner always opposed any kind of support which was unjust and dishonorable. When the government sought to carry through Congress a bill authorizing the issuing of letters of marque and reprisal, for the purpose of damaging the rebels on the ocean, Mr. Sumner strongly opposed it; and when it passed, he urged the President not to avail himself of it. His counsels prevailed.

The bill was, he said, in plain terms, "a bill to authorize *privateers*, — that is, private-armed vessels licensed to cruise against the commerce of an enemy, and looking to booty for support, compensation, and salary. It is by booty that owners, officers, and crews are to be paid. Booty is the motive power and life-spring. . . . Picture to yourselves the ocean traversed by licensed rovers seeking prey. The Dutch admiral carried a broom at his mast-head as the boastful sign that he swept the seas. The privateer might carry a scourge. Wherever a sail appears, there is a chase; the signal gun is fired, and the merchantman submits to visitation and search. Delay is the least of the consequences. Contention, irritation, humiliation ensue, all calculated to engender ill-feelings, which, beginning with individuals, may embrace country and government. . . . The speaking-trumpet of a reckless privateer may contribute to that discord which is the herald of bloodshed itself."

The war had now been waged more than two years, when rumors came that England and France designed to recognize the Southern Confederacy as an independent nation. Our foreign relations were therefore of the most critical character. Such recognition would change the whole aspect of the war, and place us in a most unfortunate position.

Mr. Sumner, as holding in the Senate so important a relation to foreign affairs, was invited to speak in New York upon the question at issue. He described our "perils from England and France," and especially the "impossibility of any recognition of a new power with slavery as a corner-stone."

"An aroused public opinion, 'the world's collected will,' and returning reason in England and France, will see to it that civilization is saved from this shock, and the nations themselves from the terrible retribution which sooner or later must surely attend it.

"No power can afford to stand up before mankind and openly vote a new and untrammelled charter to injustice and cruelty. God is an unsleeping avenger; nor can armies, fleets, bulwarks, or 'towers along the steep,' prevail against this mighty avenger. To any application for this unholy recognition there is but one word the Christian powers can utter. It is simply and austerely, 'No,' with an emphasis that shall silence argument and extinguish hope itself. And this proclamation should go forth swiftly. Every moment of hesitation is a moment of apostasy, casting its lengthening shadow of dishonor. Not to discourage is to encourage; not to blast is to bless. Let this simple word be uttered, and slavery will slink away, with a mark on its forehead, like Cain, a perpetual vagabond, forever accursed; and the malediction of the Lord shall descend upon it, saying, 'Among these nations shalt thou find no ease, neither shall the sole of thy foot have rest; but the Lord shall give thee there a trembling heart, and failing of eyes, and sorrow of mind; and thy life shall hang in doubt before thee, and thou shalt fear day and night, and shalt have none assurance of thy life; in the morning thou shalt say, Would God it were even, and at even thou shalt say, Would God it were morning.'

"And yet, British statesmen, forgetting for the moment all moral distinctions, forgetting God, who will not be forgotten, gravely announce that our cause must fail.

"Alas, individual wickedness is too often successful; but a pretended nation, suckled in wickedness and boasting its wickedness, a new Sodom, with all the guilt of the old, waiting to be blasted, and yet, in barefaced effrontery, openly seeking the fellowship of Christian powers, is doomed to defeat. Toleration of such a pretension is practical atheism. Chronology and geography are both offended. Piety stands aghast. In this age of light, and in countries boasting of civilization, there can be no place for its barbarous plenipotentiaries. As well expect crocodiles crawling on the pavements of London and Paris, or the carnivorous idols of Africa installed for worship in Westminster Abbey and Notre Dame."

CHAPTER XXVII.

Foreign Relations. — Domestic Relations. — Reconstruction of the Rebel States. — Striking at Slavery. — Rebuke to Young Men at Albany. — Final Repeal of Fugitive Slave Bills. — Happy Change. — Practical Legislation. — Treatment of Freedmen. — Freedmen's Bureau. — The Coastwise Traffic in Slaves.

During the period of the war, Mr. Sumner, as Chairman of the Committee on Foreign Relations, where he was placed in 1861, when the new era came in, held an intimate relation to the government, and was constantly consulted on foreign affairs by the President and Secretary of State. He was an authority in such matters. His profound acquaintance with international law, his accurate knowledge of European affairs, and his intimacy with foreign jurists and statesmen, preeminently qualified him to be a wise counsellor.

But, as we have seen, he was equally at home

in domestic matters. He profoundly comprehended the spirit of our government, the intent of the Constitution, as founded in universal, impartial justice, and sought to conform the actual legislation to its principles. Republicanism with him was more than a party — it was an idea. It represented simple justice as applied to government. Before the war, he had labored to expel slavery, as a foreign element; and, now that rebellion had opened the way for perfect liberty, he was constantly on the watch to follow up with new safeguards every advance towards that consummation. He would cut off the retreating foe from any way of return.

The question had arisen, What shall be done with the rebel States?

In February, 1862, he had already introduced the subject of reconstruction, in a series of resolutions, in which he declared the right of Congress "to assume complete jurisdiction" in the rebel States, and "to establish therein republican forms of government under the Constitution."

The speech which he had intended to make in defence of his views was published as an article in a magazine, October, 1863. In it he showed himself to be more practical than many who regarded him as little more than an idealist or enthusiast.

Dismissing all fine-spun theories about the status of the rebel States, he looked at the actual condition of the governments and people of those States. In fact, there existed no legal governments. The majority of the people were disloyal. Therefore, there existing no government that could be recognized, the whole region fell at once, and of necessity, under the jurisdiction of Congress. "The whole broad rebel region is *tabula rasa*, a clean slate, where Congress, under the Constitution of the United States, may write the laws."

"Behold the rebel States in arms against that paternal government to which, as the supreme condition of constitutional existence, they owe duty and love; and behold all legitimate powers, executive, legislative, and judicial, in these States, abandoned and vacated. It only remains that Congress should enter and assume the proper jurisdiction." And that, he said, would be in the interests of liberty; for slavery, being a local, a municipal institution, fell, of necessity, with the fall of the power which sustained it. The nation, through Congress, could know nothing of slavery.

To make this more secure, and to breathe the breath of freedom upon every part of the country, a constitutional amendment, prohibiting slavery throughout the national domain, was introduced in the House of Representatives towards the close of 1863. In the Senate, Mr. Sumner was its earnest supporter. It became a part of the Constitution December 18, 1865, — not, alas! till it was beyond Mr. Lincoln's power to know the result which he had looked forward to with so much interest.

But Mr. Sumner was not willing to await the slow process of a Constitutional Amendment, which, after the action of Congress, would have to be submitted to all the States.

"Beyond my general desire," he said, "to see an act of universal emancipation, at once and forever settling this great question, . . . there are two other objects ever present to my mind as a practical legislator: First, to strike at slavery, wherever I can hit it; and secondly, to clear the statute-book of all existing supports of slavery, so that this great wrong may find nothing there to which it can cling for life. . . .

"So long as a single slave continues anywhere beneath the flag of the Republic, I am unwilling to rest. For well I know the vitality of slavery, with its infinite capacity of propagation, and how little slavery it takes to make a Slave State with all the cruel pretensions of slavery."

He would therefore have immediate action, in advance of the slower method of amendment.

As a specimen of Mr. Sumner's idea of "striking at slavery wherever he could hit it," whether North or South, in its spirit or practice, we give his letter to the Young Men's Association, of Albany, within about a week after this speech. The young gentlemen, it appears, excluded from their lecture-room all persons not of the "approved color," and then invited Mr. Sumner to speak on Lafayette. His reply was as follows: —

"You invite me to deliver an address on Lafayette. . . . In view of a recent incident in the history of your Association, I am astonished at the request.

"I cannot consent to speak of Lafayette, who

was not ashamed *to fight beside a black soldier*, to an audience too delicate *to sit beside a black citizen*. I cannot speak of Lafayette, who was a friend of universal liberty, under the auspices of a society which makes itself the champion of caste and vulgar prejudice." A just rebuke to the delicate Albanians.

Three days after, Mr. Sumner followed up his attack on slavery in a bill for the "final repeal of all Fugitive Slave Acts." He had given to the Senate notice of his intention to that effect as early as December 10, 1863. About two months later (February 8, 1864) he introduced a bill. But the subject met with delay from various causes, until June 23, when it came up on a bill from the House for the repeal of all Fugitive Slave Acts, which was passed that day, and which, on the 28th, 1864, by Mr. Lincoln's signature, became the law of the land.

This was a hard blow at slavery, a glorious triumph of freedom. No more hunting of men and women through the free North, — no more dragging them trembling from their homes or hiding-places to Southern plantations, — no more converting Northern court-houses into slave-pens, and no more surrounding them with ropes and chains, under which judges must creep into the halls of justice, — no more degrading a State soldiery into the base service of helping to enslave human beings, — no more bowing the knee to imperious masters.

The nation had swept away one more relic of barbarism, and taken one more long step in the direction of universal freedom.

In urging this measure, Mr. Sumner, in the course of the debate upon it, replied to the objection, that it was not "practical." "If it be practical to relieve the people from an unconstitutional and oppressive statute; if it be practical to take away a badge of subjugation imposed by slave-masters during a brutal supremacy; if it be practical to secure the good name of the Republic, still suffering immeasurably from this outrage; if it be practical, at this moment of our own severe trial, to substitute justice for oppression, and thus secure the favor of Providence; and finally, if it be practical to strike at slavery wherever we can hit it, and to relieve ourselves of this terrible wrong, — then is this measure eminently practical. *It is as practical as justice, as practical as humanity, as practical as duty, which cannot be postponed.*"

The Union cause had now assumed a brighter aspect. The year 1863 had been one of great prosperity. The year 1864 opened hopefully, and the prospect of subduing the rebellion grew more cheering every day. General Grant, with the title of Lieutenant-General, was assigned to the command of all the Federal forces.

The rebel forces were mainly concentrated in two great armies, in Virginia and in Georgia. Against these it was the plan of the commanding general to direct the whole military power.

In consequence of our successes and the increasing prospect of crushing the rebellion, there arose a new and most important question. What shall be done with the Freedmen? It was not enough that slavery had disappeared or was departing. There must be constructed a "bridge from slavery to freedom," over which the millions who had been enfeebled and degraded by slavery might safely pass into a condition of useful citizenship. They needed guidance and protection.

Many plans were proposed by persons in and out of Congress. The one finally adopted, March

3, 1865, creating a Bureau of Freedmen under the War Department, differed in some particulars from that proposed by Mr. Sumner, May 25, 1864, but it embraced its essential features. His preference, however, was, that the bureau should be connected with the Treasury Department.

It has been supposed by some that Mr. Sumner had "a great scheme for creating a new department of the government, with a cabinet officer at its head, for the *perpetual* care of the freedmen," and tending "to perpetuate caste." Nothing could be farther from the truth. He expressly calls his plan a "*bridge from slavery to freedom.*" He sought for the freedmen "*immediate* protection and welfare *during the present transition* period." "Our *present* necessity," he said, "is to help those made free by the present war;" "to help the freedmen in their *rough passage from slavery to freedom;*" "to secure employment for them *during the transition* from one condition to another." "The *temporary* care of the freedmen is the complement of emancipation."

The sphere of the bureau was afterwards made to embrace provision for the education, as well as for the employment and protection, of the freedmen.

The bureau accomplished a most beneficent work, notwithstanding many serious mistakes in its operation, and cases of perversion of funds from their legitimate purposes.

Without it, the newly-freed would have found their transition much harder from slavery to freedom. It stood between them and their late masters, and offered help and encouragement.

The statutes for the rendition of fugitive slaves had been repealed. Another and a *last* support of slavery still remained — that which sanctioned "*the coastwise traffic in slaves* under the flag of the United States." The foreign slave-trade had been declared piracy. Why should the domestic, inter-state commerce in slavery be allowed to continue?

March 22, 1864, Mr. Sumner reported a bill for removing the "disgraceful statute." It came up again June 24 and 25, in the form of an amendment to a civil appropriation bill. It passed the Senate June 25, and on July 2, by the President's signature, the national statute-book was thoroughly purged from the stain of slavery.

Attached to the same appropriation bill was another amendment, also introduced by the indomitable "intruder" from Massachusetts, for "opening the United States courts to colored witnesses." This also was carried.

While other senators interposed objections, or were favorable to delay in these efforts for freeing the general government from all complicity with slavery, and from discriminations against the colored people, Mr. Sumner was ever on the alert with his "besom of destruction," desiring to make a "clean sweep" of all odious and oppressive distinctions. Some objected to his making use of appropriation bills for carrying through his projects; but he told them that there was "hardly ever an appropriation bill that was not compelled to take passengers in this way," and that when the "passengers" were the harbingers of justice and humanity, he had no scruples about putting them on board — if the Senate would compel him to seek for them that method of transportation.

CHAPTER XXVIII.

Nomination of Abraham Lincoln. — Reverses. — Peace Overtures. — Jefferson Davis. — Nomination of General McClellan. — Federal Successes. — Speech of Mr. Sumner at New York. — "Issues of the Presidential Election." — Chicago and Baltimore. — Election of Mr. Lincoln. — Mr. Sumner's Speech at Faneuil Hall. — Great Exultation. — Political Barbers. — Mr. Lincoln's Inaugural. — Reconstruction of Louisiana. — The Plan opposed by Mr. Sumner. — His Reception in Massachusetts. — Change of Tone. — Praise follows Blame. — Rebel Legislature of Virginia. — Mr. Lincoln's Plan. — Opposed by Mr. Sumner. — Telegram to Richmond. — Mr. Sumner's Views of Reconstruction. — Relations between Mr. Lincoln and Mr. Sumner. — Henry Clay and Dr. Channing. — Picture for the Capitol. — Tax on Knowledge.

THE war had now been prosecuted more than three years. With high hopes of its speedy termination, the Union National Convention met at Baltimore, and unanimously re-nominated Abraham Lincoln for President.

But soon reverses came, financial embarrassments increased, and a general gloom overspread the country.

Under these circumstances peace overtures were attempted. Jefferson Davis was interrogated as to his views of a peaceful settlement of the difficulties between the North and South. He would listen to no proposition of peace which did not recognize Southern independence.

The Democratic party now sounded the cry, "A four years' failure!" There were some respectable but misguided men who joined in the dirge, but with them was a large following of traitors, who now, at the first sign of ill success, crept forth from their hiding-places for a last desperate effort to save slavery from impending doom.

They came together, these enemies within the camp, of high and of low degree, in a so-called National Convention, at Chicago, August 29. There, bitter and even treasonable words were spoken against the administration, and especially its interference with slavery. General McClellan was nominated for President.

The convention had scarcely broken up when splendid successes came, under Sherman and Farragut. The public confidence and hope were strong that at last the rebellion was nigh to death.

The presidential canvass was full of importance, and awakened a profound interest. Mr. Seward stated the issues thus: "McClellan and Disunion — Lincoln and Union."

Just before the election, Mr. Sumner delivered a speech at New York (November 5, 1864) on *The Issues of the Presidential Election.* In it he said, "There is a wide-spread political party, which, true to its history, now comes forward to save belligerent slavery, — even at this last moment, when it is about to be trampled out forever. Not to save the country, but to save belligerent slavery, is the object of the misnamed Democracy. Asserting the war, in which so much has been done, to be a failure . . . this party openly offers surrender to the rebellion. I do not use too strong language. It is actual surrender and capitulation . . . in one of two forms: (1) by acknowledging the rebel States, so that they shall be treated as independent; or

(2) by acknowledging slavery, so that it shall be restored to its old supremacy over the national government, with additional guarantees. . . . Both pivot on slavery. One acknowledges the slave power out of the Union; the other acknowledges the slave power in the Union.

"Look," he said, "at the Chicago platform or candidate as you will, and you are constantly brought back to slavery as the animating impulse.

"Look at the Baltimore platform or candidate, and you are constantly brought back to liberty as the animating impulse.

"And thus again slavery and liberty stand face to face — the slave-ship against the Mayflower.

"Never was grander cause or sublimer conflict. Who is not saddened at the thought of precious lives given to liberty's defence? The soil of the rebellion is soaked with patriot blood, its turf is bursting with patriot dead. Surely they have not died in vain. The flag they upheld will continue to advance. But this depends upon your votes. Therefore, for the sake of that flag, and for the sake of the brave men who bore it, now sleeping where no trumpet of battle can wake them, stand by the flag."

November 8, Mr. Sumner was at Boston, at a meeting in Faneuil Hall. As the votes were announced giving assurance that Abraham Lincoln was elected, he spoke, as the mouthpiece of the assembly, of the free North, and of oppressed millions at the South, words of enthusiastic gratitude: —

"The trumpet of victory is now sounding through the land, 'Glory, Hallelujah!' It is the silver trumpet of an archangel, echoing in valleys, traversing mountains, and filling the whole country with immortal melodies, destined to awaken other echoes in the most distant places, as it proclaims 'Liberty throughout all the land, unto all the inhabitants thereof.'

"Such is the victory we celebrate, marking an epoch in our history and in the history of the world. . . . The voice of the people at the ballot-box has echoed back that great letter of the President, 'To whom it may concern,' declaring the integrity of the Union and the abandonment of slavery the two essential conditions of peace.

"Let the glad tidings go forth, 'to whom it may concern,' — to all the people of the United States, at length now made wholly free — to foreign countries — to the whole family of man — to posterity — to the martyred band who have fallen in battle for their country — to the angels above — ay, and to the devils below, — that this republic shall live, for Slavery is dead. This is the great joy we now announce to the world."

In merrier words, but no less serious strain, Mr. Sumner wrote, a day or two later, to the Young Men's Republican Union of New York, —

"Thank God, the pettifoggers of compromise are answered by the people, who demand peace on the everlasting foundations of Union and Liberty.

"The political barbers, who undertake to prescribe when they can only shave, are warned that their quackery is at an end."

Surely it was "at an end;" for at the next session of Congress after Mr. Lincoln's re-election, the Constitutional Amendment abolishing and forever prohibiting slavery in the United States, was passed.

Mr. Lincoln followed with his Inaugural, in which, with a solemnity and pathos, and a deeply religious strain, that seemed to betoken a consciousness that his work was almost done, and in language rather like a prophet's than like a statesman's, he spoke of the sin and woe of slavery.

"The Almighty," he said, "has his own purposes. 'Woe unto the world because of offences; for it must needs be that offences come, but woe to that man by whom the offence cometh.'

"If we shall suppose that American Slavery is one of these offences, which, in the providence of God, must needs come, but which, having continued through His appointed time, He now wills to remove, and that He gives to both North and South this terrible war, as the woe due to those by whom the offence came, shall we discern therein any departure from those divine attributes which the believers in a loving God always ascribe to Him?"

About a fortnight previous to the inauguration of the President, a resolution was introduced into the Senate, by Mr. Trumbull, recognizing the new State government of Louisiana, to be inaugurated under General Banks.

This was a favorite measure with Mr. Lincoln. "With malice towards none, and charity for all," he was anxious to have the work of reconstruction and good-will go forward.

Mr. Sumner was as earnest for this as was the President, but in this particular case, as often at other times, they differed as to means.

Mr. Sumner frankly stated his objections, in private, to the President, and also in the Senate. The new government recognized "an oligarchy of the skin;" there ought to be "no reconstruction without the votes of the blacks." He took his position against the bill. If in no other way, he would talk it down.

It was near the close of the session; most important business was pressing for action; but Mr. Sumner was resolved not to be driven from his purpose. "Such a revolutionary measure" must be defeated. To put power into the hands of men just emerged from rebellion, and full of prejudice against the blacks, leaving the latter at the mercy of the former, without a voice in the new government, was, he thought, most unsafe for the country, most unjust to one half the population of Louisiana, and a most dangerous precedent in the coming work of reconstruction. It was necessary to begin right. To prevent so great a wrong and peril was, in his view, far more important than to pass appropriation or any other bills. A mistake here might lose whatever had been gained.

And so he piled up documents upon his desk, preliminary to a determined battle. He would talk against time. He would defeat the bill. Senators beheld with dismay these formidable preparations. "Do you intend," said one member, an intimate friend, "by parliamentary tactics, to stop all the business of the Chamber?" "I do," said he; "I shall employ every parliamentary device which is allowable. I shall propose amendments. I shall talk and talk, till you are glad to surrender."

He did talk; his documental ammunition enabled him, from day to day, to keep up a running fire, which bore down all opposition, and a surrender came. That commanding presence, that resolute look, those eloquent pleas for justice, those constant discharges of facts and arguments, that determination to conquer, carried the day. The bill went by default. The country was saved from a great peril.

It was said that the President took the defeat of the bill much to heart, and it was supposed that now there was an irreparable breach between him and the sturdy senator.

MR. SUMNER'S HOUSE AT WASHINGTON.

But they were both magnanimous, and, firmly believing each in the other's honesty of purpose, could differ without malice.

"On the night of the 6th of March," says Mr. Schurz, "two days after Lincoln's second inauguration, the customary inauguration ball was to take place. Sumner did not think of attending it. But towards evening he received a card from the President, which read thus:—

'DEAR MR. SUMNER: Unless you send me word to the contrary, I shall this evening call with my carriage at your house to take you with me to the inauguration ball.

'Sincerely yours,

'ABRAHAM LINCOLN."

"Mr. Sumner, deeply touched, at once made up his mind to go to an inauguration ball for the first time. Soon the carriage arrived, the President invited Sumner to take a seat in it with him, and Sumner found there Mrs. Lincoln and Mr. Colfax, the Speaker of the House of Representatives. Arrived at the ball-room, the President asked Mr. Sumner to offer his arm to Mrs. Lincoln; and the astonished spectators, who had been made to believe that the breach between Lincoln and

Sumner was irreparable, beheld the President's wife on the arm of the senator, and the senator, on that occasion of state, invited to take the seat of honor by the President's side. Not a word passed between them about their disagreement.

"The world became convinced that such a friendship between such men could not be broken by a mere honest difference of opinion. Abraham Lincoln, a man of sincere and profound convictions himself, esteemed and honored sincere and profound convictions in others. It was thus that Abraham Lincoln composed his quarrels with his friends; and at his bedside, when he died, there was no mourner more deeply afflicted than Charles Sumner."

When, at the close of the session, Mr. Sumner returned to Massachusetts, nearly all the papers denounced him. He met with a frown everywhere. He was obstinate. He was impracticable. He was dictatorial. He was a theorist. He descended to stratagems to carry a point. He was standing in the way of reconciliation. He was anything but a wise statesman and a good son of Massachusetts. But before he resumed his seat at Washington, events which had transpired in Louisiana convinced everybody that he was right. He was no longer an idealist. He was no longer self-willed. He was proved to be the most practical and sagacious of all the great men at Washington. How often did these changes of popular opinion attend Mr. Sumner's public life!

We may here refer to a somewhat similar case of later occurrence. When, after Lee's surrender, Mr. Lincoln went to Richmond, he was solicited by persons of the vanquished party to allow the rebel legislature to convene, with a view to the reconstruction of Virginia as a loyal State. The gentlemen were submissive and courteous; they made fair promises; they moved the heart of the noble but too credulous President; and he told them to go forward. His fond dream of a restored Union seemed on the dawn of fulfilment.*

* The following is Mr. Lincoln's letter of permission: —

"CITY POINT, August 6, 1865.

"MAJOR GENERAL WEITZEL, Richmond, Virginia: It has been intimated to me that the gentlemen who have acted as the legislature of Virginia in support of the rebellion, may now desire to assemble at Richmond and take measures to withdraw the Virginia troops and other support from resistance to the general government. If they attempt it, give them permission and protection, until, if at all, they attempt some action hostile to the United

He went back. The happy news from Virginia was received with joy in Washington. There was a general approval of Mr. Lincoln's plan. But there was one most decided exception. Mr. Sumner hurried to the President. He had a hearing. "What have you done?" he asked. "A government under rebel control will undo what has been done. Slavery, in some form, will creep back into Virginia. The blood of the army will have been shed in vain. Such a legislature as you have encouraged must not be allowed to assemble."

At the door were waiting Mr. Seward and other wise Republicans. When Mr. Sumner passed out, they went in. "You have done right," said they to the President. "You have shown a noble spirit of conciliation. Your course will win back the South. You must not listen to Mr. Sumner. He is an impracticable man. His policy will irri-

States; in which case you will notify them, giving them reasonable time to leave, and at the end of which time arrest any who remain. Allow Judge Campbell to see this, but do not make it public.

"Yours, &c.,

"A. LINCOLN."

The President returned to Washington April 9. Three days after he sent to Richmond a recall of the above permission. In two days more he was assassinated.

tate the South, and endanger or delay reconstruction."

Mr. Lincoln heard them through; the telegram that was sent to Richmond the next day, ordering delay, told what Mr. Lincoln thought of Mr. Sumner and his opinions. And again the country was saved through a man who dared to stand alone.

The time is coming when the true history of events will show that, in several important crises, Mr. Sumner stood alone in the breach, and saved the nation. He had rare sagacity and courage. The country owes him a debt of gratitude which even now she cannot duly estimate.

And the South have begun to learn that even when he opposed reconstruction on their grounds, he was seeking their best interests, because seeking it on a permanent basis of justice to all. He thought it no unreasonable hardship that those who had sought to overthrow the national government should stand modestly aside until their passions had subsided, and until sure guarantees could be effected for the rights of the colored people. Peace was in his heart. But it was no deceptive peace. It was peace springing from impartial justice, involving the righteous adjustment of the relations between whites and blacks.

In this connection we may add what Mr. Schurz further remarks about the relations of these great men to each other. Speaking of Mr. Lincoln, he says, —

"Mr. Sumner he treated as a favorite counsellor, almost like a Minister of State, outside of the cabinet. There were statesmen around the President who were also politicians, understanding the art of management. Mr. Lincoln appreciated the value of their advice as to what was prudent and practicable. But he knew also how to discriminate. In Mr. Sumner he saw a counsellor who was no politician, but who stood before him as the true representative of the moral earnestness and the great inspirations of their common cause. From him he heard what was right, and necessary, and inevitable. By the former he was told what, in their opinion, could prudently and safely be done. Having heard them both, Abraham Lincoln counselled with himself, and formed his resolution.

"Thus Mr. Lincoln, while scarcely ever fully and speedily following Sumner's advice, never ceased to ask for it, for he knew its significance. And Sumner, while almost always dissatisfied with Lincoln's cautious hesitation, never grew weary in giving his advice, for he never distrusted Lincoln's fidelity. Always agreed as to the ultimate end, they almost always differed as to times and means; but while differing, they firmly trusted, for they understood one another."

Among the causes which led to the differing views of Mr. Lincoln and Mr. Sumner, and to their peculiar relations to each other, we may mention the influence, intellectual and political, upon the former, of Henry Clay, and upon the latter, of Dr. Channing. Henry Clay was the great leader of the Whig party, and his Life was read with avidity by Lincoln in his boyhood, and his example and teachings, in after years, had a powerful influence upon the formation of Mr. Lincoln's opinions on public questions. Dr. Channing was, to an important extent, the teacher and model of Sumner in his younger days, as a great foe to war and slavery.

Clay, as well as Channing, was opposed to slavery. Both the statesman and the divine desired its extermination. But while the former was largely governed in his methods by considerations of expediency, the latter viewed the subject in its profounder moral aspects, and was more earnest and radical. These differences appear in their disciples.

Mr. Lincoln and Mr. Sumner had the same hatred of slavery, and an equal desire for its extinction; but they often, as in the case just considered, differed widely as to methods. The former, though far in advance of his teacher in his attitude towards slavery, yet felt the influence of the great compromiser, and was slow and hesitating compared with Mr. Sumner. The latter, having the most intense convictions of slavery as an unmitigated wrong, would make no terms with it. He could brook no delay in dealing with it. He demanded immediate and unconditional emancipation.

They both desired emancipation, and they both reached it; but the one at a bound, the other slowly, feeling his way cautiously along; the one certain that it was always safe to do right, the other equally sure of that, but not quite sure the right time had come.

As they differed about slavery, so also about

the reconstruction of the insurgent States, and according to the different kinds of influence they had each come under, in Illinois or Massachusetts.

While the Louisiana bill was under consideration, Mr. Sumner, following up his purpose of securing a guarantee of republican governments in the rebel States, by which all, without distinction of color, might have equal rights and privileges, introduced a series of resolutions to that effect.

That, in his radical measures Mr. Sumner was governed by the highest considerations of justice, and a delicate regard to the interests and honor of the whole country, is evident from his treatment of a proposition in the Senate, February 27, "to purchase a picture for the Capitol." He offered an amendment: —

"*Provided*, That in the National Capitol, devoted to the National Union, there shall be no picture of a victory in battle with our fellow-citizens."

Here, too, Mr. Sumner stood alone. Mr. Wilson and Mr. Howe dissented from him entirely, and the amendment was rejected without a division. But here, as often, Mr. Sumner was far in advance of his countrymen.

The same day, and in the same large and liberal spirit, he opposed a proposition to lay a tax on books. The country, in its struggle with the rebellion, needed all the money she could get, but he thought it poor economy to impose a tax on knowledge.

But here also Mr. Sumner was in a small minority, and his amendment was lost.

CHAPTER XXIX.

President Lincoln and Mr. Sumner at Richmond. — Passage from "Macbeth." — Mr. Lincoln's Assassination. — Mr. Seward's Life attempted. — Mr. Sumner at the Dickens Dinner. — His Account of the Night of the Assassination. — Mr. Sumner's Eulogy on President Lincoln. — Divine Providence. — Mr. Lincoln's early Manhood. — His Departure for Washington. — His Speech at Gettysburg. — His Second Inaugural. — His Intellectual Character.

AND now we have reached a sad period of the national history.

Sherman has triumphed over the lower army of the South, Richmond has fallen, Lee surrendered, and the rebellion come to an end. It is a time of universal joy. But sorrow is at the door.

On the 6th of April, 1865, the President, attended by Mrs. Lincoln, the Vice-President, and several Senators, among them Mr. Sumner, made a visit to evacuated Richmond. It was then that the President, sitting by Mr. Sumner on the deck of the steamboat, read aloud, "from a beautiful quarto Shakspeare in his hand," those sad, prophetic words in Macbeth, —

> "Duncan is in his grave:
> After life's fitful fever he sleeps well.
> Treason has done her worst: nor steel, nor poison,
> Malice domestic, foreign levy, nothing
> Can touch him farther!"

Mr. Sumner, in his eulogy upon Mr. Lincoln, in September following, says that, "impressed by their beauty, or by some presentiment unuttered, he read them aloud a second time."

A week more, and the prophecy is fulfilled! Treason did its worst. Our noble President fell by a shot from an assassin shouting, "*Sic semper tyrannis!*" * And to think that he, so simple-hearted, so magnanimous, so true a friend to the humblest and weakest, should have been reckoned among tyrants! But this was the last frenzied shriek of the rebellion. The evil spirit went out of it, foaming and rending.

But the President was not the only object

* May such always be the fate of tyrants.

of vengeance. Secretary Seward and two of his sons came near suffering the same fate. Others, doubtless, had been marked for attack, but escaped, perhaps because of the general alarm which was immediately awakened.

Mr. Sumner was for some time thought by his friends to be in peril of his life, and he was urged to arm himself, and use other precautions against threatened danger. But he refused to do so.

The colored people of Washington were particularly concerned for his safety, and sent a committee, among whom was Rev. Mr. Grimes, of Boston, then in Washington, to urge him to accept a guard whom they would feel proud to provide, and who might, unknown to the public, watch over his person and house. He thanked them most heartily for their kindness, but firmly declined their proffer, saying that he had only done his duty in contending for their rights, and that if it was God's will that he should now go, he was ready for the event. He would leave himself in God's hands.

A friend has furnished us with some remarks of Mr. Sumner, at a little dinner-party given by him, in Washington, February, 2, 1868, in honor of Mr. Dickens, in which he gave an account of the assassination of Mr. Lincoln.

Between nine and ten of that Friday evening he was in pleasant conversation with Mr. Conners, when the door was thrown open, and a young man rushed in with his hair almost on end, and said, "Mr. Lincoln is assassinated in the theatre. Mr. Seward is murdered in his bed. There's murder in the streets!"

Mr. Sumner said he could not credit it, and replied, "Young man, be moderate in your statements — what *has happened?* Tell us!" He replied, indignantly, "I have told you what has happened," and repeated his statements.

Mr. Sumner said that he then left and went to the White House, where he found the sentinel quietly pacing before the mansion. He asked him whether Mr. Lincoln had returned. "No," was his reply, "and we have heard nothing from him."

Mr. Sumner then went to the door, and put the same question to the porter, from whom he received a similar reply.

He then said, "They say that the President

has been assassinated." Whereupon the porter rushed up stairs and told Robert Lincoln, who at once came down. As Mr. Sumner turned to go, Robert joined him. They found a hack at the door, but who sent it no one ever knew. They jumped in, and drove with great rapidity till they reached the theatre, where they found a startled crowd.

Mr. Sumner passed by the sentinels, and, as he entered the building, found where Mr. Lincoln had been carried. Mrs. Lincoln and Miss Harris were standing in the entry. Mrs. Lincoln rushed up to him with many exclamations, and asked him whether her husband was dead. He informed her that he had just come, and knew nothing of what had happened, but had brought her son. He then passed into the room where Mr. Lincoln was. He was lying on the bed, stretched diagonally across it,—for he was very tall,—his head hanging over a little to accomodate the blood, which was flowing freely from the wound. He was breathing heavily, his eyes were half open, and his face looked perfectly fresh and natural.

Mr. Sumner sat down at the head of the bed,

took the President's right hand in his, and spoke to him. One of the surgeons said, "It is of no use, Mr. Sumner — he can't hear you — he is dead."

Mr. Sumner resented the idea, and said, "No, he isn't dead — look at his face — he is breathing."

"It will never be anything more than this," was the answer.

There Mr. Sumner sat during the whole night, listening to his breathing, which sounded almost like melody, till, at twenty minutes past seven, it stopped.

He then said, "Now for Mr. Seward;" for he had heard nothing from him, and turned to go out. He found General Halleck a few feet in front of him, and as he had a carriage, Mr. Sumner asked him to take him as far as Mr. Seward's. The general said he was going to see Vice-President Johnson, and tell him not to stir out that day without a guard. After he had seen Mr. Johnson, he would carry him where he liked.

They got into the carriage, and as they passed through the crowd, people asked, "How is Mr. Lincoln? Is he alive?" He shook his head, and they drove on to the Kirkwood House, where General Halleck did an errand, and then to Mr. Seward's.

Mr. Sumner sent up his card to Mrs. Seward, and said that she might like to see him. She sent for him. As he started to go up to the third story, he found her half way down the stairs, seated, and dressed in white. She seized him by both his hands, and said, "Charles Sumner, they have murdered my husband, they have murdered my boy. Fred is dying. He will never speak to me again."

Mr. Sumner tried to say that he hoped it was not so bad, and asked how her husband was.

"Henry is doing better than I expected," she replied, "but Fred will never speak to me again." Then suddenly rising, she threw off his hands, and said, "I must fly," and disappeared.

Mr. Sumner said he never saw her again.

The city of Boston wished to do honor to the memory of the martyred President, and invited the elder of the senators of the Commonwealth to deliver a eulogy on the first day of June.

Mr. Sumner began his eulogy with these impressive words: —

"In the universe of God there are no accidents. From the fall of a sparrow to the fall of an empire or the sweep of a planet, all is according to divine Providence, whose laws are everlasting. No accident gave to his country the patriot we now honor. No accident snatched this patriot, so suddenly and so cruelly, from his sublime duties. Death is as little an accident as life. Never, perhaps, in history has this Providence been more conspicuous than in that recent procession of events where the final triumph is wrapped in the gloom of tragedy. It is our present duty to find the moral of this stupendous drama."

Speaking of Mr. Lincoln's early manhood, Mr. Sumner said, with great truth and beauty, —

"His youth was now spent, and at the age of twenty-one he left his father's house to begin the world. A small bundle, a laughing face, and an honest heart, — these were his simple possessions, together with that unconscious character and intelligence which his country learned to prize.

"In the long history of worth depressed, there is no instance of such contrast between the depression and the triumph. No academy, no university, no Alma Mater of science or learning, nourished him. No government took him by the hand and gave him the gift of opportunity. No inheritance of land or money fell to him. No friend stood by his side. He was alone in poverty; and yet not all alone. There was God above, who watches all, and does not desert the lowly. Plain in person, life, and manners, and knowing absolutely nothing of form or ceremony, for six months with a village schoolmaster as his only teacher, he grew up in companionship with the people, with nature, with trees, with the fruitful corn, and with the stars.

"While yet a child his father had borne him away from a soil wasted by slavery, and he was now a citizen of a Free State, where free labor had been placed under safeguard of irreversible compact and fundamental law. And thus he took leave of youth, happy at least that he could go forth under the day-star of Liberty."

Mr. Lincoln's departure for Washington is thus described: —

"You cannot forget how he left his village home, never to return, except under the escort of death. In words of farewell to neighbors thronging about him, he dedicated himself to his country, and solemnly invoked the aid of divine Providence.

"'I know not,' he said, 'how soon I shall see you again,' and then, with prophetic voice, announced that a duty devolved upon him greater than that which has devolved upon any other man since the days of Washington, and asked his friends to pray that he might receive that divine assistance without which he could not succeed, but with which success was certain.

"To power and fame others have gone forth with gladness and with song; he went forth prayerfully as to sacrifice."

Of that exquisite speech of Mr. Lincoln's, at Gettysburg, at the dedication of the National Cemetery, Mr. Sumner says, "The President spoke very briefly; but his few words will live as long as time. Since Simonides wrote the epitaph for those who died at Thermopylæ, nothing equal has ever been breathed over the fallen dead.

"That speech, uttered on the field of Gettysburg, and now sanctified by the martyrdom of its author, is a monumental act. In the modesty of his nature, he said, 'The world will little note, nor long remember, what we say here; but it can never forget what they did here.'

"He was mistaken. The world noted at once what he said, and will never cease to remember it. The battle itself was less important than the speech. Ideas are more than battles.

"Among events assuring to him the general confidence against all party clamor and prejudice, this speech cannot be placed too high. To some who doubted his earnestness, it was touching proof of their error. Others who followed with indifference were warmed with grateful sympathy. Many felt its exquisite genius, as well as lofty character. There were none to criticise."

"Mr. Lincoln's Inaugural Address," said Mr. Sumner, "which signalized his entry for a second time upon his great duties, was briefer than any in our history; but it has already gone farther, and it will live longer, than any other. It was a continuation of the Gettysburg speech, with the same sublimity and gentleness. Its concluding words were like an angelic benediction."

Mr. Lincoln's intellectual character was thus

portrayed: "He was original in mind as in character. His style was his own, having no model, but springing directly from himself. Failing often in correctness, it is sometimes unique in beauty and sentiment.

"There are passages that will live always. It is no exaggeration to say, that in weight and pith, suffused in a certain poetical color, they call to mind Bacon's Essays. There also was a touching reality and unconscious power, without form or apparent effort. Nothing similar can be found in State papers. How poor are kings' speeches and presidential messages by the side of such utterances, fit harbingers of the sublime era of humanity!"

How entirely in keeping with Mr. Sumner's character was his preference as to who should serve as chaplain on the occasion, as appears from the following reply to Mr. Gaffield, of the municipal government:—

"WASHINGTON, 6th May, 1865.

"MY DEAR SIR: Do as you please. The names you mention are excellent.

"If I could choose one, it would be Rev. Mr. Grimes, the colored preacher. It was for his race that President Lincoln died. If Boston adopted him as chaplain on the day when we mourn, it would be a truer homage to our departed President than music or speech. I can say nothing that could promise to be so effective on earth or welcome in heaven. Think of this, and believe me, my dear sir,

"Very faithfully yours,

"CHARLES SUMNER."

Mr. Sumner's request was granted, and the late Rev. Mr. Grimes served, with Rev. Dr. Webb and Rev. W. H. Cudworth, as chaplain upon the memorable occasion.

CHAPTER XXX.

Annexation of Alaska.—Impeachment of President Johnson.—The Alabama Question.—Johnson-Clarendon Treaty.—Mr. Sumner's Views.—Project for Annexing Dominica.—Mr. Sumner's Opposition.—Unfriendly Relations with the President.—Joins the Liberal Party.—His Reasons.—His Feelings.—Letter to a Friend.—Removal from Chairmanship of Committee on Foreign Relations.—His Disinterestedness.

THE year 1867 added more than five hundred thousand square miles to our national territory, by the purchase from Russia, for seven million two hundred thousand dollars, of her possessions in North America—the region that now bears the name Alaska.

Mr. Sumner took much interest in this purchase, and made an elaborate speech in the Senate in favor of the treaty to that effect.

In 1868 Mr. Sumner was much engaged in the case of the impeachment of President Johnson. He firmly believed that the chief magistrate was seeking to execute a plan of reconstruction of the revolted States which would restore unrepentant rebels to their old power, and revive slavery, and that for this purpose he was setting at defiance the Constitution and laws of the land, and usurping power which belonged to Congress.

Let us hope that the President was not so great an offender as he was charged with being.

In the year 1869 Mr. Sumner took decided ground against the Johnson-Clarendon treaty for the settlement of the "Alabama question" and other difficulties between the United States and Great Britain, growing out of the war of the rebellion, especially from rebel cruisers.

But it does not appear that he intended to press to an extremity the full amount of claims. He hoped to effect, out of a full and frank examination of the whole case, a better understanding between the two countries, and great reforms in the international code. He most of all sought security against future causes of disagreement, and firmer guarantees of peace.

In a speech at Worcester, in September, he said, —

"Who shall fix the measure of this great accountability? For the present it is enough to expose it. I make no demand — not a dollar of money, not a word of apology. I show simply what England has done to us. It will be for her, on a careful review of the case, to determine what reparation to offer. It will be for the American people, on a careful review of the case, to determine what reparation to require.

"On this head I content myself with the aspiration that out of this surpassing wrong and the controversy it has engendered, may come some enduring safeguard for the future, some landmark of humanity. Then will our losses end in gain for all, while the law of nations is elevated.

"But I have little hope of any adequate settlement until our case, in its full extent, is heard. In all controversies, the first stage of justice is to understand the case; and, sooner or later, England must understand ours."

In 1870 and 1871 Mr. Sumner engaged in

another contest, which proved to be one of great bitterness. It concerned a favorite project of President Grant — the annexation of a part of St. Domingo to the United States. Mr. Sumner took decided ground in opposition to the measure.

Baez, the alleged ruler of Dominica, with whom negotiations for its purchase had been carried on, Mr. Sumner regarded as an unprincipled usurper, who was attempting to sell his country for gold, "in violation of its constitution." The relations between the two governments of Hayti and Dominica were of so disturbed a character, that Mr. Sumner deemed it especially censurable in our government to pursue a course of "menace" for the acquisition of a part of the island, to the offence and humiliation of the Haytien Republic.

Such was Mr. Sumner's view of the matter, the correctness of which recent events have most abundantly vindicated. Honestly entertaining it, he could do nothing less than vigorously oppose the presidential scheme. He did so with his usual thoroughness, and with that force of language of which he was master. Of course there was a tempest, and the relations between the Senator and the President were far from pleasant.

Every day the clouds gathered blackness, until they found vent in a drenching rain of denunciation, President Grant being arraigned before the bar of the country in the famous speech, "Republicanism *versus* Grantism: Reform and Purity in Government," delivered in the Senate, May 31, 1872. In this speech Mr. Sumner renewed his attack upon the presidential plan for annexing Dominica, and freely commented upon various points of the administrative policy.

In all this he declared that he was not warring with the Republican party. He simply wanted reform, in the direction of honesty and justice. Of the party he said, "I stood by its cradle; let me not follow its hearse."

The party, however, disregarded Mr. Sumner's appeals, and renominated President Grant.

Mr. Sumner, finding his efforts fruitless within the old organization, joined in a separate movement, which aimed at the election of Horace Greeley, professedly a Reform candidate.

How far he was mistaken in his allegations

against the administration, or how far time has proved their correctness, it is not the province of this volume to inquire.

But we cannot believe that the man who had heretofore labored with singular disinterestedness for lofty ends, had now, at last, descended to the mean gratification of personal spite, willing to rend the party which had cherished him, and which had given freedom to the whole country. Concede that he erred in judgment; still his high purpose was to serve his country in what seemed to him the only practicable way that was left him.

It was said that in siding with the Liberal party, he showed too much sympathy with the South. In reply, he appealed to his course from the first, through the whole contest against slavery, in proof that his eye had ever been upon peace.

"Such," he said, "is the simple and harmonious record, showing how, from the beginning, I was devoted to peace; how constantly I longed for reconciliation; how, with every measure of equal rights, this longing found utterance; how it became an essential part of my life; how I discarded all idea of vengeance and punishment; how reconstruction was, to my mind, a transition period; and how earnestly I looked forward to the day when, after the recognition of equal rights, the people should again be one, in reality as in name. If there are any who ever maintained a policy of hate, I never was so minded; and now, in protesting against any such policy, I act only in obedience to the irresistible promptings of my soul."

In these contests for Truth and Right, as he understood them, he suffered the keenest sorrow. Writing to a friend about this time, he unbosomed himself with unaccustomed fullness: —

"I do not deserve the praise of my friends, nor do I deserve the censure so freely lavished by others. In what I have done I have acted always under irresistible promptings, which I could not disobey, being the voice of conscience within — thinking little, asking never, how it might affect me personally. . . . I am no stranger to sorrow. But is not this the lot of life? Sometimes I feel that I have had more than my share. There have been fountains of tears for me that few know of and the world cannot divine. Besides these, I have felt keenly the trials of my position, and the perils of the truth which I love. Never have I seen my way more clearly than in these late conflicts, which have disturbed some of my associates, and never was my course more simple or conscientious. To suppose that I am under the influence of personal motives, whether of ambition or anger, on a great question of national and international duty, is an absurdity which can come from those only who find my motives in their own."

Mr. Sumner's removal from the chairmanship of the Committee on Foreign Relations, which he had held and honored since 1861, was to him a great source of pain. This displacement was occasioned by his altered relations to the President, which, in the opinion of many, rendered a change necessary for the public interest. But he felt it keenly, not so much as involving the loss of a distinguished place, as indicating, in his view, a rude change of feelings towards him on the part of friends with whom he had long labored on terms of mutual esteem and affection, and as taking him from a position where he felt entirely at home, and where he had so long been trusted with questions of the highest concern to the country.

That Mr. Sumner's views about the St. Domingo affair were unchanged to the very last, is shown by a letter written to a friend, three days before his death, and received after that event: —

"SENATE CHAMBER, 9th March, '74.

"MY DEAR ——: I am against capital punishment, but if ever a man deserved a halter it is Baez, who proposes to visit Boston.

"I know his history intimately, and he is a usurper, whose hands have been red with innocent blood, and who had the terrible audacity to conceive the idea of keeping an American citizen in prison to prevent his return to New York, where it was feared he would write against the treaty; and this crime he actually perpetrated!

"If he goes to Boston, he ought to be driven out by an indignant public sentiment.

"Sincerely yours,

"CHARLES SUMNER."

CHAPTER XXXI.

Battle Flags and Army Register. — Proposition to erase Names of Battles. — First Resolution. — General Scott. — Picture for the Capitol. — Second Resolution. — Censured by the Legislature of Massachusetts. — Mr. Sumner's Feelings. — Letters. — Efforts for rescinding the Vote of Censure. — John G. Whittier. — The Resolution rescinded. — Mr. Sumner's Views. — Broad Patriotism. — Opinion of Carl Schurz.

PERHAPS none of Mr. Sumner's acts has been more entirely misunderstood, and at last more thoroughly vindicated, than his attempt to erase the names of battles won during the war of the rebellion, from the regimental colors of the army and from the army register.

This subject was first introduced into Congress by Mr. Sumner, May 8, 1862, on the occasion of a despatch from General McClellan, in which that officer inquired whether, like other generals, he should direct the names of battles to be placed on the colors of regiments. Upon this, Mr. Sumner moved the following resolution: —

" *Resolved,* That, in the efforts now making for the restoration of the Union, and the establishment of peace throughout the country, it is inexpedient that the names of victories obtained over our fellow-citizens should be placed on the regimental colors of the United States."

The resolution was not received with favor, and no action was taken upon it. General Scott, however, said of the resolution, " This was noble, and from the right quarter."

It may seem strange that a proposition which, when renewed ten years later, excited intense feeling against its author, should at this time, in the very midst of the war, have attracted scarcely any notice, so that Mr. Sumner was re-elected by an almost unanimous vote, nine months after he had introduced it. But at the latter period there were immediate causes of hostility to Mr. Sumner; and so his action with reference to the national flags was seized upon as a means of still further prejudicing the public mind against him.

On February 27, 1865, two years after his re-election without any censure, there being a resolution before the Senate authorizing a contract with W. H. Powell for a picture at the Capitol, Mr. Sumner proposed an amendment: —

"*Provided*, That in the National Capitol, dedicated to the National Union, there shall be no picture of a victory in battle with our fellow-citizens."

In connection with this, Mr. Sumner said, —

"Are you sure that the subject selected at the present time would be such as a maturer and more chastened taste could approve? This is a period of war. We are all under its influence. But I doubt if it be desirable to keep before us any picture of war, especially of a war with fellow-citizens. There are moral triumphs to which art may better lend its charms. I need only refer to the Proclamation of Emancipation, which belongs to the great events of history."

The amendment was opposed and rejected; but still we hear no note of rebuke from Massachusetts.

Again, December 2, 1872, Mr. Sumner brought the subject before the Senate, without a thought, probably, of rousing a tempest of denunciation against himself for what he had done twice before unrebuked: —

"*Whereas*, The national unity and good-will among fellow-citizens can be assured only through oblivion of past differences, and it is contrary to the usage of civilized nations to perpetuate the memory of civil war: Therefore,

"*Be it enacted by the Senate and House of Representatives of the United States of America, in Congress assembled*, That the names of battles with fellow-citizens shall not be continued in the army register, or placed on the regimental colors of the United States."

At once, as though guilty of some recent offence, there arose a cry against the senator, which found official expression in the passage of a resolution of censure, December 18, by the legislature of Massachusetts, sixteen days after the offence had been committed.

"*Resolved by the Senate, &c.*, That, whereas a bill has been introduced into the Senate of the United States by a senator from Massachusetts, providing 'that the names of battles with fellow-citizens shall not be continued in the army register, or placed on regimental colors of the United States;' and

"*Whereas,* The passage of such a bill would be an insult to the loyal soldiery of the nation, and depreciate their grand achievements in the late rebellion;

"*Therefore, resolved,* That such legislation meets the unqualified condemnation of the people of this Commonwealth."

This action was hasty and ill-considered. It was done at a special session called to consider measures of relief for the city of Boston under the losses sustained by the great fire. It did not represent Massachusetts.

The injustice of this act was keenly felt by Mr. Sumner, and it threw a gloom over the last years of his life. It seemed to him that he was cast off by the State which he loved so well, whose honor he had ever sought to uphold, and which he had thought held him in true esteem. It was not enough that he was told that the act was a hasty one — that it was not the real act of Massachusetts. There stood the censure upon her records! He was deeply touched by assurances given him that it would be annulled. He almost died without the sight.

To an intimate friend, who had assured him

that the censure would soon be removed, he wrote, February 23, 1873, —

"My dear ———: Your letter surprises me. I never doubted that, sooner or later, justice would be done me; but I thought it would be later. Your own action is another proof of that unbroken friendship which has so long subsisted between us. Thanks! many thanks! I send you my bill introduced by two allegations of fact which nobody can dispute.

"You will find in vol. vi., p. 499, of what booksellers call 'Works of C. S.' the first appearance of the official resolution, as long ago as May 8, 1852. Massachusetts did not condemn me then, but soon thereafter re-elected me. General Scott, once commander-in-chief of our army, and perhaps as well informed in history as any army officer, thanked me (see vol. i., pp. 155–190 of his autobiography), as also did General Robert Anderson of Fort Sumter.

"Thanks to Mrs. ———, also, and believe me, dear ———,

"Ever sincerely yours,

"Charles Sumner."

To the same friend he wrote, March 11, —

"Thanks again, dear ———. Never was I more sure of any proposition than that for which I am assailed. When well enough, I will

Washington 11th March

Thanks again, dear Mr Claflin.

Never was I more sure of any proposition than that for which I am assailed. When well accepted it will place it beyond all question.

[illegible] sharp reaction [illegible] history. [illegible] civilized nations ever [illegible] it. The Emperor of Germany has just adopted it.

Ever sincerely yours,
Charles Sumner

place it beyond all question, — showing reason, history, and every civilized nation for it. The Emperor of Germany has just adopted it."

To another personal friend he wrote, March 20, —

"If persons would only consider candidly my original convictions on this question, they would see how natural and inevitable has been my conduct. As if in such a matter I could have 'hostility' or 'spite' to any body! I am a public servant, and never was I moved by a purer sense of duty than in this bill, all of which will be seen at last. Meanwhile men will flounder in misconception and misrepresentation, to be regretted in the day of light."

John G. Whittier was foremost among those who were deeply grieved by the vote of censure. By his pen and in conversation, his noble heart appealed to the sense of justice and magnanimity of the members of the legislature, to rectify the grievous wrong done to the high-minded and patriotic son of Massachusetts by hasty action taken in a moment of excitement.

Early in 1874, soon after the opening of the session, numerous petitions, from John G. Whittier, Vice-President Wilson, Henry L. Dawes, Ex-

Governors Emory Washburn and William Claflin, Henry L. Pierce, and very many other citizens of the highest standing, representing the intelligence and honorable feelings of the Commonwealth, were presented to the Senate. These were at once referred to the Committee on Federal Relations, who, January 29, reported, that, "finding an unmerited censure had been inflicted upon a representative of the State in the Senate of the Union," they submitted the following resolution: —

"*Resolved*, That the resolution passed on the eighteenth day of December, eighteen hundred and seventy-two, at the extra session of the legislature of that year, relating to a bill introduced in the Senate of the United States concerning the army register and regimental colors of the United States, be and hereby is *rescinded and annulled*."

This resolution was carried, and being intrusted to a special messenger, Joshua B. Smith, of the House, was borne to Mr. Sumner. It reached him just before his death. Who is not rejoiced to know that it greatly gladdened a heart oppressed with heavy sorrow? After all, the "dear old Commonwealth" had done him justice. The heart of Massachusetts and the heart of her great son once again beat in perfect unison.

Whatever opinion may be held as to the expediency of Mr. Sumner's proposition, this is certain — that it was in perfect consistency with principles declared by him as early as 1847, twenty years before his first resolution. In an oration before the literary societies of Amherst College, August 11 of that year, speaking of *civil* wars, he said, —

"Even if countenanced by justice or dire necessity, they were none the less mournful. *No success over brethren of the same country could be the foundation of honor.* And so firmly was this principle embodied in the very customs and institutions of Rome, that no *thanksgiving* or religious ceremony was allowed by the Senate in commemoration of such success; nor was the *triumph* permitted to the conquering chief whose hands were red with the blood of fellow-citizens. Cæsar forbore even to send a herald of his unhappy victories, and looked upon them with *shame.* . . . [The Christian] would . . . pray that the recording angel would blot with tears all recollections of the fraternal strife in which he was sorrowfully engaged."

In a learned note appended to the address, Mr.

Sumner gave many historical illustrations of his position. He quoted from Dion Cassius, that Pompey, after his success over Cæsar at Dyrrachium, "did not speak of it boastfully, nor did he wreathe his fasces with laurel, feeling a repugnance to doing anything of this sort on account of a victory over citizens."

Mr. Sumner knew that it was the uniform practice of all civilized, Christian nations to remove all national memorials of civil war. To his generous and comprehensive mind, informed as to universal custom elsewhere, it seemed both just and magnanimous to efface from the national, the common flag, all traces of our fraternal strife. If North and South were ever to be united, it must be by meeting on common ground, by oblivion of past differences, and by putting away all memorials of former hate.

Mr. Sumner was said to be wanting in patriotism; but his was the highest, broadest patriotism, embracing the whole country, and not a moiety. It was national, not sectional. It was based on the principles of Christianity. Surely it were better that the different parts of the country should be of one heart, than that sectional pride should be perpetually gratified. Here, in his view, was an opportunity for the noblest self-sacrifice, to gain a great national advantage.

"I am for peace," said he, on another occasion, "in reality as in name. From the bottom of my heart I am for peace, and I welcome all that makes for peace. With deep-felt satisfaction I remember that no citizen who drew his sword has suffered by the hand of the executioner."

Urging the "enduring fellowship of a common citizenship," he said, "To this end there must be reconciliation; nor can I withhold my hand. Freely I accept the hand that is offered, and reach forth my own in friendly grasp. I am against the policy of hate; I am against fanning ancient flames into continued life; I am against raking in the ashes of the past for coals of fire yet burning. Pile up the ashes; extinguish the flames; abolish the hate — such is my desire."

It was such noble sentiments as these that dictated Mr. Sumner's policy. Was he the man to be pronounced by a legislative body worthy of "unqualified condemnation," as offering "an insult to the loyal soldiery of the nation?" This was a blow aimed at as pure a patriot as America was ever blessed with. Who is not thankful that a stigma which could not attach to him was removed from Massachusetts?

The position of Mr. Sumner was well expressed by a fellow-senator, Carl Schurz, in his noble eulogy upon Mr. Sumner, in Boston, April 29:—

"Should the son of South Carolina, when at some future day defending the republic against some foreign foe, be reminded by an inscription on the colors floating over him, that under this flag the gun was fired that killed his father at Gettysburg? Should this great and enlightened republic, proud of standing in the front of human progress, be less wise, less large-hearted, than the ancients were two thousand years ago, and the kingly governments of Europe are to-day? Let the battle-flags of the brave volunteers, which they brought home from the war with the glorious record of their victories, be preserved intact as a proud ornament of our State Houses and armories. But let the colors of the army, under which the sons of all the States are to meet and mingle in common patriotism, speak of nothing but union, — not a union of conquerors and conquered, but a union which is the mother of all, equally tender to all, knowing of nothing but equality, peace, and love among her children.

Do you want shining mementos of your victories? They are written upon the dusky brow of every freeman who was once a slave; they are written on the gate-posts of a restored Union; and the most shining of all will be written on the faces of a contented people, reunited in common national pride."

Mr. Sumner's patriotic act is bearing the fruit of peace. The South is touched by his generous purpose. "Let the grave," says the New Orleans Picayune, "cover all that was inimical to Southern ideas and sentiments in the deceased senator, and let us only remember that he would have put away from the federal archives all show and sign of the triumph of countrymen over countrymen."

Said Mr. Lamar, of Mississippi, in the House of Representatives, "It was certainly a gracious act towards the South . . . to propose to erase from the banners of the national army the mementos of the bloody internecine struggle, which might be regarded as assailing the pride or wounding the sensibilities of the Southern people. That proposal will never be forgotten by the people so long as the name of Charles Sumner lives in the memory of man."

CHAPTER XXXII.

Religious Views of Mr. Sumner. — Dr. Channing. — Mr. Sumner's Faith in God. — Seeking Help from the Highest Source — Gratitude to God. — Divine Providence. — Justice of God. — Regard for the Scriptures. — Belief in Christianity. — The Christian Standard.— The Christian Hero. — Familiarity with the Bible. — Advice to a Young Clergyman. — The Good Shepherd. — Mr. Sumner's Character. — The Chief-Justiceship. — Mr. Sumner's Disinterestedness. — His Writings.

In his youth, and for some time after he entered upon the practice of his profession, Mr. Sumner was a regular attendant at King's Chapel. During this period, Rev. Dr. F. W. P. Greenwood and Rev. Dr. Ephraim Peabody were the pastors, the latter beginning his pastorate in 1846. They were men of fine gifts and eminent worth.

Mr. Sumner's character was formed under the decided influence of religious principles. All his writings, as well as his life, show that he had a reverent faith in God. Indeed, the constant recognition of a Supreme Being of infinite justice, truth, and love, is a conspicuous feature of his speeches.

"True greatness," he says in one place, "consists in imitating, as nearly as possible, the perfections of an Infinite Creator — above all in inculcating those highest perfections, Justice and Love."

The references to God, scattered through his political speeches, as well as his literary and other addresses, carry with them every appearance of sincerity and profound conviction.

This is corroborated by some remarks by Rev. E. E. Hale, in an address at Faneuil Hall: "Mr. Sumner said to a young man, who repeated it to me, that, when there was any new subject of debate; when there was any new course to be adopted; when there was any policy which seemed strange or difficult; when there were any of those clouds of which we have been speaking; when that track was to be found and was hard to find; he never took counsel with men, but separated himself from men, and went alone and consulted the Highest Authority; and when he was assured by the Highest Authority, then he always went forward, and asked no question more."

How reverent his mention of God's care over him, in the opening words of his speech on the Barbarism of Slavery!

How grand and impressive that opening paragraph in the eulogy on President Lincoln, in which he speaks of divine Providence!

He speaks of the injustice of ending the war against the rebellion, without also putting an end to slavery, as "challenging the judgments of a righteous God." "If," said he, "the instincts of patriotism did not prompt this support (emancipation), I should find a sufficient motive in that duty which we all owe to the Supreme Ruler, God Almighty, whose visitations upon our country are now so fearful."

Mr. Sumner also made frequent references to the Scriptures of the Old and the New Testament, and always in the spirit of reverence. He heard God speaking in them, and summoning us to obedience. "Amidst the thunders of Sinai God declared, 'Thou shalt not kill;' and the voice of these thunders, with this commandment, is prolonged in our own day in the echoes of Christian churches."

Of the Fugitive Slave Act he says, "With modesty, and yet with firmness, let me add, it offends against the divine law."

Mr. Sumner was a believer in Christianity. He speaks of it in one place as "our faith." In his view, Christianity was the "true" religion, in contrast with heathen religions, which he calls "false."

Conversing at one time with Rev. Dr. Neale, who often met him in educational meetings, as well as elsewhere, Mr. Sumner, in answer to a question designed to draw out his religious views, declared his full belief in the Christian religion. "My way of looking at it," he said, "may differ somewhat from yours, but it is the same religion. The sun shines in a different way upon different persons, his rays striking some vertically, and others obliquely, according to their respective localities; but it is the same glorious sun. So with Christianity — it comes to me in a way somewhat peculiar, but it is the same glorious faith."

Mr. Sumner regarded Christianity as presenting the highest, even a perfect, standard of right. He constantly speaks of " Christian duty " as presenting duty in its purest and most authoritative form. When discoursing upon arbitration for the settlement of difficulties between nations, after other reasons in its favor, he adds, " Above all, it is consistent with the teachings of Christianity," and implies " a lofty Christian statesmanship."

He speaks of " that sublime revelation of Christianity, the brotherhood of man." " Are we not all," he asks, " in a just and Christian sense, brethren of one household ? " " To the Christian, every fellow-man, whether remote or near, is 'neighbor' and 'brother.' "

Speaking of slavery as a barbarism, and not a civilization, he says, " In the Christian light of the nineteenth century there can be but one civilization." Slavery he calls " an infraction of God's great laws of right and love, and of the Christian precept, 'Whatever ye would that men should do to you, do ye even so to them.' "

The highest commendation he gives to Washington Allston is, to call him "a Christian artist."

Thus, every private and public act and institution was tested by the Christian standard.

He speaks of "the irresistible might of Christian institutions," and of the encouragement derived from "the promises of Christianity." "With this faith, we place our hands, as those of little children, in the great hand of God. He will guide and sustain us — through pains and perils it may be — in the path of progress."

"In the clear eye of that Christian judgment which must yet prevail, vain are the victories of war." "He is the benefactor, and worthy of honor, who carries comfort to wretchedness, dries the tear of sorrow, relieves the unfortunate, feeds the hungry, clothes the naked, does justice, enlightens the ignorant, unfastens the fetters of the slave, and finally, by virtuous genius in art, literature, science, enlivens and exalts the hours of life, or by generous example, inspires a love for God and man. This is the Christian hero." "Christianity inculcates patience, forbearance, forgiveness of evil, even the duty of benefiting a destroyer."

In one place he declares his belief in the future universal prevalence of Christianity. "Nor do we doubt that Christianity will yet prevail over the whole earth, as the waters cover the sea."

Mr. Sumner was very familiar with the Scriptures. This is evident, not only in his frequent and most apposite quotations, but in those incidental allusions and in that happy use of Scripture phraseology which flavor and dignify his writings.

As an instance of this, take a sentence in his address to the governor at the time of his public reception in Boston, in 1856, where, speaking of his efforts to regain his health, he said, "I listened to the admonitions of medical skill, and I courted all the bracing influences of Nature, while time passed without the accustomed healing on his wings."

The uniform correctness of his references to the Bible forms a noteworthy contrast with the sorry work which politicians are apt to make in their awkward attempts at Scripture citation.

The Christian spirit that animated Mr. Sumner appears in a little incident. He was once present at the ordination of a young clergyman. At the close of the services he went up to him, and said, in a pleasant tone, "He prayeth well who loveth well."

A few weeks before Mr. Sumner's death, a party of ladies and gentlemen from Boston visited his house at Washington, in company with a common friend. Mr. Sumner was even more than usually genial and animated, and took great pains to point out and explain objects of interest in his apartments. Among other things to which he called the attention of his guests, was a small and rude *terra cotta* figure of the Good Shepherd, in relief, bearing a lamb, the lost one, now recovered, upon his shoulders. Mr. Sumner said to his visitors that this was the way in which the shepherd in Eastern countries was accustomed to carry home his sheep when infirm or disabled. He repeated the passage in the gospel about the lost sheep, and the owner leaving the ninety and nine to seek that one, giving a touching explanation of it. He spoke with deep feeling of Jesus as the Good Shepherd, and of his great compassion to mankind. The company were much struck with the earnestness and tenderness of his manner, and they remember the scene as one of uncommon interest.

Who that considers the character of his life, his ruling purpose to do good, can doubt that a spirit was breathed into him from above, from the Father of all truth and goodness, to prepare him for the great work of mercy which he was a chief instrument in accomplishing?

He had faults and weaknesses, but they were not the faults and weaknesses of an ignoble and selfish character. He sometimes showed hauteur in his manner, — though this was not the habit of his nature, — but it was always in a good cause. It largely grew out of his profound convictions, his intense hatred of all wrong, indirectness, sham, and double-dealing. These things aroused his ire, and sometimes made him pass over the bounds of a proper moderation. But he was not a man to harbor petty grudges; he was not a self-seeker; he was not jealous or envious; he never sought to supplant others to make a place for himself. Above any casual infelicities of temper or manner, arising in part, no doubt, from nervous infirmity brought on by his brave exposure of wrong, shone forth his genuine love of truth and justice, his indomitable patriotism, his sincere purpose to benefit his race. George William Curtis calls him "conscience incarnate in politics."

Mr. Caleb Lyon, in some personal reminiscences of Mr. Sumner's life in Washington, gives one instance of his remarkable disinterestedness. "Soon after Chief Justice Taney's death," says the account, "he showed me a card from the President, upon which was written, 'Hon. Charles Sumner: The vacant chief justiceship is placed at your disposal. A. Lincoln.' He then said, 'There was a time when this office would have been the realized dream of my youth; but now it must not, cannot be. The breach between Mr. Chase and the President is growing wider and wider, and this will close it. No personal sacrifice is too great, nor can anything tempt me to desert my post. The Republican party must remain intact until its mission is fulfilled.'

"It is well known that only the great senator's persistency accomplished the appointment of Mr. Chase, after a tedious delay from October to December. Mr. Chase through life remained unconscious of Mr. Lincoln's offer to Mr. Sumner, and his refusal."

Persons who knew Mr. Sumner intimately in Washington for years together, bear uniform testimony to his great kindliness of spirit in private life, and to his thoughtful regard for the comfort of those who were in any way dependent on him. They relate how patiently he would often listen to a long story of trouble from some humble unfortunate, while he also well knew how to shake off mere intruders upon his time.

CHAPTER XXXIII.

Mr. Sumner's Purity of Life. — Political Integrity. — Conversational Peculiarities. — A French Dinner.

Mr. Sumner we have seen to be a man of the purest principles. He was, also, a man of unblemished life. Political venom never assailed his character.

Profanity — that vice too common among public men — was always repulsive to him, as also was the slightest approach to vulgarity or coarseness in conversation. A gentleman, who was one of his warm supporters and personal friends, and who often entertained him as his guest, says that he has met him in all places where gentlemen meet without restraint, and heard him converse on all topics with men of various classes; but has never heard him tell a story or make an allusion, that would have offended the ear of the most dainty lady.

He once said to a clergyman of this city, speaking of his somewhat limited means, "I have never had the art to get my hand into the treasury."

The boldest schemer of evil never dared to approach him with plans for robbing the people; and his hand remained to the last unsullied by the touch of unholy gain. So great was the gulf between him and the men who play traitor to their trusting constituents, that he could say with truth, "People talk about the corruption at Washington. I have been here all these years, and have seen nothing of it." He had not seen it, because he never looked in that direction.

He never pledged an offering to Freedom which he did not lay, freely and without reserve, on her altar. He never held out an unmanly allurement for votes; never spent a dollar in the effort to gain an election; never used any of the low trickery which degrades alike the elections of England and America. He could not stoop either to buy from, or to cajole a vote out of, any man. He was the same dignified gentleman during a political campaign, that he was in the Senate Chamber and the drawing-room.

Mr. Sumner talked, rather than conversed, when in company. One who knew him well, and was frequently in his society, expresses it thus: "He either led the conversation or remained silent."

Mr. Sumner was an inimitable story-teller. That minuteness of detail which in another would have amounted to tediousness, only kept up the interest of the listener, as every word gave a new charm. It would be impossible to give any adequate illustration of this, but to convey some idea of the way in which he related scenes and events, we will give, as nearly as it can be done from memory, his account of a dinner to which he was invited at the mansion of one of the most noted among European rulers, the last time he was abroad.

It required a real diplomatist to make himself agreeable to foreigners at that time. They were hungry to hear all about republics; but being, as he felt himself, under a ban which the world knew, he realized the great importance of steering clear of American politics; as, should "the battle flag matter" come up, he could not defend himself without censuring "dear old Massachusetts" — and that he would not do.

He had a habit of constantly throwing the words "you will observe" into his conversation, particularly when describing persons he had met, or scenes through which he had passed.

He had been courteously received by the gentleman in question, and was now invited to a dinner at his elegant mansion. Having arrayed himself with that care which all who knew him will remember, he ordered a cab to convey him thither; and he tells the story of the dinner thus: —

"When I left my hotel, I told the cabman I wished him to drive me to the residence of ——.

"'Yes, sir,' he replied, 'I will gladly do so; we all love him.'

"After a short drive, we turned into the elegant grounds, and drove up the avenue which leads to the mansion, at the door of which a servant received me.

"I saw no one in the halls as I was conducted up stairs to my room by the man who carried my bag for me. Entering the apartment assigned me, — a most luxurious one, — I found an open fire glowing in the grate, a table fully furnished with writing materials, and an easy-chair beside it — a very beautiful welcome for a stranger. The servant then asked for my key, opened my bag, and laid out, over a chair, the articles I had brought to complete my toilet, and then retired, saying, 'I will wait at your door until you are ready, sir; when you call me I will conduct you to the drawing-room.'

"This, you will observe, is the custom in such circles.

"When I was ready, I went to my door, where I found the man awaiting me. I descended the stairway, and was ushered into the saloon, where I found Madame —— and her guests, — the custom of my host being, you will observe, not to appear until just before dinner is announced.

"The house was gorgeous and elegant, and the company very distinguished-looking, and of course most richly dressed. Madame ——, who was a large and rather coarse-looking person, received me with courtesy, and introduced me to the company.

"We conversed for some time before our host joined us; and very soon after he did so, a man-servant threw open the doors which led to the dining-room, and gravely announced, 'Dinner is served.' The gentleman of the mansion then offered his arm to the most distinguished lady of the party, and led the way to the dining-room. But the custom, you will observe, is, not for the lady of the house to give her arm to the gentleman she wishes to honor, and follow her husband, but to remain with him behind, till she sees that all the ladies are provided with escorts, and have left the saloon, when she and her escort follow them, and take their places at table. I had given my arm to my hostess, taking care, you will observe, that it should not be in a way which would oblige her to place me at her right hand at table unless she desired to do so. This, however, she did.

"The table and its appointments were elegant and costly beyond description, all the service, even to the plates, being either of solid gold or of solid silver. The style of serving was in accordance with the elegance and costliness of the arrangements of the table.

"I was still careful, as you will observe, to avoid every topic strictly American, lest it might lead us towards politics. Knowing, as I did, that my host was a great connoisseur in art, and the owner of rare collections, and remembering that he lost many beautiful pictures and statues in the barbarism of the revolution, I opened this subject with Madame ——. But on art in general I met no response. I then said to her, 'I am very glad, madame, to hear that some of your husband's rare treasures, which he lost in your troubles, have been returned to him;' feeling sure that that must be a matter of interest. She manifested not the least interest in the matter, and her only reply was, 'If he has recovered any of them, I never heard of it before.'

"I found it impossible to keep up any conversation with her.

"The elegant and refined tastes of the gentleman found, you will observe, no sympathy in his wife. She is very rich, but not a woman of culture or polished manners, while he is a model of an elegant and polite French gentleman.

"At one time during dinner, my host cast an anxious look on the lady, who, perhaps, to his practised eye, looked out of humor, and said very kindly, — what with us would be regarded as a breach of politeness, — 'You look very weary, my dear;' but she did not reply. She took no more notice of the remark than if she had been deaf.

"On returning to the long saloon, the hostess and all the ladies gathered at one end of the room, and the gentlemen at the other. The entertainment then partook rather of the form of a lecture than conversation. The host stated his views on points which were then occupying the public mind, and gave his reasons for them, discoursing at some length, to the great enjoyment of his guests. It is in this way that he prepares the speeches, which he afterwards delivers.

"Having finished his remarks, my host turned to me and asked, 'What, sir, is the opinion of American statesmen in regard to the electoral college system?'

"That was a question I had no delicacy in answering. 'They regard it as an utter failure, sir,' I replied. He then turned to a gentleman near him, and said, 'Mr. Secretary, note that statement of the American gentleman.'"

CHAPTER XXXIV.

Wide General Information.— Talk at a Stock Club.— Talk on Laces.— Mr. Sumner and his little Namesake.— Interest in the Work of others. — Letter of Hon. G. W. Warren.

GREAT men are too often wise only in their own sphere, and ignorant of all beyond it.

Mr. Sumner was remarkable for his general information. Nothing escaped his eye, and no subject was too great or too small for his investigations.

Being once on a visit at the country house of a friend, when a "stock club" was to meet there, Mr. Sumner entered heartily into the matter, and expressed pleasure at meeting the gentlemen.

But he was not a listener only; he surprised both host and guests by his familiarity with the subject, and by finally giving what amounted to a dissertation on the various breeds of cows, and the varieties of cheese. He knew all about the English and Scotch cows, and dwelt with interest on their marked peculiarities. He introduced to their notice a breed of Highland cows, of which none of the stock club had ever heard before.

On another occasion, at the same house, a fellow-guest, one of our most honored public men at the Capitol, was entertaining the company with an account of the way in which he had been duped in the purchase of lace when abroad, — buying miserable cotton stuff in place of the rich fabric he wanted — by the statements of "half-price" and "poverty," from the glib-tongued daughters of Erin, near Queenstown.

At this Mr. Sumner took up the subject of lace, and went into it minutely. He described the different varieties, told how and where they were made, — from the rich altar-pieces and other laces of antiquity down to the manufactures of our own day. He knew the name of each style, and in whose possession the laces were which had come down as heirlooms in royal and noble families.

When surprise was expressed that a gentleman should know so much on a subject which would naturally interest ladies only, he said that he once sat at a dinner party next Mrs. General F——, when this subject was brought up. She then told him the name of the lace worn by each lady at table, calling his attention to the fact that some of the least showy were the most rare and expensive. After that, he felt an interest in the subject, and read about laces, and examined the different kinds when abroad; so that now he was really a judge of the article, and proof against imposition.

Mr. Sumner's manner towards little children shows that there was a fountain of tenderness sealed up beneath what many regarded his stern and cold exterior. What he might have been, surrounded by family love and schooled by sweet home influences through life, we can only imagine.

Mr. H. Vincent Butler, of Boston, having asked Mr. Sumner's permission to name a little son for him, received the following reply: —

"WASHINGTON, 25th February, '72.

"DEAR MR. BUTLER: I have never expressed my gratitude that you should have thought my name worthy of your son, but I have not been insensible to the kindly appreciation which prompted the parents.

"But pardon me. Is it right to call a child after a living person? Only when death has set its seal on a name, can it be given to another without peril. Who knows what may come in the vicissitudes of life? But I will not follow these hints.

"I have expected you for several days. Meanwhile the days are charming. Accept my best wishes for the boy, and believe me, my dear sir,

"Sincerely yours,

"CHARLES SUMNER."

And so the beautiful little fellow was named Charles Sumner Butler; and afterwards, whenever the senator had an opportunity, he always asked, with much interest, "How is that boy?"

When this baby was about seven months old, he was taken by his parents to visit Mr. Sumner at his rooms in the Coolidge House. The senator was engaged with his books when they entered, but arose at once, and gave them a most cordial greeting. He then took the babe, and

MR. SUMNER'S ROOM AT THE COOLIDGE HOUSE, BOSTON.

carried it about the room in his arms, while the little one gazed up with infantile wonder into the strange but noble face of him who was so kindly caressing it. He then apologized for not having called on the baby.

Just then two gentlemen came in, friends of Mr. Sumner, to whom he said, after having introduced the parents, and holding the baby up towards them, "And this gentleman is Master Charles Sumner Butler!"

At this moment the senator, being unskilful in the art of holding babies, accidentally snapped the elastic cord that held the cap, against the little one's cheek, which made it cry out with pain.

"Is that so?" said one of the gentlemen. "We must admit that he has early commenced, like his honored predecessor, to 'cry aloud and spare not,' since he does not hesitate to express his mind in this illustrious presence."

CHAPTER XXXV.

Routine of Life in Washington. — Home at Washington. — Aunt Chloe's "God bless him!" — Giving Autographs. — Honor in Money Matters. — The Malachite Table. — The Hard-earned Vases. — Bust of Psyche.

MR. SUMNER'S tastes were elegant and refined, but his manner of life was remarkably simple for one in his public position. He rose about seven o'clock, breakfasted at eight, and read his letters and papers, and received visitors, often conversing with friends while at breakfast.

He was remarkably prompt as a correspondent, answering all letters in the order of their dates, and very generally with his own hand. He dined at six o'clock, after which he conversed with his guests till their departure, when he put himself earnestly to his work, amid what seemed to others a wild confusion of books, papers, magazines, and manuscripts, but what was to him the poetry

Senate Chamber
5th Jan '74

Dear Mrs Claflin,

To-day we begin again & I am once more at my desk. I miss W. with whom I have so often conferred here. His absence makes a perceptible gap. I hope that he is prudent but I fear the contrary.

A happy New Year to you & yours!

Sincerely yours,
Charles Sumner

The tea came in season: but I have not yet commenced with it. — as some of the old remained, & I feared lest it would suffer in comparison with the new.

of order, as he knew where to lay his hand on anything he wanted. Much of Mr. Sumner's brain-work was done after his guests had retired.

He was genial and pleasant with his servants, and courteous to all those who served or aided him in a higher capacity. A gentleman who was for two years his secretary, and companion at table and in the library, says he never once saw him out of temper. When assailed or misrepresented, he seemed grieved, but never angry. Very frequently, in the case of a violent attack, he made no reply whatever.

It is not our intention to give a full description of Mr. Sumner's home, nor a list of his art treasures. We shall, however, give a private letter from a lady who visited the senator, and was shown through the rooms by him, and heard descriptions and anecdotes of these things from his own lips, only a few weeks before his death: —

". . . We passed through La Fayette Square to Mr. Sumner's house. It was a lovely morning, so summer-like that we wondered the grass and flowers did not forget it was January, and peep out.

"The birds were out in full force, filling the

place of leaves on the bushes, and singing with all their power. There were large, smooth, glossy leaves, like magnolia leaves, scattered about the paths.

"Mr. Sumner's house stands on a corner, the Arlington House on either side, making it look as if it were a part of the hotel.

"When we entered, Mrs. —— sent up her card, and while the servant was gone we sat in the charming parlor, furnished in gold-colored satin, and filled with pictures and articles of virtu.

"Mr. Sumner asked us, at once, up stairs into his study, where we found Vice-President Wilson. When we entered the room, there was a little flurry about seating us, as the chairs were all filled with newspapers and manuscripts.

"I am accustomed, as you know, to sitting on sermons and manuscripts of that sort in the study at home; but I confess that I hesitated a little before taking a chair already occupied by senatorial speeches, public orations, and the like.

"As soon as we were seated, Mr. Sumner returned to his reclining-chair. He was dressed in a *robe de chambre* of dark, bluish-purple cloth, richly trimmed with crimson, and confined about the waist by a crimson cord and tassels. He is a grand-looking man, tall and broad-shouldered. He has a splendid head, crowned with what I should call — although I have never seen Jupiter — 'ambrosial locks.' His smile is very beautiful, lighting up his usually stern face, and melting away all its coldness. I never saw a face before which was so changed by a smile. I was particularly struck with his hands, which were very white and beautifully formed.

"Mr. Sumner had just received a letter from a friend, asking a favor of him. He spoke of it to Mr. Wilson, saying he hoped he should be able to arrange the matter. Mr. Wilson volunteered to attend to it for him, and soon left the room for that purpose. The large, sunny study in which we were, extends over the library and part of the dining-room. It has three windows, in one of which hangs a beautiful transparency. There was a large desk in the centre of the room, and another by one of the windows. Photographs were tacked all over the walls and the doors, and everywhere about were lying books, books — papers, papers.

"Very soon Mr. Sumner showed us his copy of Pope's 'Essay on Man,' with interlined and marginal corrections by the author's own hand. We read them, and found they were improvements as well as alterations.

"He next showed us his copy of Erasmus, with pen-and-ink etchings on the margin by Holbein, and John Bunyan's Bible. Mrs. —— remarked, that Bunyan's Psalm-book (which she owned), which bore his autograph and that of his wife, Elizabeth Bunyan, seemed to her more valuable than his Bible.

"'I had my choice between the two when they were for sale, and preferred the Bible,' said Mr. Sumner. 'There is something about the Bible, you know,—his Bible,—which inclined me to it.'

"He had the daintiest of cases for these rare books, into which they just fitted. He alluded to them, and said there was nothing like them made in this country.

"He then brought out from careful paper wrappings two small wood-cuts he had recently received, according to his order, from an English sale.

"One was a head of Prester John, and as I, in

common with others, have rather a vague idea of this semi-mythical gentleman, I was not surprised to see a good-looking colored man.

"The other was Salvator Rosa's 'Jonah's Deliverance from the Whale.' The prophet seemed coming out of his prison in a terrible hurry, on all fours. The 'great fish' was a fearful-looking animal, resembling a Japanese griffin more than anything else.

"I remarked that the artist had carried out the words of the Scripture by making a *great fish* instead of the traditionary *whale.*

"'Why, was it not a whale'?" asked Mr. Sumner, smiling. 'I was brought up to believe it was a whale, and always thought it was.'

"I referred him to the English Bible, and felt surprised and glad to find that I knew one thing which Charles Sumner did not know!

"We chanced, in the course of conversation, to speak of 'A Week in a French Country-House,' when he told us that he had met Madam Sartori, the author of it, abroad, and was once invited to the house of a friend to hear her sing. She was at that time studying for the stage, but married Mr. Sartori soon after, and so never entered on a public career. This lady, I may remark, is the mother of the young man who is, at the time of writing, engaged to be married to the daughter of President Grant.

"Mr. Sumner then spoke of Fanny Kemble, who is Madam Sartori's sister. He said he knew her well, and that some years ago he boarded near her, and used to take long rides with her on horseback, during which they conversed much on the topics of the day. He said that he greatly admired Mrs. Kemble.

"Mr. Sumner spoke very feelingly of Agassiz. He said that, when he was last in Cambridge, Agassiz showed him the manuscript of his article on the Darwinian theory, — or rather, the three manuscripts, — for he first dictated the matter to Mrs. Agassiz, then corrected and interlined the writing, which she afterwards re-wrote. This copy he corrected and added to, after which she made a third transcript, which was sent to the printer.

"While on this subject, Mr. Sumner said that Mrs. Agassiz was in entire sympathy with her husband in his scientific work, and rendered him great assistance; and added, with much earnestness, 'She is a true woman and a true wife.' He had not heard till then of the gift Agassiz had received from his daughter, for the carrying out his cherished plans. When Mrs. —— told him about it, he seemed greatly pleased, and said, 'How happy that it came in such good time, while she could enjoy the pleasure of giving and he of receiving.' He and Mrs. —— then talked of various people, and of the interests of the country, in a most interesting way.

"Mr. Sumner was to make a speech that day; but, unfortunately for us, it was in a secret session. We rose to leave. But he asked us to go down stairs and wait till he should join us.

"When he came down, he went to the library, opened a drawer, and showed us a Latin book of John Dryden's, with his name scrawled on the fly-leaf in a school-boy's hand. While we were examining it, Mr. Sumner told us that once, when he was showing it to two ladies, one of them looked at the writing, and exclaimed to the other, 'Isn't that just like our John's?' He showed us Wickliffe's Bible, with its long chain and padlock.

"Among his valuable autographs was this most interesting one: —

'If Virtue feeble were,
Heaven itself would stoop to her.
'JOHANNES MILTON.
'COMUS, 1637.'

"When, after showing us many other beautiful things, he was obliged to leave, he asked us to remain and look at the pictures. In the dining-room we saw the picture of St. Mark coming down with flying mantle to rescue a slave who was lying prostrate in the public square. He had used this tradition as an illustration in one of his earliest speeches, and afterwards, seeing the picture, had bought it. Mr. Whittier has made the story the foundation of a poem. In this room were many very beautiful pieces of china, and on the door leading to the china closet hung a picture suggestive of the place. Indeed, all the pictures were in keeping with the rooms where they hung. On the side of the stairs were pictures of famous stairways. In the study were engravings of the House of Lords, the French Assembly, the United States Senate, and heads of eminent statesmen. The richer pictures, with statues, elaborate tables, vases, and rare curiosities, were in the parlor and library, and presented work for more than one morning.

MR. SUMNER'S LIBRARY AT WASHINGTON.

From Harper's Weekly.

"Then we went through the hall, where a large Dutch clock stands at the foot of the stairs, out into the noisy street, and across the sunny park, towards the White House."

A lady who was visiting in Washington, not long before Mr. Sumner's death, was talking with "Old Chloe," a colored woman in whom she had long been interested, when Senator Sumner, who was a warm personal friend, sent up his card. Rising, she said, "I shall not be able to talk with you any longer now, Chloe. Mr. Sumner is down stairs, and I must go to see him."

Then poor Chloe broke out in rapturous strains, and extolled Mr. Sumner's character as the friend and helper of her race. "I's often wished," she said, "dat I could shake hands wid him, but I don't suppose I ever shall. I wish you would tell him how we all loves him, and den shake hands wid him for me; and tell him dat every time I sees him in de street, I says, 'God bless him.'"

Those who had been present when Mr. Sumner opened his morning mail say that, amid all his duties, he often took time to send autographs to boys who had written for them.

A young lad once came in possession of a

"frank" of his, on a coarse envelope; but he wanted a well-written autograph, not imagining that so great a man could write so blindly, except when in haste. So he wrote to him of the one he had, that he only had succeeded in making it out by consulting a congressional directory, a legal friend, and the superintendent of a manufacturing corporation. To this communication Mr. Sumner sent the following holograph note: —

"BOSTON, 21st September, '61.

"DEAR SIR: I am glad you have so good a committee to help you in learning to read.

"Faithfully yours,

"CHARLES SUMNER."

Ten years afterwards the recipient of the note reminded Mr. Sumner of the incident, whereupon the senator laughed heartily, and said, "I declare, I was not aware before that I ever said anything quite so Spartan as that!"

One of our Boston Latin School boys gives an account of the way in which he secured Mr. Sumner's autograph, thus: —

"When returning one evening from one of the Lowell lectures, in the horse car, a gentleman of imposing appearance attracted my attention

He looked as I imagined the old Roman senators did. I was watching him closely, when it flashed across my mind that he could be no other than Charles Sumner. I found I was not mistaken. I had always felt a great desire to see him, and I could not have had a better opportunity.

"I was much interested in making a collection of autographs, and was soon questioning whether or not it would be rude to ask him for his, when he arose to get out of the car. I thought, 'Now is my time,' and immediately rushed from the car, just in time to overtake him. He noticed me approaching, and inquired the way to James Freeman Clarke's church. I said I should be very happy to walk to the church with him. Coming, just then, to a lamp-post, I asked him if he would be willing to give me his autograph. He answered so pleasantly, that I felt almost as if I had conferred a pleasure on *him*. Having a book with me, I took from it a scrap of paper, and with a pencil he wrote, —

'Yours truly,
'CHARLES SUMNER.
'In the Street, Nov. 17, 1873.'

"We then continued our way to the church, he

talking very familiarly with me. As I left him at the door, he shook hands with me, and lifting his hat, bade me 'good by,' while I scarcely realized that I had had a walk and talk with the 'great and good Sumner.'"

Mr. Sumner did not love money enough to do an ungenerous thing to secure it.

In November, 1856, Albert Sumner, who, like his illustrious brother, was a splendid specimen of a man, of noble bearing and courteous manners, was lost, with all his family, in the wreck of the Lyonnese.

Mrs. Albert Sumner was a lady of fortune; and dying without a will, her property went by law to her husband's relatives; but such was the honor of Charles Sumner, that he insisted that this estate, as far as it could be disentangled from that of his brother, should be passed over to the relatives of the unfortunate lady.

Surely this was an act of noble unselfishness rarely met with in the world where so many—even men who have more money than they can take care of—seem playing at the game which children call "grab," the motto of which is, "Keep all you've got, and catch what you can."

Mr. Sumner's stern principle prevented his living in a style beyond his means. He enjoyed only what he could pay for at the time of purchase. One of his friends says that some years ago, while Mr. Sumner was living very modestly in the suburbs of Washington, he visited him. He occupied at the time a room and bedroom, and took his breakfast there, but dined in the city. He was about to pay his landlady, and holding out his hand towards his friend, with seven ten dollar gold pieces in it, he said, "That is for my monthly rent and my breakfast." His guest expressed surprise that he did not live in a little more style, when he replied, "The country cannot pay me any more, and I cannot live beyond my means."

Even to the last, when he had a home of his own, elegantly furnished and rich with gems of ancient and modern art, he used the democratic horse-car in going to and from the Senate, and always, except in taking drives for pleasure, when he hired a carriage from a livery stable.

A gentleman from Boston asked him, not long ago, why he did not keep horses.

"Because," he replied, "if I did so, I could

not indulge my taste for pictures, statuary, rare books, and manuscripts. I can live without horses, but I cannot live without the other things." They had become necessities with him.

A lady of Boston, who was one of his most familiar friends, and who, with her honored husband, has been true to him through all his trials, was among his last visitors. In attracting her attention to a malachite table of rare value and beauty, he said, "This, Mrs. ——, is the result of my lecture in Brooklyn, and those vases (he pronounced the word *väzes*) are the result of my Philadelphia lecture. He called attention to a Psyche, and said, "I bought that on account of the strong resemblance it bears to my twin sister;" thus showing that he had carried the memory of her sweet face, as well as of her lovely spirit, through life with him.

Beneath what seemed Mr. Sumner's cold and unimpressible manner, there lay a warmth of heart of which we now and then catch a gleam, and that shows the man as he really was.

One of those who knew him best, who was a confidant in hours when he threw off his public burdens and laid aside the veil which usually hung between his heart and the world, says, "When Mr. Sumner's brother George lay suffering at the hospital, whither he had gone for treatment, and where he died, it was the senator's custom to visit him every morning.

"He always entered the room with his natural high bearing and kingly tread, and asked in deep tones the usual questions, and said whatever of interest he had to say. He then bade the sufferer good morning, and went out, apparently as unmoved as a stone.

"But the attendants reported that as soon as he had passed the screen that shielded his brother, his heart gave way, and he manifested deep feeling, the great tears rolling down his cheeks as he passed out of the room."

He was then, doubtless, carried back to the days of his childhood. The statesman was lost in the brother; ambition for the future was dimmed by regrets for the past; and his sympathy for all, concentrated in a yearning desire to save the partner of his childhood from pain and death.

CHAPTER XXXVI.

A Struggle for Life. — Opposition to the Centennial Bill. — Speech against the Bill. — Insults from the Projectors. — Leaves the Senate Chamber for the Last Time. — Last Hours. — His Dying Charge. — Announcement of Mr. Sumner's Death. — A Mourning Nation. — Funeral at King's Chapel. — Procession to Mount Auburn. — The Closing Scene.

CHARLES SUMNER received his death-blow in 1856; but he was long in dying. A man of weaker nerves, or one without a high purpose in life, would have yielded to the power of disease rather than endure a slow martyrdom for years. But as long as there was work for him to do, he bravely struggled on, compelling himself to undertake what was really beyond his strength.

It was in this spirit that he set himself to perform what proved to be his last public act.

As he had never learned the art — unfortunately easy to so many — of putting his hand into the public treasury, neither had he learned that of letting other men do so, if he knew their purpose.

Believing that the "Centennial Bill" was a huge scheme for benefiting a private corporation at the public expense, Mr. Sumner delivered a speech on the subject Friday, March 6. In the part we quote he was more humorous than was his wont: —

"But I have something more to say — very briefly, however — on the way in which these corporators, if I may so express myself, worked into their present position. They came here for their bill; they obtained it with the condition that I have mentioned — a condition openly announced and accepted by their representatives on this floor, and also in the other House accepted fully; and the venerable senator from Pennsylvania on my right was so jubilant that he announced at once that they would obtain the money without delay. Ah, sir, does not the poet tell us, —

'Fair laughs the morn, and soft the zephyr blows'?

It was so with them. Their morning laughed, and the zephyr fanned their cheeks. They were confident of success. They began with their own immediate fellow-citizens, and there they failed. They then turned to the States; there again they failed; and now, sir, morning no longer laughing, and zephyr no longer blowing, they turn to the United States, and ask us to assume this great expense. There should have been more frankness originally. If the United States were at any time to be called to assume this expense, they should have known it in advance.

"Nor is this all. The United States should have had the conduct of the whole business. It should not have been entered upon by a private corporation of stockholders. Permit me to say, in a certain sense they are usurpers; occupying a supreme national function. Thus far, all world's fairs have been governmental in origin and conduct, and I see no reason in our national condition why we should be an exception. I do not find that we have facilities for massing capital and obtaining the means for a great world's fair that should make us an exception to the received rule and practice of other nations. The world's fair should have been in the hands of the nation.

"And now, still further, I am about to say that, in my judgment, a proper celebration of the one hundredth natal day of the republic should have been by the nation, and not by any private corporation. But these private corporators have worked themselves into the business. The authentic story of the Siberian bear is revived. You all remember it. The bear leaped upon a horse, and he ate so furiously that he absolutely ate his way into the harness and drew the sledge. I know not if our Philadelphia bear has not already eaten itself into the harness. But has not the time come to stop? I think we must give the bear notice to quit; at least let him know that he cannot drag this nation into any world's fair."

Monday evening, March 9, was the last time that Mr. Sumner conversed sociably on matters of the day. A writer in a Washington paper, who passed several hours with him, and found him free from actual pain, gives the following account of the interview: —

"At eight o'clock on Monday evening I made

my last call on Senator Sumner. He greeted me, saying, 'I am so weary thinking over my speech on finance! I wanted a change, — a ray of sunlight, — and I am glad you have come.' He at once began to talk on European politics, which, to him, was an outspread map, and whose kaleidoscopic changes he always viewed with absorbing interest. He spoke of Gladstone — his noble struggle in the cause of liberalism, his success, his failure, and his fall; he gave a sketch of a breakfast with him, and summed up by expressions of his firm faith in the ultimate triumph of those principles which Gladstone so nobly championed. 'A great man, under the shadow of defeat,' said he, 'is taught how precious are the uses of adversity; and as an oak tree's roots are strengthened by its shadow, so all defeats in a good cause are but resting-places on the road to victory at last.' He spoke of the patchwork empire of Germany; of Bismark and De la Marmora; of truth, stranger than fiction, viz., of the Italian statesman's assertion of Bismark's offer to cede to France a portion of German territory; of the impolicy of the annexation of Alsace and Lorraine; of the differences with the

Catholic church, the imprisonment of her prelates — and then, taking a volume of Milton, he read, in deep, rich tones of tender melody, his famous sonnet upon the persecution of the Waldenses, during Cromwell's protectorate, as follows: —

'Avenge, O Lord! thy slaughtered saints, whose bones
Lie scattered on the Alpine mountains cold;
Even them who kept thy truth so pure of old,
When all our fathers worshipped stocks and stones,
Forget not; in thy book record their groans,
Who were thy sheep, and in their ancient fold
Slain by the bloody Piedmontese, that rolled
Mother with infant down the rocks. Their moans
The vales redoubled to the hills, and they
To heaven. Their martyred blood and ashes sow
O'er all the Italian fields where still doth sway
The triple tyrant; that from these may grow
A hundred fold, who, having learned thy way
Early, may fly the Babylonian woe.'

"In closing, he added, 'Thus History revenges herself.'

"About this time his evening mail was brought; whenever he came to an interesting note or letter, he would look it over and then hand it to me to read. The first was from an art association in Boston, saying that the Duke de Montpensier, of Spain, had agreed to loan his valuable collection of pictures, valued at five hundred thousand dollars, to the association, provided they paid packing, transportation, and insurance; and as the laws of the United States limit the time of international loan free of duty to six months, it needed a special act of Congress to keep the paintings two years, so as to pay expenses by their exhibition, and he desired speedy legislation. He asked me if I had seen them when in Spain. I answered him, I had, and described several of those I remembered best. He said, 'In the Senate I do not think there will be much difficulty; but in the House,' he added, smiling, 'Ben Butler can put it through, as he does, with his white horse, everything else. Why, he is a political Cagliostro.'

"The next letter was from Philadelphia, an anonymous attack of the bitterest description, impugning his motives concerning his speech on the International Centenary Exposition, winding up with a threat of violence, which I forbear to transcribe. As he handed it to me, he said, good humoredly, 'I am used to such letters.' I read it, and as I did so, consigned it to the blazing grate. The next letter was from Indiana; one of those good, whole-souled letters, full of sympathy and admiration, with an urgent, earnest invitation for him to visit the writer next summer, and an offer of generous and unstinted hospitality. 'There,' said he, 'you have burned the bane, and here is the antidote.' His next letter was from Boston, full of hearty thankfulness for his restoration to health and cheer for the future. It was closely written, and as he handed it to me, he said, 'This is no summer friend.'

"The last of many letters was one of congratulation about the Massachusetts legislative resolutions, rescinding the vote of censure. I never saw him look more happy than when he was reading it. He then arose and showed me with satisfaction the legislative resolutions, beautifully engrossed on parchment. I asked, 'Will you address the Senate when they are presented?' He replied, 'The dear old Commonwealth has spoken for me, and that is enough.'"

Tuesday, March 10, at two o'clock, he took a seat in the Senate Chamber beside a brother senator, also a prominent opponent of the Centennial Bill, and told him, with an evident feeling of annoyance, of the offensive anonymous letters which had been sent him.

His friend turned his mind from this by alluding to the recent action of the Massachusetts legislature, at which Mr. Sumner expressed great pleasure.

He talked with Senator Ferry, of Connecticut, a fellow-sufferer from spinal disease, and told him of his intense pain the night before, which had forced him to send for his physician, who relieved him by injecting morphine under the skin.

Mr. Sumner realized that day that he was going far beyond his strength. "I want to talk with you about my health, for I fear I am working too hard," he said to a friend a few hours before he was attacked with the spasm which proved fatal.

Tuesday evening he entertained a few friends at dinner. That was the last time he sat down at his table. That night the summons came for him to lay aside his armor, and to receive his discharge from a long and toilsome warfare. His friends and physicians did all that mortals could do to ward off the mightiest of foes — but in vain.

There were no kindred present to smooth his dying pillow; but he was not without love and sympathy in his parting hour. There were the men of mind and culture, whose hearts had been knit to his by common labors and sufferings in behalf of humanity; and there were there, also, friends representing the race for whom he had lived and toiled.

Even while dying, he still pleaded for the cause that was dearer to him than life. Almost his last words were an appeal to those about him, who held positions in the national councils, to consummate the last great act of justice to the colored race.

Judge Hoar, of Massachusetts, who stood beside his bed, received the great senator's dying charge, "Do not let the Civil Rights Bill fail!"

Solomon said, "I sleep, but my heart waketh." So Sumner, when lulled to sleep by necessary opiates, was awake to his life-work, and murmured his charge to all who had any influence in the government, "Don't let the bill fail!"

Again he begged with earnestness that the bill might not be lost. Judge Hoar stooped, and with much emotion kissed the cold hand of the senator.

Again Mr. Sumner spoke, and said, "I should not regret this, if my book were finished. My book! my book is not finished; but the great account is sealed."

About nóon on the 11th he raised his head, and said to Senator Schurz, "Why! I can't see! What does this mean?" After hours of agony he moaned, "I am so tired, I am so tired! I can't last much longer!"

Just before he died, Judge Hoar gave him a message from Ralph Waldo Emerson, to which Mr. Sumner replied, with some difficulty, "Tell Emerson that I love and revere him."

To a colored friend who stood chafing his cold hand in the vain effort to restore the lost circulation, he said tenderly, "My poor Johnson, you can soon rest." To one who said, "I wish I could do something to warm your hands," he replied, "You never can."

Being told that his friend, Hon. Samuel Hooper, had come, he looked at him, waved his hand, and said, "Sit down."

At that moment his heart ruptured, a terrible convulsion shook his frame, and he was no longer among the living.

The great Irish Liberator exclaimed, when he heard that Wilberforce was dead, "He has gone up to heaven with a million broken fetters in his hands!" May not as much be said of our departed senator?

When it was announced that Charles Sumner was dead, a pall seemed to fall over the Capitol; and as the sad news flew over the wires there was a nation of mourners. Even his enemies were at peace with him now, and all differences were forgotten in presence of that mighty reconciler — Death.

Previous to the removal of the remains to Massachusetts, appropriate funeral services were held in the Capitol.

There was a continued funeral service on the route, and as the train neared Boston the crowds assembled to meet it. In the shadows of evening, he who had so often entered his native city in the triumph of success, was borne into its streets for the last time, in silence; and when the procession arrived at the State House, the remains were formally delivered by the committee of Congress into the keeping of the Governor of Massachusetts, and lay in state in the Doric Hall over the Sabbath, during which time they were visited by fifty thousand people.

No funeral since that of Abraham Lincoln has

been to our people so much like the burying of their own dead as that of Charles Sumner.

On Monday, Boston seemed lost to everything but the fact that it was the burial-day of her great son.

The funeral procession, which consisted of the dignitaries of the State and City, moved at about ten o'clock down Beacon Street to King's Chapel, which was elaborately draped with black, relieved by flowers and vines. The services were conducted by Mr. Foote, pastor of the church, and consisted of scriptural readings, music, and a prayer, one sentence of which should be preserved in letters of gold: "Teach us to honor only those who honor Thee, and to trust only those who put their trust in Thee."

The shadows were beginning to fall when the imposing cortege reached Mount Auburn, and wound up the avenues and paths through which Charles Sumner had so often followed his dead with an aching heart. The personal friends of the deceased, with the committees of Congress and the Legislature, and the few surviving members of the class of 1830 at Harvard, gathered beside the open grave, while thousands of spectators stood on the hillocks and all around, waiting for the closing scene.

The clergyman read another portion of Scripture, the friends around the grave joined with him in repeating the Lord's prayer, and then all that remained of this mighty man of valor was lowered into its silent bed, to slumber till the day of the great awakening.

John G. Whittier, who loved Mr. Sumner with a brother's heart, wrote to a beloved friend of both, on hearing of his death, —

"I was in the act of mailing this, when the telegram announced the death of our dear and noble Sumner. My heart is too full for words. In deepest sympathy of sorrow I reach out my hand to thee, and to Mr. ——, who loved him so well.

"He has died as he wished to, at his post of duty, and when the heart of his beloved Massachusetts was turning towards him with more than the old-time love and reverence.

"God's peace be with him."

A few months before his death, Mr. Sumner met Pastor Fliedner at the residence of a friend. Their conversation turned upon war. The two gentlemen expressed their views, which closely agreed, on the barbarity of war, and the great wrong in nations, professedly Christian, perpetuating it, in the light of the nineteenth century. At parting, they clasped hands, when Pastor Fliedner said, "I hope we shall meet in the land of peace!" "Let us hope so!" replied Mr. Sumner, in those deep tones which gave such power to every utterance of his.

The Germans have added another beatitude to those given by our Lord in the sermon on the mount: "Blessed are the homesick, for they shall reach home." May we not say of Charles Sumner, who followed the apostolic injunction, "Seek peace and ensue it;" "Blessed is the peace-lover, for he has reached the land of peace"?

APPENDIX.

A.

As showing the kind of influence under which the children of Sheriff Sumner were brought up, we insert below a paper written by one of the daughters, at the age of sixteen, a year before her death.

The delicate conscientiousness which is here seen also formed a striking characteristic of Charles Sumner.

"May 1, 1836.

"It is now nearly a year since I first wrote my character; and the self-examination necessary for it, I found so useful, that I will try it again. I have hoped, and even believed sometimes, that that fault (vanity), which was so predominant in my character then, was partly cured; but in the very act of allowing that thought to take possession of my mind, I was, perhaps, indulging the very thought which has given me so much distress, and throwing myself off my guard when temptation should arise. 'Watch and pray therefore.' I have done these, but not enough, and my mind is still far too much engrossed with the follies and vanities of the world. I have too great a desire to appear well, and I fear, to show off how much I know. It is hard to own this to myself; but I have need of being humbled.

"I have not enough moral courage — courage to tell the simple truth at all times, and in spite of everybody. I have not guarded this carefully enough, and vanity is at the bottom here. I thought I was conscientious, I had been so often told so, and my vanity persuaded me to believe it, at least in part.

"I have a great lack of charity, that virtue which I feel should be exercised towards me. My own failings should teach me this. Prejudice and pride, too, form a part of my character. I am still sometimes cross and fretful, and I fear my temper is not at all improved. My own selfishness shocks me, sometimes.

"The only thing in which I have improved this past year, is that I have a greater desire to grow good, and I am more thoughtful and watchful. I have wept and prayed over these faults; and will they never be eradicated? Must I always endure this state of anxiety, this longing for pure feelings? I will persevere, for I know that He who has helped me so far, will continue his aid.

"How much reason I have to be thankful for my long illness and the moments of delighful intercourse with God which I then enjoyed, and how grateful ought I to be for being kept so long from the enticements which we are subject to, who mix with the world. But I have not improved it enough. How happy should I be if I had! I fear that when I am again well, all the impressions which my sickness has given me will vanish like a mist. Ungrateful shall I be if they do.

"This is what I am just at sixteen."

A lady who was intimate with Mrs. Sumner says that she remembers talking with her one day about her son after he had received his injuries from Brooks, and saying, "How proud I should be if I had such a son!" "Yes," was the reply, "but I tremble."

Speaking of the father, the lady said that he would sometimes buy tickets to lectures on useful subjects, and give them to his children, with the remark, "I shall be busy myself this evening, and I wish you, when you return, to give a correct account of what you hear." In such ways he cultivated in them habits of attention, and the power of communicating what they knew.

B.

The following letter, written by Mr. Sumner, just on the eve of his setting sail for Europe, in 1837, was addressed to one of his sisters, then a little girl. It reveals the future man.

"My dear ——:

"I don't remember that I ever wrote you a letter. I feel confident, however, that your correspondence cannot be very extensive; and, therefore, I may flatter myself that what I write you will be read with attention, and, I trust, also, deposited in your heart. Before trusting myself to the sea, let me say a few words to you, which shall be my *good by*. I have often spoken to you of certain habits of personal care, which I will not here more particularly refer to than by asking you to remember all that I have told you, and to endeavor to follow my advice. I am very glad, my dear, to remember your cheerful countenance. I shall keep it in my mind, as I travel over the sea and land, and hope that when I return, I may still find its pleasant smile ready to greet me. Try never to cry. But, above all things, do not be obstinate or passionate. If you find your temper mastering you, always stop till you can count *sixty*, before you say or do anything. Let it be said of you that you are always amiable. Love your father and mother, and brothers and sisters, and all your friends; cultivate an affectionate disposition. If you find that you can do anything which will add to the pleasure of your parents, or anybody else, be sure to do it. Consider every opportunity of adding to the pleasure of others as of the highest importance, and do not be unwilling to sacrifice some enjoyment of your own, even some dear plaything, if, by doing so, you can promote the happiness of others. If you follow this advice, you will never be selfish or ungenerous, and everybody will love you. Besides this, my dear, always tell the truth. Nobody was ever hurt who told the truth;

while many who told falsehoods have been struck down, like Ananias and Sapphira, whose history you have undoubtedly read in the Acts of the Apostles. If you have ever done anything wrong, always tell of it at once, and your parents and God will forgive you; whereas, they never will if you try to conceal it, or tell a falsehood with regard to it.

"Study all the lessons given you at school, and when at home, in the time when you are tired of play, read some good books which will help to improve the mind. If you follow all this advice you will be amiable, good, and happy, and will contribute very much to the happiness of others. Let me know, on my return from Europe, that you have followed all my dull advice. I should feel grieved very much if I should understand that you had not followed it. If you will let Horace read this letter, it will do the same, perhaps, as one addressed to him, and perhaps he will follow my advice. Give my love to mother, and Mary, and the rest.

"Your affectionate brother, CHAS."

"ASTOR HOUSE, Dec. 7, 1837."

www.ingramcontent.com/pod-product-compliance
Lightning Source LLC
LaVergne TN
LVHW021312110826
845150LV00003B/551

* 9 7 8 1 4 2 5 5 5 8 1 0 9 *